A Book of Blue Flowers

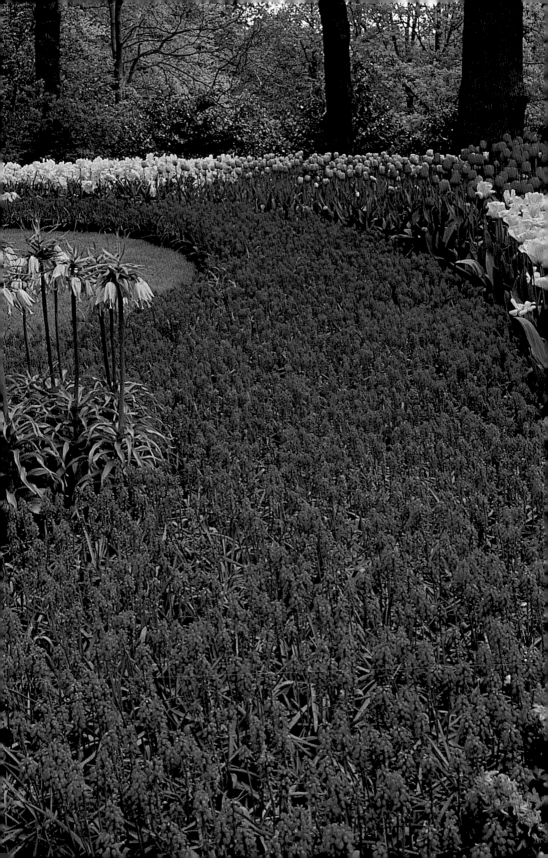

A Book of Blue Flowers

Written and photographed by
ROBERT GENEVE

Timber Press
Portland, Oregon

Half-title page and page 6: *Muscari armeniacum.* Frontispiece: *Muscari armeniacum* mass planting in Keukenhof, Lisse, The Netherlands.

Published in 2000 by
Timber Press, Inc.
The Haseltine Building
133 S.W. Second Avenue, Suite 450
Portland, Oregon 97204, U.S.A.

Designed by Susan Applegate
Printed in Hong Kong

Library of Congress Cataloging-in-Publication Data

Geneve, R. L.
    A book of blue flowers/Robert Geneve.
      p. cm.
    Includes bibliographica references (p.).
    ISBN 0-88192-487-3
Plants, ornamental. 2. Plants, Ornamental—Pictorial works. 3. Flowers—Color. I. Title.

SB407.G46 2000
635.9'68—dc21

00-026330

To my supportive and loving parents,
Louis and Regina

Contents

Preface

Why write a book about plants with blue flowers? That is a question I asked myself for some time before starting this manuscript. I finally decided it would be an interesting project, because there was not a similar work that specifically looked at the diversity of flowers with blue color. I also felt that "blue" as a garden feature can be underrepresented in gardens, especially in the United States. One striking difference I have observed between European and U.S. gardens is the more common integration of blue flower color into European landscape gardens. Of course, this statement is a generalization and is not meant to suggest that plants with blue flowers are not used in the United States. One advantage the gardeners in northern Europe have is the milder summer climate that suits so many blue-flowering plants of alpine origin. The climate of northern Europe also brings out the best in plants from the Boraginaceae (borage family), which contains so many wonderful "true blue" flowering plants. These plants can be difficult for many gardeners in the hotter summer regions of the United States; however, many blue-flowered plants do well in even difficult regions of the United States and deserve a more prominent place in gardens.

As is true in other works of this type, I have tried to include enough species to represent the subject, but this book is not meant to be a comprehensive treatise on all the plants that have blue flowers. I have tried to include all the commonly available plants sold in easily obtained garden catalogs or at nurseries. I also intentionally have included species that are unfamiliar to many gardeners. Some are not commonly available because they are difficult to grow, but others are worthy of a garden trial. I apologize if your favorite blue-flowering plant was not included among the many found in this book.

The plant descriptions are arranged in alphabetical order by genus. Each entry begins with a general discussion of the genus, followed by a specific discussion of those species within the genus that contain individuals with blue flowers. This treatment seems appropriate because not all members of a genus have blue flowers. I also have included a reference to the number of species within a particular genus. These numbers are not meant to be "exact" as they can differ widely depending on the reference consulted. I have included an estimate to give some idea of the size of the genus relative to the number of cultivated species. It is amazing to think of how many plants with ornamental potential are still waiting to be selected for garden use! I applaud the recent efforts to introduce (or sometimes reintroduce) plants from South America and Australia that broaden the palette of new plants for gardens.

Salvia farinacea (mealy-cup sage), *Salvia splendens* (scarlet sage),
and *Rudbeckia fulgida*

Is That Really a Blue Flower?

It is very difficult for me to be definitive on the criteria for whether the color of a flower is "blue enough" to be really blue. The flowers on some plants are obviously blue. The common grape hyacinth (*Muscari armeniacum*) is one such example. It has "true blue" flowers with no hint of pink or purple in the petals. It is the species with flowers that are "almost" blue that give me the problem. Stop to notice all the different shades of blue in flowers! You can find lavender-blue, violet-blue, purple-blue, sky blue, pale blue, and gentian blue. There are also azure, cerulean, and turquoise. I once read that men can be at a disadvantage for discriminating subtle differences in shades of color. In this respect, my wife has been a great help to me. On one of our many garden trips I asked her, "Is that flower blue?" She replied (after 50 such inquiries), "If you want it to be, dear." I have come to believe that her response was not a bad one.

Although blue can be in the eye of the beholder, it turns out that there is a science to color. By definition, color is the property of light reflecting off a surface as different wavelengths. Wavelengths in the visible range appear to us as color. As the wavelengths become shorter, there is a progressive change in color (a spectrum) that proceeds from red to orange, yellow, green, blue, indigo, and violet. Red is considered a "warm" color, and blue is considered a "cool" color. Colors, therefore, can be described by the size of the corresponding wavelength. For the average gardener, describing color as having a wavelength of 450 nanometers does not hold much appeal. It also does not take into account some of the other optical properties of color that change the way we see flowers.

Several systems have evolved to categorize the various shades and nuances of color. These make it possible for artists, photographers, and plant people to communicate about color in everyday terms. The Munsell color order system was developed by Albert Munsell from the United States. It attributes three qualities to color—hue, value, and chroma. Hues are the major colors like red, yellow, and blue. Value is the brightness or how light a color appears. Chroma is the degree of saturation in the color. The Royal Horticultural Society color chart is an outgrowth of this system and has become the standard for those serious about describing flower color. It also ascribes three attributes to color that correspond to Munsell's color order system. They are hue, brightness, and saturation. These attributes lead to an array that can be used to describe color. The example on the facing page is for colors that are near blue.

This system can be used then to create a vocabulary of vernacular terms for color. No where is this more evident than in the variety of terms used to describe "blue." The list on the facing page can be used as a guide to correlate common terms for describing blue flowers with the qualities of "blue."

HUES

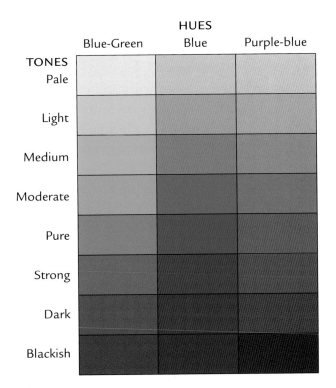

	Blue-Green	Blue	Purple-blue
TONES			
Pale			
Light			
Medium			
Moderate			
Pure			
Strong			
Dark			
Blackish			

BLUES	COMMON TERMS
Pale blue	Baby blue, grayish blue, light blue, powder blue, sky blue
Light blue	Flax blue, forget-me-not blue, porcelain blue
Moderate blue	Gentian blue
Pure blue	Cerulean, ultramarine
Strong blue	Cornflower blue
Dark blue	Princess blue, sapphire
Blackish blue	Navy blue

BLUE-GREEN	
Pale blue-green	Aquamarine
Light blue-green	Turquoise
Strong blue-green	Azure

BLUE-PURPLE	
Light blue-purple	Lilac blue, wisteria blue
Pure blue-purple	Purplish blue, violet blue
Strong blue-purple	Violet

We are interested in describing blue as a color not only to provide an adequate language for cataloging flowers and color, but also to develop pleasant color schemes for the garden. Invariably any discussion about using color in the garden must begin with the artist's color wheel. The color wheel is also an outgrowth of reflected light as a continuous spectrum of colors. In simple terms, colors opposite each other on the color wheel evoke strong contrast, while colors adjacent to each other blend more harmoniously.

Color combinations that blend well or are "harmonious" with blue include blue-violet-white, blue-mauve-violet, blue-pink-white, and blue-pink-violet. Those combinations that tend to contrast and highlight each other include blue-yellow, blue-orange, blue-red, blue-pink-yellow, and blue-violet-yellow. These combinations may consist of flowers only or flowers plus foliage color.

One concept for blending colors is to form a "triad" of colors equally spaced around the color wheel. If you start with the blue-green found

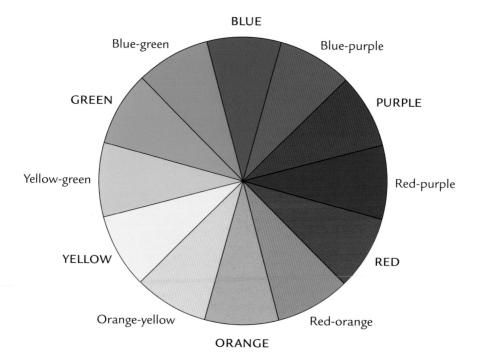

in many attractive foliage plants, the combination would be blue-green, blue-purple, and red-purple.

The classic herbaceous flower border schemes tend to blend flowers from warm to cool colors. The warm colors (red, orange, and yellow) tend to be a more dominant presence in the garden and these need to be blended together. Blue and violet are cool colors and need a contrast to make a bold statement. White and gray are considered achromatic (without color), but they can bring out the vibrant color in blue. Deep blue flowers work well with white flowers or with plants having silver-green foliage. Pale yellow flowers also combine well with "true blue" flowers. Silvery blue foliage like that found in rue (*Ruta graveolens*) or certain *Hosta* species can repeat or "echo" the blue found in flowers. Repeating images or colors is a wonderful garden technique to provide harmony to a design and set up focal points.

The perception of blue as a color can be affected by the quality of light (shade versus full sun) as well as the other colors immediately associated with a blue flower. Strong primary colors like red or yellow can accentuate the intensity of the blue color. Flowers that are not "true blue" but have tints of purple or red are not as noteworthy in the garden as individual plants, but they tend to be easier to combine with other colors in the mixed flower border. Here again, associated flower colors can accentuate the blueness of the flower or bring out its redder shades. I find that purple-blue or red-blue flowers mix well with flowers of other primary colors. For instance, *Campanula glomerata* 'Superba' has a purple-blue flower that to me appears bluer in the presence of the bright yellow flowers of *Lysimachia punctata*.

Blue is also an emotional color in our culture. Everyone recognizes the feelings associated with having the "blues." Blue color in the garden also can be evocative. Viewing a mass, naturalized planting of *Chionodoxa* blooming in spring among the yellow, early blooming individuals of *Corylopsis* evokes a tranquil feeling, while coming upon a *Meconopsis* species blooming in front of a red *Rhododendron* species calls forth sudden elation.

In many cases, blue in the garden is subtler than the bright yellows and reds. This unevenness in intensity requires closer inspection, but also can provide for some interesting patterns and color combinations. I enjoy photographing blue flowers in different ways. Many times, blue flowers have a lighter center that provides movement to the image. This movement can be accentuated with the camera. It is easy to follow in the graceful petals of *Chionodoxa* species. The tiny flowers of *Hedyotis* (bluets) species, when viewed close up with the camera, can appear to repeat each other in a cloud of color.

Meconopsis betonicifolia (Himalayan blue poppy)

Anchusa azurea 'Dropmore' (Italian alkanet)

What Is in a Name?

The "name game" can be very interesting to the professional botanist and increasingly frustrating to the gardener. In defense of the taxonomist who may suggest a new name for a familiar plant, we need to remember that many genera with large numbers of species may not have been thoroughly studied. Significant differences may become apparent to the professional observer that make splitting a genus into two or more genera sensible to follow a more natural order. In many cases, these studies have been long overdue and make garden associations among species more understandable. One example might be the separation of the evergreen, woody members of *Hebe* from the larger genus *Veronica*.

I find more frustrating the odd time when an older genus name is used. Under the standards for nomenclature for cultivated plants, the first name published for a particular species after 1753 (the publication date for Carl Linnaeus's landmark book—*Species Plantarum*) should be the accepted name. This Rule of First Priority makes sense but is subject to the exception of conserved names. Under this exception, about 400 species retained the name by which they were known in the nineteenth century because they were so well known, regardless of the priority of publication. I think the new millennium may be the right time to declare the conservation of current names for those plants common in commerce. It does not make commercial sense for a well-known plant to change names because of an obscure prior publication. Germane to our discussion are changes like renaming Virginia blue-bells from *Mertensia virginica* to *M. pulmonariodes* or the genus *Coleus* to *Solenostemon*. This type of nomenclatural change serves only to confuse the gardener searching for plants from commercial sources. In the current work, I have tried to cross-reference the names of genera and species used most often in commerce with the current acceptable botanical names. I realize this can be confusing, but often the only recourse a gardener has is to associate a name in a catalog with one found in more scholarly references.

When botanists want to describe a species as blue, they use a number of Latin descriptors including derivations of *caerulea, coerulea, cyanea,* or *azurea*. Some feel so strong about describing the blue color accurately that they resort to combinations like *purpureocaeruleum*. It also becomes apparent when compiling a list of plants with blue flowers that horticulturists have run out of novel names for cultivars. At least 12 species include 'Blue Bird' as a cultivar name for blue-flowering selections. I am not sure if this reflects some common feature inherent in these cultivars, or if this is simply a name with good sales appeal. Next most popular is 'Blue Star' found in at least 11 species and 'Heavenly Blue' with 10 citations. 'Sky Blue' is used in 8 species and 'Sapphire' in 7. This naming phenomenon suggests that blue is a special color.

Blue is the color most often sought after if it does not normally occur in a species. Hybridizers are trying to engineer blue roses and to breed deeper blues in geranium. Of course with carnation, breeding is not necessary; soaking the cut flowering stems in blue food coloring achieves what nature cannot. I just hope blue remains unavailable in daylilies!

Mertensia primuloides

Family Relationships

Relative to other flower colors, blue is not widespread throughout plant families. In this book only 44 families are represented with blue-flowering species. In some cases, it is possible to place a species into its family based on the shade of blue color in the flower. For instance, members of the Boraginaceae (borage family) frequently have pink flower buds that open into blue flowers, while members of the Solanaceae (nightshade or potato family) tend to produce blue flowers with a purple tint.

The genera included in this book are listed by family. It becomes obvious how some families dominate the ornamental species grown for their blue flowers.

Acanthaceae
    Thunbergia
Amaryllidaceae
    Worsleya
Apiaceae
    Eryngium

    Trachymene
Apocynaceae
    Amsonia
    Vinca
Asclepiadaceae
    Oxypetalum

Asteraceae
    Ageratum
    Aster
    Brachycome
    Catananche
    Centaurea

Asteraceae, cont.
   Cichorium
   Cynara
   Echinops
   Felicia
   Senecio
   Stokesia
Boraginaceae
   Anchusa
   Borago
   Brunnera
   Buglossoides
   Cynoglossum
   Echium
   Lindelofia
   Lithodora
   Mertensia
   Moltkia
   Myosotis
   Omphalodes
   Pentaglottis
   Pulmonaria
   Symphytum
Brassicaceae
   Heliophila
Bromeliaceae
   Aechmea
   Tillandsia
Campanulaceae
   Adenophora
   Campanula
   Codonopsis
   Laurentia
   Lobelia

   Phyteuma
   Platycodon
   Trachelium
   Wahlenbergia
Commelinaceae
   Cochliostema
   Commelina
   Dichorisandra
   Tradescantia
Convolvulaceae
   Convolvulus
   Evolvulus
   Ipomoea
Dipsacaceae
   Scabiosa
Fabaceae
   Baptisia
   Clitoria
   Lathyrus
   Lupinus
   Sophora
   Wisteria
Fumariaceae
   Corydalis
Gentianaceae
   Eustoma
   Exacum
   Gentiana
Geraniaceae
   Geranium
Gesneriaceae
   Achimenes
   Ramonda
   Saintpaulia

   Streptocarpus
Globulariaceae
   Globularia
Goodeniaceae
   Scaevola
Hydrophyllaceae
   Nemophila
   Phacelia
Iridaceae
   Babiana
   Crocus
   Gladiolus
   Iris
   Neomarica
   Patersonia
   Sisyrinchium
Lamiaceae
   Agastache
   Ajuga
   Coleus
   Hyssopus
   Lavandula
   Meehania
   Nepeta
   Perovskia
   Plectranthus
   Rosmarinus
   Salvia
   Teucrium
Liliaceae
   Agapanthus
   Allium
   Camassia
   Chionodoxa

Hyacinthoides
Hyacinthus
Ipheion
Muscari
Puschkinia
Scilla
Tecophilaea
Tricyrtis
Triteleia
Linaceae
 Linum
Loganiaceae
 Buddleia
Malvaceae
 Hibiscus
 Malva
Nolanaceae
 Nolana
Nymphaeaceae
 Nymphaea
Papaveraceae
 Meconopsis
Passifloraceae
 Passiflora
Plumbaginaceae
 Ceratostigma

Limonium
Plumbago
Polemoniaceae
 Phlox
 Polemonium
Polygalaceae
 Polygala
Pontederiaceae
 Pontederia
Primulaceae
 Anagallis
 Primula
Ranunculaceae
 Aconitum
 Anemone
 Aquilegia
 Clematis
 Delphinium
 Hepatica
 Nigella
Rhamnaceae
 Ceanothus
Rubiaceae
 Hedyotis
Saxifragaceae
 Hydrangea

Scrophulariaceae
 Collinsia
 Hebe
 Nemesia
 Otacanthus
 Parahebe
 Torenia
 Veronica
 Wulfenia
Solanaceae
 Browallia
 Brunfelsia
 Iochroma
 Nierembergia
 Petunia
 Salpiglossis
 Solanum
Verbenaceae
 Caryopteris
 Clerodendrum
 Duranta
 Petrea
 Verbena
 Vitex
Violaceae
 Viola

Delphinium 'Summer Skies'

Technical Aspects of Blue as a Flower Color

The diversity of flower colors found in plants is probably an adaptation that signals or attracts pollinators. Flower color is the result of the accumulation of chemicals called flavonoids in cells of the flower. The flavonoid pigments most responsible for flower color are known as **anthocyanins**. The term is derived from the Greek words for "flower" and "dark blue." The pigments that appear red, pink, purple, and blue in flowers are usually anthocyanins. Other pigments besides anthocyanins occur in flowers. Yellow, for example, comes from a different pigment (usually a carotenoid).

Technically, anthocyanins are made by adding a sugar (usually glucose) to a group of compounds called **anthocyanidins** and derived from the flavonoid biosynthesis pathway. What makes anthocyanidins interesting is that they are named for the plants where they were first discovered and so their names are familiar to almost all gardeners. The most common of these compounds was first found in bachelor button (*Centaurea cyanus*) and is called **cyanidin**. It has a crimson-red color. Other common anthocyanidins include the scarlet **pelargonidin** (from geranium, *Pelargonium*); the rosy red **peonidin** (from peony, *Paeonia*); the purple **petunidin** (from *Petunia*); and the blue-violet **delphinidin** (from larkspur, *Delphinium*). Anthocyanidins are unstable in the plant until they are converted to the many (hundreds of) anthocyanins found in different species of plants.

Combinations of anthocyanins in petals provide an almost endless array of red through blue color tones. Factors that impact the type of anthocyanin produced or the amount of anthocyanin will influence the color of the flower. Environmental stress, plant nutrition, and even insect attack can modify anthocyanin production. A good example is the intensity of color often associated with plants exposed to a chilling temperature. Anthocyanins also explain why some plants grown in climates with cool summer nights can show more intense color compared with the same cultivars grown in warmer areas where flower color can be duller.

Additional factors can influence the intensity of flower color. These include co-pigmentation, the shape of petal cells, and changes in vacuolar pH. When anthocyanins are accompanied by flavonols (yellow pigments) or flavonoids (colorless pigments), they present another range of colors in a process known as co-pigmentation. Co-pigmentation tends to shift the color into the blue range. It not only affects the way we see flower color but can change the way a pollinator sees a flower. Flavonols and flavonoids have strong ultraviolet absorption that is perceived by insects. It is important to recognize that insects see color different from human vision. To a bee, red flowers do not appear pigmented, while white or yellow flowers can appear light blue. White flowers that also contain flavonols appear creamier to us, but are dark blue to insect pollinators.

The impact of petal cell shape on flower color is just beginning to be understood. Cell shape on the surface of the petal influences optical properties of the cell and changes the way a color is seen. Conical cell shape gives higher light absorption and a velvety sheen to the flower. Flat cells give a duller color.

Anthocyanins are stored in the vacuole of the cells in a petal. The pH of the vacuole strongly influences the pigmentation of the petals. Some individual flowers change color as they age or develop, which may signal prospective pollinators that the flower is fertilized already and no longer has any nectar. In larkspur (*Delphinium*), this color change is caused by a change of pH in the cell's vacuole. In general, higher pH (more alkaline) causes a shift to blue coloration. In the case of larkspur, an increase in pH changes the pigment from red-purple to purplish blue. This change in cellular pH can be very important in controlling blue color pigmentation. For example, blue flower color was not available in pansies until plant breeders were able to modify the cellular pH of the plants. Red pansies have a pH in their vacuoles that is under 5. Blue pansies are the result of increasing the pH to just over 6.

A change in flower color is a characteristic feature of members in the Boraginaceae (borage family). These plants have predominantly blue flowers; however, in the same flower cluster, one or more flowers may be pink. Blue and pink flowers on the same plant! Actually these flowers change from pink to vivid blue as the flowers become older. Although this feature is unique to this family, it shows how closely related blue and pink pigments are in plants. Plants in the borage family with blue

Blue and pink flowers of *Borago officinalis* (common borage)

flowers include borage (*Borago officinalis*), Virginia bluebells (*Mertensia virginiana*), and forget-me-nots (*Myosotis sylvatica*).

Another plant with flowers that range from shades of pink to blue is *Hydrangea macrophylla*. Depending on the garden location, plants might be pale pink to azure blue. Growers observed this phenomenon as early as the late eighteenth century, although the cause was unknown at that time. In general, plants grown in acidic soil have blue flowers, and those grown in neutral or alkaline soils have pink. This fact seems contradictory to the previous discussion on the influence of vacuolar pH on flower color, where an alkaline cell pH shifted petals into the blue color range. It is understood now that the major factor associated with deeper shades of blue hydrangeas is the availability of aluminum ions in the soil. Acid soil (between pH 5 and 6) has an increased availability of aluminum that can be taken up by the plant roots. It is the association of this metal ion with the anthocyanin pigment that leads to the blue coloration.

Scientists believe that if they understand the flower color biosynthetic pathway, they will be able to bioengineer plants with new flower

Blue florets of *Hydrangea macrophylla* (florist's hydrangea)

colors not available in some species. For years, plant breeders have been able to incorporate a diversity of flower colors into plants based on the genetic diversity for color found in that genus. This principle is nicely shown in the range of colors offered by petunias and impatiens. Biotechnology may extend the natural range of flower color for several popular plants lacking the natural genetic diversity for novel colors.

The objectives of commercial efforts to use biotechnology to engineer flower color are threefold: to add new colors to a species where that color does not exist (for example, the attempt to create a blue rose), to intensify colors that are already present in elite plants (for example, in roses and chrysanthemum; see below for examples), and to produce unique color patterns in flowers (for example, pinwheels in petunia). The three major crops being targeted by genetic engineering for commercial flower color modification are rose, chrysanthemum, and carnation; however, flower color also has been modified successfully in petunia, gerbera, eustoma, and geranium. One good example of successful bioengineering for flower color has occurred with petunia. In this case, a gene for production of the anthocyanidin pelargonidin (scarlet pigment) from corn was introduced into petunia to create a novel orange flower color not previously available in petunia.

Creating blue flowers in species that do not normally produce blue pigments will prove to be difficult. Evidence suggests that many species without blue flowers lack the ability to make the anthocyanidin delphinidin. Using biotechnology, it should be possible to insert the gene for the key enzyme in delphinidin production into these species. The gene for delphinidin (blue-violet pigment) has been engineered into carnation to begin to extend its color range into the blue area; however, additional information on how the cell controls the subtle interplay between co-pigmentation and vacuolar pH is necessary before species like rose and chrysanthemum can be modified to include blue pigmentation.

Crocus speciosus (showy crocus) mass planting

Use of Blue Flowers in the Garden

I enjoy many different kinds of gardens. Talk to me today and I might be enamored with alpine gardens, tomorrow, the stoic elegance of a Japanese tea garden. I am garden fickle, and since I am writing this section in winter, my immediate response for a favorite use of blue flowers in the garden is for early spring blooms. Several species with blue flowers can naturalize to form impressive blue carpets of flowers, especially in the spring. This feature is not restricted to blue-flowering plants, but it does seem that many of the best species for naturalizing are also blue flowering. Plants that are exceptional at this include the small, spring-flowering bulbs like *Chionodoxa*, *Muscari*, *Puschkinia*, and *Scilla*. Thoughts of the bright blue drifts these species can make under the high shade of large trees can help a gardener make it through a long winter. Other blue-flowering species with the colonizing spirit belong to the genera *Camassia*, *Collinsia*, *Delphinium*, *Endymion*, *Lupinus*, *Mertensia*, *Myosotis*, *Phlox*, and *Viola*. Wow! The mass flowering of blue Texas bluebonnet (*Lupinus texensis*) combined with the red-flowering Indian paintbrush (*Castilleja*) has created a thriving tourist industry for areas of Texas.

Perennial bed featuring *Veronica australis* subsp. *teucrium* 'Kapitan' (Hungarian speedwell), Allan Bloom's Dell garden, Bressingham, England

Muscari (grape hyacinth) and *Buxus* (boxwood) species in formal garden,
King's Garden, Het Loo Palace, Apeldoorn, The Netherlands

Myosotis (forget-me-nots) in a rock garden planting,
in Fayette County, Kentucky.

Spring is not the only time when blue-flowering plants can have mass appeal. A naturalized swath of showy crocus (*Crocus speciosus*) suddenly appearing in the early autumn from a tired summer lawn is a delight. Planning for these kinds of grand garden features requires patience, but what a lovely gift to leave your grandchildren.

Most plants covered in this book are herbaceous perennials. Use of blue flowers has a long tradition in both formal and less formal perennial beds. Attempts have even been made to create theme gardens with only blue-flowering plants. These are no longer as fashionable as white theme gardens. Blue flowers tend to provide focal interest in the garden. They combine well with other primary colors to form areas in perennial beds with strong interest. Reds and blues are a favorite color combination for my garden. This combination is not meant to blend into the perennial border but rather to form bright focal points. In the part of the United States where I garden, it can be difficult to have an exclusively perennial garden that remains in color for the entire season. The hot summers can reduce flowering in many perennial plants. Especially vulnerable are the blue-flowering perennials that prosper in Europe or the Pacific Northwest but "melt" in the Midwest heat. In warmer regions gardeners must ask annual flowering plants to fill in and provide color in the summer border. Various evolvulus, lobelias, and sages (*Salvia*) can keep blue color in the summer garden.

A special relationship exists between the many diminutive species with blue flowers and rock gardens and alpine collections. The blue flower color is very well represented in the mountain meadows and streambeds that abound above tree line, especially in the Himalayan Mountains of Asia and the Rocky Mountains of North America. Many of these species can be difficult to grow, but are delightful where the environment is forgiving. I think the word *delightful* is the proper way to describe many of these plants. I particularly enjoy the smaller plants that flaunt their oversized flowers. Gentians, campanulas, and columbines (*Aquilegia*) are wonderful tucked in among the stones or peat blocks of a rock garden or rising above containers in the alpine house. I usually regret not budgeting enough time to completely explore the better rockeries in major botanic gardens.

Anemone coronaria De Caen strain (poppy anemone)

Blue Is for Flowers

Blue is not a common color in plant organs other than flowers. Our view of the world would be quite different if a segment of deciduous plants had brilliant blue-colored leaves included with the reds and yellow that dominate fall. Red as a fall color is the result of unmasking and intensifying anthocyanins as chlorophyll breaks down in the leaf. Since blue is one manifestation of anthocyanin pigments, I am not sure why it is not found in fall colors except that it may be related to the cellular pH in senescing leaves. It suggests that blue as a flower color has advantages for attracting pollinators that warranted its evolution in flowers.

Even so, some types of plants normally have bluish leaves. These can complement species with blue flowers by repeating their color in the garden. Blue foliage color is more common in certain plant groups than others. It is most common in conifers such as fir (*Abies*), juniper (*Juniperus*), cedar (*Cedrus*), and spruce (*Picea*); ornamental grasses such as fescue (*Festuca*) and oatgrass (*Helictotricon*); and desert species such as *Agave*, *Echeveria*, and *Euphorbia*. It is even found in perennials like hostas

and rue (*Ruta*). The blue coloring is not always due to additional anthocyanin pigmentation in the leaf. Rather, many of these plants have
a glaucous bloom made of waxes. This bloom provides a "cloudy window" over the leaf. When seen through this covering layer, the normal
green color of the leaf appears blue. This ecological adaptation helps
the leaf to reduce water loss in harsh environments.

Blue color also can appear in fruits. These are not as common and
have more subtle appeal than the boisterous claims of red or orange
fruits. My favorite choice in this category is the porcelain berry (*Ampelopsis brevipedunculata*). I first saw this plant trained in a zigzag pattern
atop a broad railing alongside descending steps at Dumbarton Oaks
Gardens of Georgetown, Washington, DC. This arrangement was a
wonderful way to "tame" this vine to provide close inspection of the
multicolored berries that appear in late summer into fall. Other plants

Helictotricon sempervirens

with ornamental blue fruit include barberry (*Berberis*), fringe tree (*Chionanthus*), *Clintonia, Clerodendrum, Juniperus,* privet (*Ligustrum*), Oregon grape (*Mahonia*), Solomon's seal (*Polygonatum*), skunk cabbage (*Symplocos*), *Vaccinium,* and arrowwood (*Viburnum*).

Cedrus atlantica 'Glauca Pendula'
(Atlas cedar)

Ampelopsis brevipedunculata
(porcelain berry)

Woodland area with *Phlox divaricata* (woodland phlox) and *Delphinium tricorne* (dwarf larkspur), Raven Run Nature Sanctuary, Lexington, Kentucky

Descriptions A–Z

Achimenes
Cupid's Bower
GESNERIACEAE

Achimenes is a group of tender, herbaceous perennials developing from an underground rhizome. These plants are grown for the large saucer-shaped flowers that are available in many bright colors including white, yellow, pink, red, purple, and blue. Cupid's bowers can be used as bedding plants for a shady location, but they are seen most often in containers or hanging baskets. They also make good greenhouse displays. Plants develop best in an organic soil that is moist but well drained; they must be well watered and not allowed to dry out. They prefer partial shade in the garden or bright, filtered light in the greenhouse. Plants go dormant in the autumn, and the small, scaly rhizomes can be overwintered just like the tubers of *Dahlia* in a cool, dry area. The genus name is a derivation of the Spanish word for "to suffer from the cold" and refers to the plant's aversion to cold weather.

Propagation: Plants are propagated by seed, division of the dormant rhizome, and leaf cuttings taken in the summer.

Representative species and cultivars: *Achimenes* is a genus of approximately 25 species native to Mexico and Central America. *Achimenes longiflora* with its long flower tubes and *A. patens* with shorter flower tubes have violet-blue flowers; however, *Achimenes* species are seldom cultivated. In most cases, *Achimenes* is represented by its large-flowered hybrids. These are commonly available as F_1 hybrid strains or as individual colors. Some are compact plants growing to 8 inches (25 cm) and suited for bedding out, while others are trailing plants that perform better in hanging baskets. Cultivars with blue flowers include 'Paul Arnold' with deep purple-blue flowers and 'Gloria' with violet-blue flowers. The Palette mixture has white, red, blue, and violet flowers.

Aconitum
Monkshood
RANUNCULACEAE

Monkshoods are hardy, herbaceous perennials that provide a tall-flowering feature to the late summer and early fall perennial bed. Plants can reach 5 feet (1.5 m) tall with a terminal flower spike that contains unique individual flowers. The showy pigmented sepals form a "hood," creating a flower resembling a monk's hood. Monkshood is used as an upright-flowering feature in the perennial garden, where it grows 2 to 6 feet (60 cm to 2 m) tall. It is a popular commercial cut flower used to decorate fall dried flower arrangements. Plants prefer light shade and a well-drained, organic soil. Taller plants may need staking. Monkshoods do not tolerate transplanting and should be planted in a permanent location if possible. They do best where summer nights are cool. The genus name is the ancient Greek name for the species and may be derived from the Greek word for "a dart," alluding to the use of the plant in making arrow poison. Monkshood was recognized since early times for its toxic and potentially medicinal properties. All parts of the plant are poisonous, especially the root. An older common name for monkshood is wolf's bane, possibly because arrows dipped in the poison of these plants were used to hunt wolves. *Aconitum napellus* is the commercial source of the heart medication called aconite.

Propagation: Plants are propagated by seed or division. Seed germination is improved by cold moist stratification at 41°F (5°C) for 6 weeks. Most cultivars are propagated by division of the dormant tuberous root.

Representative species and cultivars: The approximately 100 species of *Aconitum* are native to temperate areas of Asia, Europe, and North America. Two species are commonly cultivated along with hybrids mainly from crosses with *A. napellus* and *A. variegatum*.

Aconitum ×bicolor (bicolor monkshood; synonym *A. ×cammarum* 'Bicolor') is probably of hybrid origin with *A. napellus* as one parent. Plants grow 4 feet (1.2 m) tall and bloom in late summer. They have appealing blue and white flowers. 'Bressingham Spire' is a compact plant growing to 3 feet (1 m) tall with violet-blue flowers. 'Newry Blue' is a seed-produced cultivar reaching 3 to 4 feet (1 to 1.2 m) tall with deep blue flowers.

Aconitum carmichaelii (azure monkshood) is a native of Russia and China and produces large flower spikes in early fall that can be 12 inches (30 cm) long. Plants can grow 4 to 5 feet (1.2 to 1.5 m) tall. 'Arendsii' (possibly a hybrid) has deep purple-blue flowers, and 'Barker's Variety' has violet-blue flowers.

Aconitum henryi is native to western China. It can grow to 5 feet (1.5 m) tall and produces dark purple-blue flowers in late summer and early

Aconitum ×bicolor (bicolor monkshood)

fall. It is a good companion of *A. napellus* to continue bloom into fall. 'Sparks' (synonym 'Spark's Variety') is a violet-blue selection.

Aconitum napellus (common monkshood) is from northern Europe and blooms in late summer. Plants are 4 feet (1.2 m) tall with indigo blue flowers.

Aconitum wilsonii, from China, grows more than 5 feet (1.5 m) tall and produces purple-blue flowers in early fall. It probably is a subspecies of *A. carmichaelii.*

Adenophora
Ladybells
CAMPANULACEAE

Adenophora is a group of hardy, herbaceous perennials closely allied to *Campanula*. Plants display similar nodding, bell-shaped flowers that can be blue or lavender-blue in color. The major distinction between these genera is a disk at the base of the protruding style (female part) in *Adenophora*. Ladybells are useful in mixed perennial borders to provide flower interest in summer. Smaller species can be used in the rock garden. Plants prefer full sun or partial shade and a moist, well-drained soil with some organic matter. They can spread aggressively in the garden. The genus name is Greek for "having glands" and refers to the nectaries in the flower.

Propagation: Plants are usually propagated from seed. Because they have fleshy roots, plants are difficult to transplant or divide.

Representative species and cultivars: The approximately 40 species of *Adenophora* are native to northern regions of Europe and Asia. In general, these very winter hardy plants are long-lived in the garden. Blue is the dominant flower color in this genus.

Adenophora bulleyana is native to western China and forms upright, 3- to 4-foot (1- to 1.2-m) tall plants. Pale blue to purple-blue flowers appear in summer on upright spikes (racemes). The nodding, bell-shaped flowers can occur in small groups at each node in the spike.

Adenophora confusa (Reginald Farrer's ladybells) is among the better ladybells for the garden. The common name sometimes applied to this species honors the famous plant hunter who collected the plant in western China. This species is similar to *A. bulleyana,* but shorter, growing less than 3 feet (1 m) tall. Flower color is blue, and flowers last a long time in the garden. The species name is appropriate, as *A. confusa* is sold interchangeably with *A. bulleyana* in garden catalogs.

Adenophora liliifolia is from Siberia and grows to about 2 feet (60 cm) tall. It is very winter hardy, but also tolerates the heat of southern gardens. It is a good choice where other bellflowers (*Campanula* spp.) fail because of hot weather. Flower color is pale blue, and flowers are fragrant.

Adenophora potaninii is another western China native. It produces blue bell-shaped flowers that are fairly open at the tips. It can grow more than 3 feet (1 m) tall and spreads rapidly.

Adenophora stricta (synonym *A. aurita*) is from Japan and China. It is late flowering with lavender-blue flowers produced in abundance. Plants grow about 3 feet (1 m) tall.

Adenophora takedae is also from Japan and produces blue flowers on short 1-foot (30-cm) tall plants. It blooms in late summer and has a white form.

Aechmea

BROMELIACEAE

Aechmea is the most popular member of the bromeliad family used as an ornamental. It consists of unique plants that grow as epiphytes in treetops. They produce a rosette of thick, leathery leaves that retains water in the central "cup" formed by the leaves. The leaves are very ornamental: they are often pigmented or striped and can be toothed along the leaf margin. From the center of the rosette, a flowering spike emerges that carries many tiny flowers. The flower spike can be very attractive and long lasting. The bright colors on the flower spike may be due to showy bracts, petals, or persistent fruit. Colors include pink, red, yellow, and blue. After flowering, the rosette usually dies and several offshoots called "pups" take its place. Aechmeas are tropical plants usually grown in a warm greenhouse or indoor location. They also can be used outdoors as bedding plants or located in trees as epiphytes during frost-free times of the year. They are easy to grow if given bright light and a moist, well-drained potting medium similar to an orchid mix. Where appropriate, the central cup should be kept full of water. Plants also need minimal fertilization during the growing season. The genus name is derived from the Greek word for "spear tip" or "a point" and refers to the sharp tips of the sepals.

Propagation: Plants are multiplied by seeds or offshoots. The easiest method of propagation is to remove and root one of the offshoots or pups. Seed can be sown as soon as the fruit is mature. The fruit surrounding the seed should be removed before sowing.

Representative species and cultivars: *Aechmea* is native to South and Central America and constitutes about 200 species. Most of the cultivated species originated from Brazil and were introduced in the early nineteenth century. They were selected for their showy leaves and bright, usually pink-, yellow-, or red-flowering and fruiting spikes. Sev-

Aechmea fasiata (urn plant, vase plant)

eral species have blue flowers, which, although small, emerge from the bright bracts to provide interesting color.

Aechmea distichantha is a native of Brazil and Argentina. It produces narrow, straplike leaves that can reach 3 feet (1 m) long. The flowers are arranged pyramidally with pink bracts from which emerge violet-blue flowers. *Aechmea distichantha* f. *glaziovii* grows naturally at higher elevations than the species, is a smaller plant only reaching about 1 foot (30 cm) tall, and produces flowers that are a brighter blue.

Aechmea fasciata (urn plant, vase plant; synonym *Billbergia rhodocyanea*) is a commonly cultivated aechmea from Brazil that was introduced around 1825. The 2-foot (60-cm) tall plants are prized for the colorful green leaves crossed with silver. The blue flowers are embedded in the showy pink bracts on a densely packed flower stem. The common names refer to the overall shape of the plant.

Aechmea fendleri was named for Andre Fendler who collected it in Venezuela in 1956. Plants can reach 3 feet (1 m) tall and produce showy violet-blue petals against pink bracts that are held on a 1-foot (30-cm) tall branched inflorescence.

Aechmea miniata var. *discolor* is another Brazilian native. It produces blue flowers that open above 2-foot (60-cm) tall plants. The key ornamental feature of this plant is the red fruit that persists for several months.

Aechmea phanerophlebia is a distinctive bromeliad with lower leaves that droop and upper leaves that are closely gathered together. It is a native of Brazil and reaches about 3 feet (1 m) tall. The cylindrical flower spike is held high above the foliage and has blue flowers that emerge from showy rose-pink bracts.

Agapanthus
Blue African Lily
LILIACEAE

African lilies are tender perennials producing blue flowers in rounded umbels that rise several feet above fleshy, straplike leaves. They are commonly grown as container plants. In milder climates, they are also

used in the perennial bed or are grown for cut flowers. Plants complement architectural features and bloom most of the summer if grown
properly. It is common to see large containers dressed with African
lilies around formal water features. Large containers are recommended
to allow development of the fleshy tuberous roots. African lilies require
full sun, and the growing medium should be well drained, but not allowed to dry out. Plants do not tolerate winter temperatures below
10°F (−12°C). They can be overwintered in cool conditions, where they
go dormant when the amount of water in the container medium is reduced. The genus name is Greek for "love flower."

Propagation: Plants are easily propagated by seeds, and volunteer seedlings appear in the garden. These seedlings, however, do not come true
to type for cultivars, which must be propagated by division of the fleshy
root in the early spring before growth resumes.

Representative species and cultivars: At one time *Agapanthus* was
thought to be a variable genus. Today, it constitutes 10 species native to
Africa. Hybrid selections of African lily are more commonly cultivated

Agapanthus Headbourne hybrids (blue African lily)

than the species. Many of these have bright blue flower color, but flowers also may be white or shades of purple. The most popular selections are the Headbourne hybrids, a group popular partly for their violet to pale blue flower color but also because they are the hardiest of the African lilies. 'Baby Blue', a hybrid selected in New Zealand, is a compact 2-foot (60-cm) tall plant with pale blue flowers. 'Blue Giant' produces a large, rounded flower cluster on 4-foot (1.2-m) tall plants. 'Midnight Blue' has a very deep blue flowers and is more winter hardy, surviving temperatures to 0°F (−18°C). 'Pinocchio' has deep violet-blue flowers.

Agapanthus africanus (African lily) is native to South Africa and has been cultivated in Europe since 1679. It bears deep blue flowers starting in late summer. Plants grow 2 to 3 feet (60 cm to 1 m) tall and are evergreen in frost-free climates. 'Peter Pan' is a compact selection only reaching 1.5 feet (45 cm) tall; it is better suited for bedding out than the taller species and hybrids.

Agapanthus inapertus var. *hollandii* is native to South Africa and differs from the other *Agapanthus* species described here because it produces nodding flowers in a round umbel. Plants reach 3 feet (1 m) tall, and seedling plants produce blue or white flowers.

Agapanthus praecox (synonym *A. orientalis*) is also from South Africa, but is late blooming. It grows 2 feet (60 cm) tall and has white and blue selections.

Agastache
Giant Hyssop
LAMIACEAE

Agastache species are interesting herbaceous perennials gaining in popularity due to cultivar introductions. Plants grow rapidly to form 2- to 3-foot (60-cm to 1-m) tall clumps topped in the summer and fall with terminal spikes of pink, purple, or blue flowers. Plants do best in full sun or light shade in well-drained soil and require very little special care other than division when they become crowded. These are not the showiest plants nor do they have the brightest blue flowers in the garden, but they are very good companions for a mixed perennial garden. The genus name is Greek for "many ears of wheat" and refers to the shape of the flowering spike.

Propagation: Plants are multiplied by seed, cuttings, or divisions. Seed is often used because plants flower the same season they are sown.

Representative species and cultivars: The approximately 30 species of *Agastache* are mostly native to eastern or western North America, but also Asia. Two species produce cultivars with blue flowers.

Agastache foeniculum (anise hyssop) is the most commonly cultivated species. It produces a bushy, upright plant to 4 feet (1.2 m) tall. The leaves are aromatic and smell like anise, suggesting the common name. In summer, the plants are covered with terminal spikes of blue flowers emerging from showy violet bracts. 'Blue Fortune', 'Butterfly Delight', and 'Fragrant Delight' have pale blue flowers.

Agastache scrophulariifolia (purple giant hyssop) is a large perennial growing to 4 feet (1.2 m) tall. Flower color is usually purple, but 'Liquorice Blue' has blue flowers and an anise fragrance to the foliage.

Ageratum
ASTERACEAE

Ageratum species are mostly herbaceous annual and perennial plants. Flower heads consist of many small florets, making the flower look like a fuzzy button. Flower color is light blue, pink, or white. One species has become a popular edging plant in the front of the annual border. Plants prefer full sun, but tolerate light shade and need a relatively fertile soil that is moist, but well drained. They are among the easiest bedding plants to grow The taller selections make excellent long-lasting cut flowers. The genus name comes from the Greek word for "long lasting" and refers to the persistent flowers.

Propagation: Plants are multiplied by seed or cutting. Seed propagation is the most common method for commercial growers, but stem cuttings root easily as well.

Representative species and cultivars: The approximately 60 species of *Ageratum* are native to North or South America. The most commonly cultivated species is *A. houstonianum,* which is represented by numerous cultivars and hybrids. *Ageratum houstonianum* (floss flower) is a herbaceous annual native to Mexico. It has been extensively selected for compact, well-branched plants with good garden performance. They are usually 6 to 12 inches (15 to 30 cm) tall and used as a common edging plant for annual beds. Flower color is white, pink, and various shades of blue. Representative blue-flowering F_1 hybrids include 'Blue Blazer', pale blue flowers; 'Blue Danube', lavender-blue flowers; 'Blue Horizon', purple-blue flowers; 'Blue Lagoon', bright mid-blue flowers, heat resistant; 'Hawaii Blue', mid-blue flowers; and 'Neptune Blue', pale blue flowers. Unlike the dwarf bedding plants, 'Cut Wonder' grows more than 2 feet (60 cm) tall and is excellent for cut flowers.

Ajuga
Bugleweed
LAMIACEAE

Bugleweed is a spreading plant used as a ground cover or in the foreground of perennial beds. Plants are usually less than 6 to 10 inches (15 to 25 cm) tall even in flower and spread rapidly by stolons either above or below the ground that can be very aggressive in the right conditions, sometimes competing with turf for a place in the lawn. Flowers usually occur in the spring on short spikes of blue, pink, or less commonly white blossoms. They are the typical two-lipped flowers found in the mint family. Some cultivars rebloom in summer. Plants bloom best in full sun, but they also grow well in partial shade. Cultivation is easy and plants prefer a moist soil. The origin of the genus name is not known.

Propagation: Plants are multiplied by seed and division. Seedlings tend to volunteer in the garden, but these plants spread naturally by stolons. Propagation is easiest from division of rooted stolons that can be separated from the main plant almost any time of year.

Representative species and cultivars: The more than 40 annual and perennial species of *Ajuga* are native to most temperate regions of the world. Of these, three species are commonly cultivated but even so, plant nomenclature can be confusing. Most selections have been made for unique foliage color or texture rather than blue flower color; however, bugleweed at peak bloom in late spring can carpet a large area with deep blue flowers.

Ajuga genevensis (blue bugleweed) is native to Europe and Asia. It is not as commonly known as *A. reptans,* but it is becoming popular because it does not spread as aggressively. It can reach 12 inches (30 cm) tall and bears large upright spikes of indigo blue flowers.

Ajuga reptans (common bugleweed)

Ajuga pyramidalis also has bright blue flowers on slow spreading plants. The most well-known cultivar, however, is 'Crispa' (synonym 'Metallica Crispa'), which is grown for its interesting crinkled foliage.

Ajuga reptans (common bugleweed) is the most widely available bugleweed. It reaches 6 inches (15 cm) tall and spreads rapidly from stolons. 'Catlin's Giant' has dark purple-green foliage and blue flowers; it is almost twice the size of the species. 'Bronze Beauty', 'Burgundy Glow', and 'Multicolor' have blue flowers, but are grown for their foliage. 'Bronze Beauty' has dark maroon foliage; 'Burgundy Glow' and 'Multicolor' produce multicolored leaves that include pink, bronze, and cream.

Allium
Flowering Onion
LILIACEAE

Allium may not be the first genus you think of when contemplating blue flowers, but several delightful species have blue flowers. In general, flowering onions make good additions to the bulb or perennial garden. Many produce bold flowers that attract considerable attention. Most produce flower clusters that are rounded or somewhat pointed atop long flower stems. Flower color can be white, yellow, shades of purple, or blue. Plant height ranges from creeping species less than 4 inches (10 cm) tall to giant plants more than 4 feet (1.2 m) tall during bloom. Flowering onions grow best in full sun in a well-drained, fertile soil. The foliage should be allowed to die back naturally to ensure next season's flowers. Most species develop from underground bulbs, but some spread by rhizomes. Bulbs should be divided and respaced as they become crowded. Species with a smaller growth habit are excellent rock garden plants. The genus name is the old Latin word for "garlic."

Propagation: Plants are multiplied by seed or bulb offsets. They can be raised easily from seed just like the common vegetable onion. Most flowering onion species are propagated by offsets from the bulb. Species that produce rhizomes are propagated by division.

Representative species and cultivars: The more than 500 species of *Allium* are distributed throughout the Northern Hemisphere and include common vegetables like onion, leek, and garlic. Several species are grown for their blue flowers. Although these are less commonly grown than the larger-flowered lavender and white types, they deserve to be more popular with gardeners.

Allium beesianum produces blue or white flowers in late summer on small 8-inch (20-cm) tall plants. It is native to China.

Allium caeruleum (synonym *A. azureum*) was introduced from Asia in 1830. It is a hardy perennial, developing from a bulb that grows to 2 feet (60 cm) tall. The rounded clusters of pale blue flowers appear in early summer.

Allium cyaneum is native to China and is a wonderful addition to the alpine or rock garden. It produces a prostrate plant only 6 inches (15 cm) tall. Numerous nodding, blue flowers cover the plant in summer. A selection with sky blue flowers is available. I first saw this

Allium cyaneum

species in the rock garden at the Denver Botanic Garden in Colorado. The flower shape is unmistakably that of a flowering onion, but the prostrate growth and blue flower color make this species an uncommon addition for the garden. It spreads by rhizomes.

Amsonia
Amsonia, Blue Star
APOCYNACEAE

Amsonia species are hardy, herbaceous perennial plants. Pale blue, star-shaped flowers appear in clusters in late spring and early summer. Plants form substantial clumps and are about 3 feet (1 m) tall. They can be used in mixed perennial borders and are equally at home in a less formal wildflower planting. They make an excellent background for shorter, summer-blooming annuals or perennials. The bright yellow fall color on some species can be a real bonus, adding interest in the fall garden. These easy-to-grow plants do well in full sun or partial shade. If overfertilized, they become "leggy." Every 3 or 4 years they need to be divided. The genus name commemorates the eighteenth-century American physician Charles Amson.

Propagation: Plants are multiplied by seed, cuttings, or divisions. In the home garden, plants are easily propagated by division in the spring before growth begins. Commercial growers use stem cuttings taken in the summer after the plants flower.

Representative species and cultivars: The 25 species of *Amsonia* are native to North America, Europe, and Japan. All the cultivated species are similar in appearance, but *A. tabernaemontana* is the most winter hardy and best suited for northern gardens. It is hardy to −40°F (−40°C), while the other species are hardy only to −20°F (−29°C). An excellent collection of *Amsonia* species can be found in garden settings at Louis Ginter's Garden in Richmond, Virginia.

Amsonia ciliata (blue star, blue milkweed, downy amsonia; synonym *A. angustifolia*) is native to the southeastern United States and produces pale blue flowers. The 2-foot (60-cm) tall plants tend to be stiff and upright in appearance.

Amsonia hubrichtii is similar to other *Amsonia* species, producing light sky blue flowers on 3-foot (1-m) tall plants. Native to the East Coast of North America, it is gaining popularity in the Southeast because it has the best yellow fall color.

Amsonia illustris is the tallest *Amsonia* species in cultivation, growing to more than 4 feet (1.2 m) tall. Otherwise it is similar in flower to the other species. It is also a North American native.

Amsonia jonesii is native to the mountains of the southwestern United States. It is a floriferous selection growing to around 3 feet (1 m) tall. Flowers are pale blue.

Amsonia orientalis (synonym *Rhazya orientalis*) is native to Turkey and Greece and resembles its North American relatives in plant habit

Amsonia tabernaemontana (willow amsonia)

and flowering. Plants grow to 3 feet (1 m) tall. This species is not cultivated as commonly as the other *Amsonia* species.

Amsonia tabernaemontana (willow amsonia, willow-leaved amsonia) has been the most commonly cultivated species. Native to eastern North America, it produces the pale blue flowers typical of the genus. It can form large clumps 2 to 3 feet (60 cm to 1 m) tall. *Amsonia tabernaemontana* var. *salicifolia* has a narrower leaf and is more commonly grown than the species. The species name commemorates James Tabernaemontanus, a sixteenth-century German physician and botanist. The common names allude to the shape of the leaf, which resembles a willow leaf.

Anagallis
Pimpernel
PRIMULACEAE

Pimpernels are a group of herbaceous annual and perennial plants growing to 1.5 feet tall (45 cm) with red or blue flowers. They are not as commonly cultivated as they once were, but make nice summer-blooming additions to the annual or perennial bed. Pimpernels also can be grown as greenhouse pot plants for seasonal interest. Plants require full sun for best flowering. They do best in a moist but well-drained soil with good fertility. The flowers are five-petaled, bright, and attractive, but if that is not enough to renew interest in these plants, then the names should reserve a place for those gardeners looking for special interest plants. The genus name comes from the Greek word "to make laugh" and refers to a use of the plant to relieve sadness. One common name for *Anagallis* is "poor man's weather glass," referring to the tendency for the flowers to close before an approaching storm.

Propagation: Plants are multiplied by seed, stem cuttings, or division. Seed propagation is most common for annual species. Cultivars are propagated from softwood stem cuttings.

Representative species and cultivars: The approximately 20 species of

Anagallis are native to Europe and Africa. The most commonly available species, *A. arvensis,* is usually a red-flowering plant and has escaped as a weed in parts of North America. Its two botanical varieties produce plants with deep blue flowers on low-growing plants: *A. arvensis* var. *caerulea* and *A. arvensis* var. *latifolia.*

Anagallis monellii (blue pimpernel)

Anagallis monellii (blue pimpernel) is a tender perennial with blue saucer-shaped flowers. It can be treated as an annual bedding plant. The intense blue color is not available in other sun-loving bedding plants and is becoming more common in display gardens. Plants are low growing to 6 inches (15 cm) tall and spreading. The trailing habit of this plant also makes it a good candidate for hanging baskets. 'Pacific Blue' and 'Skywalker' have abundant gentian blue flowers.

Anchusa
Alkanet, Italian Bugloss
BORAGINACEAE

This group of herbaceous annual and perennial plants has typical "forget-me-not" blue flowers produced in terminal, upright panicles. Most plants are short lived in the garden. They bloom in the late spring and early summer, but some can repeat bloom throughout the summer. They are a welcome blue-flowering addition to the early summer perennial border. Plant height ranges from 1 to 5 feet (30 cm to 1.5 m) tall depending on the cultivar. These plants flower best in full sun in a deep, well-drained soil. They respond to additional fertilizer, but can become lanky. Taller cultivars may require staking. The genus name comes from the Greek word for "paint on the skin" and refers to an Old World cosmetic made from this plant. The common name alkanet refers to the use of some species to produce a red dye. Bugloss is Greek for "ox tongue" and may refer to the appearance of the leaves.

Propagation: Plants are multiplied by seed, division, and root cuttings. Root cuttings are most common for taller cultivars.

Representative species and cultivars: The approximately 35 species of *Anchusa* are native to Europe, Asia, and Africa. Only a few are grown as ornamentals. Because their flowers are similar in appearance to those of *Brunnera* and *Pentaglottis, Anchusa* species are sometimes misrepresented in these genera.

Anchusa azurea (Italian alkanet, bugloss; synonym *A. italica*) and its cultivars are the most popular perennials in this genus. The species is native to southern Europe and northern Africa. The old garden favorite 'Dropmore' is the most readily available cultivar. It is a 4-foot (1.2-m) tall plant with hairy stems and deep amethyst blue flowers,

Anchusa capensis 'Blue Angel'

but may not be as good a garden plant as newer cultivars like 'Royal Blue' and 'Loddon Royalist' that produce deeper blue flowers on sturdier stems. 'Opal' is also an old cultivar with a plant habit similar to that of 'Dropmore', but with pale blue flowers. Cultivars of Italian alkanet combine well with Siberian iris of contrasting flower colors. 'Little John' and 'Blue Bird' are dwarf cultivars less than 2 feet (60 cm) tall; they do not require staking and work well in the front of the perennial border or as features in the rock garden.

Anchusa caespitosa is a mat-forming perennial only 4 inches (2.5 cm) tall. It is native to the mountains of Greece. Its blue flowers hug the ground during summer in the rock garden. This species is similar in appearance to *Lithodora* species.

Anchusa capensis is a smaller plant from South Africa. It is usually grown as an annual. Plants grow about 10 inches (25 cm) tall and have many terminal, blue flowers with a light center in summer. 'Blue Angel' and 'Blue Bird' are compact selections with light blue flowers; they are usually grown from seed.

Anemone

Windflower

RANUNCULACEAE

Windflowers are herbaceous perennial plants, many growing from an underground tuberous root. Flower color ranges from white to pink and shades of lavender-blue. The showy part of the flower is actually the sepals. Windflowers are a diverse group of plants ranging from 6 inches to 5 feet (15 cm to 1.5 m) tall. Various species are useful as rock garden plants, perennials, cut flowers, and greenhouse pot plants, or naturalized in a woodland garden. Plants bloom in the spring or fall depending on the species, but blue flowers are seen only in spring-flowering species. Winter-hardy species spread easily and should be divided only if crowding reduces blooming. Tender species should be grown as pot plants or lifted from the garden in fall and overwintered as dormant tuberous roots. Most species benefit from well-drained soil in full sun to partial shade. As expected, woodland species do best in an organic soil, while species native to rocky, mountain sites prefer a sandy, well-drained soil. The genus name comes from the Greek word for "the wind" and also suggests the common name windflower.

Propagation: Plants are multiplied by seed, division of the tuberous roots, or root cuttings, depending on the species. Seed germination can be erratic and is improved by chilling stratification prior to sowing. Autumn-flowering species are easy to propagate from root cuttings taken in the early spring before growth starts.

Representative species and cultivars: *Anemone* is a diverse genus containing more than 120 species native to northern latitudes throughout the world. Some are arctic or inhabit high mountain locations. Several species contain blue flowers. These include the hardy *A. blanda, A. nemorosa, A. obtusiloba, A. trullifolia,* and the tender *A. coronaria* hybrids.

Anemone blanda (Grecian windflower) is native to southern Europe, especially Turkey. Most garden centers offer it for fall planting as a dormant tuber along with tulips and daffodils. It produces a spread-

Anemone blanda (Grecian windflower)

ing plant less than 10 inches (25 cm) tall with large flowers that appear above the foliage in early spring. Plants are winter hardy to −20°F (−29°C). They are often sold in mixed flower colors that include white, pink, violet, and blue. Blue-flowering selections like 'Blue Shades', 'Blue Star', and the deep blue 'Ingramii' are also available. Grecian windflower is an excellent choice for the rock garden or naturalized with other bulbs.

Anemone coronaria (poppy anemone) hybrids are not hardy in northern gardens, but can be planted in the fall in milder southern locations. They are native to the Mediterranean area, but only cultivars or seed-grown strains are planted in gardens. The large-flowering cultivars are showstoppers in the spring garden. Plants reach 18 inches (46 cm) tall, with large, single or double flowers that can be 3 inches (7.5 cm) in diameter. Flower colors are available in shades of white, pink, red, and blue. Most gardeners treat these as annuals, replacing them each year as flower production can decline after the first year. The De Caen strain produces large, single flowers on long stems in vibrant red, rose, white, and blue. 'Blue Poppy' is the De Caen selection with violet-blue flowers. The St. Brigid strain, called peony-flowered anemones, is semi-double flowering and available in the same color range as the De Caen strain. 'The Admiral' is a good violet-blue selection from the St. Brigid strain.

Anemone nemorosa (European windflower) is available, but not as common in U.S. gardens as other windflowers. It is well worth trying if you can find it in specialty catalogs. Native to European mountain slopes, it produces pink, white, or blue star-shaped flowers in early spring above compact 6-inch (15-cm) tall plants. European windflower works well in the rock garden or for naturalizing. White-flowering cultivars are more readily available, but 'Blue Beauty', 'Blue Bonnet', and 'Royal Blue' have blue flowers. 'Bowles' Purple' has purple-blue flowers. 'Bracteata Pleniflora' is not a blue cultivar, but is a remarkable plant in flower, producing white flowers subtended by several layers of frilly, white and green bracts.

Anemone obtusiloba and *A. trullifolia* are not commonly available, but both are well suited for the front of the perennial border or the rock garden. Native to the Himalayan mountains, they remind me of plants from the closely related genus *Hepatica*, but the flowers are held above the foliage on longer stems. They produce dainty, solitary yellow, white, or blue flowers above rounded plants in the spring. *Anemone obtusiloba* is about 2 inches (5 cm) tall, while *A. trullifolia* grows to 6 inches (15 cm) tall.

Aquilegia
Columbine
RANUNCULACEAE

Columbines are popular plants for perennial beds, naturalizing, and rock gardens. The flowers are recognizable for their unique structure: five spreading sepals form the pigmented face of the flower, while the petals form the center and projecting spurs behind the flower. The white, red, blue, yellow, or bicolored flowers are held singly or in panicles usually high above the foliage. Depending on the species, plants can be between 1 and 3 feet (30 cm and 1 m) tall. Columbines make elegant garden plants, blooming in late spring and early summer. They prefer full sun to light shade in a moist, well-drained, organic soil. Although they are perennial, plants can be short lived. Most cultivars self-sow in the garden but may not be true to type. The genus name is derived from the Latin word for "eagle" and refers to the unique flower shape.

Propagation: Plants are multiplied by seed or division. The most common form of propagation is by seed, which benefits from chilling stratification. Most cultivars are offered as strains or mixtures. Double-flowering forms require isolation during pollination for seeds to provide a high percentage of double-flowering seedlings.

Representative species and cultivars: *Aquilegia* has a wide distribution in northern temperate areas. Many of the more than 60 species come from mountainous areas. Several blue-flowering species and hybrids are available.

Aquilegia alpina (alpine columbine) is native to the Swiss Alps. It produces nodding, blue flowers that are not as large as the hybrid cultivars, but are abundant on compact, 18-inch (46-cm) tall plants. Unfortunately, this fine garden perennial is often overlooked for the larger-flowered hybrids.

Aquilegia caerulea (Rocky Mountains columbine) is familiar to anyone who has hiked in the western mountains of the United States. Large flowers with blue sepals and white petals are borne on 2-foot (60-cm) tall plants. This species is usually considered a wildflower, but it makes a good garden perennial.

Aquilegia flabellata (fan columbine) is a wonderful, small plant from eastern Asia and Japan. *Aquilegia flabellata* var. *pumila* is the form grown most often and produces nodding white or blue-purple flowers on small 8-inch (20-cm) tall plants. Fan columbine is suited for rock gardens or alpine dish gardens.

Aquilegia ×hybrida represents the many columbine hybrids, most of which are widely grown for home gardens. Columbines hybridize readily and many of the best columbines are offered as hybrids of *A. canadensis, A. longissima,* and *A. vulgaris.* Several common hybrids contain blue or blue and white flowers: Angel series ('Blue Angel'); Biedermeier mixture; McKana Giant mixture; Music series; Song Bird series ('Blue Bird' with light blue sepals and white petals, 'Blue Jay' with dark blue sepals and white petals, and 'Bunting' with light blue sepals and white petals); Mrs. Scott Elliott's strain; and Star series ('Blue Star'). All are robust plants, growing 20 to 30 inches (50 to 60 cm) tall and producing very large flowers. Columbines self-sow in the garden, but seedlings may not resemble the original hybrid parents depending on the proximity of other columbine species during pollination.

Aquilegia vulgaris (common columbine, granny's bonnet) is a European native characterized by shorter spurs than many of the other species, leading to the common name of granny's bonnet. Plants grow to 3 feet (1 m) tall and flower color can be white, pink, violet, or blue.

Aquilegia vulgaris (common columbine, double form)

Most often this species is represented in gardens by the double-flowering forms. The Barlow series includes fully double, nearly spurless flowers in pink, rose, white, and blue. 'Blue Barlow' has violet-blue flowers, and 'Christa Barlow' produces dark blue flowers with white edges.

Six other blue-flowering species are lesser known but available from specialty catalogs: *Aquilegia bertolonii,* a 4-inch (10-cm) tall dwarf from Europe; *A. discolor,* a 6-inch (15-cm) tall species from Spain with blue and white flowers; *A. jonesii,* the best-known western U.S. columbine after *A. caerulea,* with deep blue flowers that tip upwards; *A. ottonis,* a 1.5-foot (45-cm) tall species from Greece and Italy with pale blue and white flowers; *A. pyrenaica,* a 1-foot (30-cm) tall species from Europe with nodding flowers and short spurs; and *A. scopulorum,* a sky blue, large-flowering species from western North America.

Aster

ASTERACEAE

Asters are a group of mostly long-flowering perennial plants that bloom in late summer and fall. They are a prominent feature of the fall landscape. Plant habit varies from 6 inches to 8 feet (15 cm to 2.4 m) tall. All asters have the characteristic daisylike flowers typical of the family. Flower color is as variable as plant habit and includes various shades of white, red, lavender, and blue. Asters should be included in perennial borders for fall interest. Some species are prized as cut flowers. Cultivation of asters is fairly easy. They flower best in full sun in a well-drained soil that has moderate fertility. Larger species need staking for support and benefit from pinching in the spring and again in early summer to promote compact branching and to increase the number of flowers. Plants should be divided frequently as they become crowded. The genus name is derived from the Latin word for "star." In Greek mythology, Virgo scattered stardust over the earth and it became asters.

Propagation: Plants are multiplied by seed, division, or stem cuttings.

Cultivars are most easily propagated by division while plants are dormant or by stem cuttings during the growing season.

Representative species and cultivars: Depending on the reference consulted, the genus *Aster* includes between 250 and 600 species native to temperate areas throughout the world. Numerous species and cultivars have flowers that display various shades of blue.

Aster ×*alpellus,* a cross between *A. alpinus* and *A. amellus,* is represented by the cultivar 'Triumph' that produces purple-blue flowers on 2-foot (60-cm) tall plants.

Aster amellus (Italian aster) is native to Europe and western Russia. Abundant purple-blue ray florets are produced around yellow central disk florets. Plants grow between 1 and 2 feet (30 and 60 cm) tall and bloom from late summer into fall. 'Blue King' and 'King George' have been selected for flowers that are a paler blue than the species.

Aster diplostephioides is native to China and is an early summer blooming aster with large flowers composed of blue ray florets and orange-brown inner disk florets. Plants grow to 18 inches (46 cm) tall. This relatively underused aster deserves wider use in the perennial garden.

Aster ×*frikartii,* a cross between *A. amellus* and *A. thomsonii,* is a deservedly popular aster with several blue cultivars. 'Monch' has lavender-blue ray florets and 'Wonder of Staffa' produces light blue florets surrounding yellow disk florets. Both are long-blooming, summer cultivars on 2- to 3-foot (60-cm to 1-m) tall plants.

Aster novi-belgii (New York aster, Michaelmas daisy) is, as its first common

Aster ×*frikartii* 'Monch'

name implies, native to eastern North America. It is called Michaelmas daisy because it is in full bloom in Europe during St. Michael's
day on 29 September. Plants were introduced into England by Mark
Catesby in 1720, which left just enough time to select superior cultivars and make them popular garden plants before Pope Gregory
changed the Roman calendar to make St. Michael's day earlier in the
year—at aster time. This very popular fall-blooming aster has several
pale blue cultivars. Plant size ranges from 2 to 4 feet (60 cm to 1.2 m)
tall. 'Buxton's Blue', the most readily available of the blue cultivars,
has small pale blue flowers. 'Eventide' is a vigorous cultivar with lavender-blue flowers. Other cultivars with flowers containing various
shades of blue are 'Ada Ballard', 'Blue Eyes', 'Lady in Blue', 'Marie Ballard', and 'Professor Anton Kippenberg'.

Aster tongolensis (East Indies aster) produces flowers with lavender-blue
outer florets and an orange or yellow center on 1.5-foot (46-cm) tall
plants. Available blue cultivars include 'Berggarten', 'Napsbury', and
'Wartburg Star' (synonym 'Wartburgstern').

Babiana
Baboon Flower
IRIDACEAE

Babiana species are herbaceous perennials grown from corms. They are
among the Cape bulbs from South Africa and resemble *Freesia* species
when in bloom. Flowers have six tepals and are produced on upright
simple or branched flowering spikes. Flower color can be white, yellow,
purple, red, or blue. These tender plants are suitable for the cool greenhouse conservatory or outdoors in a mixed perennial border. They are
not reliably hardy and must be lifted for overwintering like *Gladiolus*.
Greenhouse-grown plants bloom in early spring. Outdoor plantings
bloom in summer if dormant corms are planted in spring. Plants prefer full sun and a light, well-drained soil. The genus name is derived
from the Afrikaans (Dutch) name for "baboon" and was given to this
group of plants because baboons eat the corms.

Propagation: Plants are multiplied by seed or offshoots. Offsets (cormels) can be removed from dormant corms.

Representative species and cultivars: *Babiana* consists of up to 60 species from the grasslands of South Africa. Several species are available commercially, including some with blue flowers.

Babiana rubocyanea is a small plant only reaching 8 inches (20 cm) tall. The flowers are interesting because they are predominantly blue with a red center.

Babiana stricta is the most commonly cultivated baboon flower. It grows to 12 inches (30 cm) tall and resembles a small *Freesia* species. Flower color can be purple, white, yellow, or blue. The Kew hybrids constitute a strain of baboon flower selected for its range of rich colors.

Baptisia
False Indigo, Wild Indigo
FABACEAE

False or wild indigo is a wonderful group of herbaceous perennials in the pea or legume family. They produce upright flower spikes above stout 2- to 3-foot (60-cm to 1-m) tall plants. Flowers are pealike in white, yellow, or shades of blue. These durable plants require little attention except division every 5 years. Plants bloom best in full sun, but tolerate light shade. They seem to thrive even in poor soils and are choice plants for the perennial bed. The genus name comes from the Greek word "to dip" and alludes to the use of flower extracts as a substitute for the blue dye of true indigo (*Indigofera*).

Propagation: Plants are multiplied by seed and division of dormant roots. Be-

Baptisia australis (blue wild indigo)

cause of its hard coat, the seed must be scarified to allow water uptake. It also may benefit from chilling stratification.

Representative species and cultivars: Of the approximately 30 species of *Baptisia,* only one is usually cultivated with blue flowers. *Baptisia australis* (blue wild indigo) is native to the eastern United States, although the species name seems to suggest otherwise. It is usually propagated by seed, and the flower color varies from lavender-blue to deep indigo blue. A cultivar should be selected with deep blue color. Rounded plants reach about 3 feet (1 m) tall when not in bloom and remain handsome throughout the growing season.

Borago
Borage
BORAGINACEAE

Borago is the type genus for a family that contains many plants with "true blue" flowers. It contains annual and herbaceous perennials between 6 inches and 2 feet (15 and 60 cm) tall. The interesting flowers contain petals that usually emerge pink and turn blue as they mature. Flowers have five fused petals, and the stamens fuse to form a dark, pointed cone in the center of the flower. Borage flowers are very attractive to bees and seed freely in the garden. Most gardeners use borage only in the herb garden, but it can be effective in the perennial bed and small species can be used in the rock garden. Borage prefers full sun and is tolerant of other growing conditions. Seedling volunteers can present a weed problem. The genus name comes from a Latin word for "rough hair" and describes the hairiness of borage plants.

Propagation: Plants are multiplied most commonly by seed but division is also used. Seed can be started directly in the garden or earlier in the greenhouse and then transplanted outdoors. The perennial types can be divided.

Representative species and cultivars: Although *Borago* lends its name to the Boraginaceae, which contains more than 2400 species, it only contains 3 species.

Borago laxiflora (synonym *B. pygmaea*) may surprise gardeners. It is a perennial species (annual in colder climates) that is appropriate for use in the perennial bed or more usually the rock garden. It blooms deep blue with many tiny flowers covering compact 1-foot (30-cm) tall plants throughout the summer. It is much smaller than *B. officinalis*.

Borago officinalis (common borage) is used primarily in herb gardens. It has been referenced since the earliest herbals as a plant that brings gladness and remedies melancholy. It is less commonly used as a blue feature in mixed annual and perennial beds, because its tendency to seed freely in the garden can make it weedy. The flowers are bright blue and produced for a long period during the summer.

Borago laxiflora

They are edible and taste a bit like cucumber. Coating borage flowers with sugar is a fun activity for children. Plants reach about 2 feet (60 cm) tall.

Brachycome
Swan River Daisy
ASTERACEAE

Swan River daisies are a group of herbaceous annual and tender perennials grown as summer annuals. They are used either as bedding plants or in hanging baskets. Plants are 1 to 1.5 feet (30 to 46 cm) tall, but the trailing stems are best used in containers or hanging baskets. The flowers have light blue outer ray florets and yellow, white, or black inner disk florets forming typical daisylike flowers. Plants need full sun and a well-drained soil or potting medium. The genus name is derived from the Greek word for "short hairs" and refers to the hairs on the seeds.

Brachycome iberidifolia (Swan River daisy)

Propagation: Plants are multiplied by seed or cuttings. The most common method of propagation is seed sown in early spring for transplants.

Representative species and cultivars: The approximately 75 species of *Brachycome* (also *Brachyscome*) come from Australia and New Zealand. Several species are in cultivation, but only *B. iberidifolia* is well known.

Brachycome iberidifolia (Swan River daisy) is among the many interesting plants introduced from Australia. The outer ray florets are usually blue, but can be pink or white. This species is useful mixed with other annuals in containers or hanging baskets. 'Blue Splendor' with purple-blue flowers is the blue representative from the Splendor series. 'Blue Star' is an interesting cultivar with rolled outer ray florets rather than the flat florets of the species; it has mid-blue flowers.

Brachycome multifida (rock daisy) is another annual species from Australia growing to 1.5 feet (46 cm) tall. Flower color can be white, pink, purple, or blue. Rock daisy is taller than Swan River daisy and makes a good bedding plant.

Browallia
Amethyst Flower
SOLANACEAE

Browallia is a small group of herbaceous annuals or tender perennials used mostly as bedding plants or for hanging baskets. Five fused petals typical of the nightshade family form white or bright blue flowers on 1- to 3-foot (30-cm to 1-m) tall plants. Plants can tolerate full sun, but prefer partial shade and a well-drained soil. They should be fertilized for continued blooming. These plants are excellent in a hanging basket for shady locations and are complementary with impatiens; both flowers respond to similar cultural conditions, but blue is a color lacking in impatiens. Plants may require pinching to increase branching. The genus name commemorates Abo Johan Browall, a sixteenth-century Swedish botanist.

Propagation: Plants are multiplied most commonly by seed but also by cuttings. Seed needs light to germinate and thus should not be covered; it also needs a moist medium. Although not commonly used by commercial growers, stem cuttings also root easily.

Representative species and cultivars: The six species of *Browallia* are native to South America and the West Indies. Two are commonly cultivated.

Browallia speciosa (amethyst flower, sapphire flower) is the most commonly grown species in the genus. Native to South America, it produces bright blue flowers on 2-foot (60-cm) tall plants. 'Amethyst' and 'Heavenly Blue' are common cultivars, but the newer F_1 hybrids are beginning to dominate the market because of their uniformity for basal branching and their color range. 'Blue Troll' has large flowers on 10-inch (25-cm) tall, rounded plants that are excellent in containers. Selections of the Bell and Starlight F_1 hybrid series have flower colors in white or various shades of blue. 'Blue Bells Improved' is lavender-blue; 'Marine Bells' is deep indigo blue; 'Powder Blue Bells' is light blue; and 'Sky Bells' is a light pale blue. The Starlight

Browallia speciosa 'Heavenly Blue' (amethyst flower)

series produces compact plants that are day neutral for early and continued flowering. 'Starlight Blue' is lavender-blue, and 'Starlight Sky Blue' has a paler blue flower.

Browallia viscosa is similar to *B. speciosa* but smaller, reaching 6 inches (15 cm) tall. Flowers are blue with a distinct white eye in the center. 'Sapphire' is a common cultivar.

Brunfelsia
Yesterday-today-tomorrow
SOLANACEAE

Brunfelsia is a group of tender evergreen shrubs and small trees. Where climates are mild, these species are suitable for landscape use. In temperate climates, they are grown as greenhouse specimen plants. The large flowers have fused, saucer-shaped petals. Flower color is violet-blue fading to white. Plants prefer full sun or partial shade and a moist, organic soil that is well drained. When grown in the greenhouse, they need ample water during the growing season. To promote branching, plants should be pinched. This genus has one of the longest common names; the name refers to how the flowers seemingly change from violet-blue to white almost overnight as the flowers fade. The genus name commemorates Otto Brunfels, a noteworthy German herbalist from the sixteenth century.

Propagation: Plants are propagated most commonly from stem cuttings that root easily in spring or summer.

Representative species and cultivars: The approximately 40 species of *Brunfelsia* are native to Central and South America. Two species with bluish flowers are commonly grown as pot plants or in ground beds in large greenhouse conservatories.

Brunfelsia australis is from Brazil and Argentina. It is similar to *B. pauciflora,* but has smaller fragrant flowers often in clusters of two or three.

Brunfelsia pauciflora 'Macrantha' (yesterday-today-tomorrow)

Brunfelsia pauciflora (yesterday-today-tomorrow) is also from Brazil and produces a lavender-blue flower with a distinct white eye in the center. Plants can reach 10 feet (3 m) tall and are best trained as small trees. The species is cultivated less commonly than its two cultivars with larger flowers, 'Macrantha' and 'Exima'.

Brunnera
Siberian Bugloss
BORAGINACEAE

Brunnera is an important group of herbaceous perennial for shady gardens, growing alongside *Hosta* and *Astilbe* species. In spring, plants produce 2-foot (60-cm) tall flower clusters containing blue "forget-me-not" flowers. After flowering, *Brunnera* produces handsome, heart-shaped leaves on spreading plants. Excellent variegated leaf forms are available. Plants do best in shade, with a moist, organic soil that is well drained. The genus name commemorates the seventeenth-century Swiss botanist Samuel Brunner.

Propagation: Plants are multiplied by seed, root cuttings, and division. The preferred method of propagation for all but the variegated types is to take root cuttings in winter. Because plants with variegated leaves lose their variegation if propagated by root cuttings, they must be propagated by division.

Representative species and cultivars: *Brunnera* is native to Europe and Asia and was once listed under *Anchusa,* which it resembles. Today, three species constitute *Brunnera,* but only *B. macrophylla* is commonly cultivated. It produces airy, "forget-me-not" flowers in late spring followed by large, heart-shaped leaves. Several cultivars are available, but all have been selected for white leaf variegation. 'Variegata' is an older selection with a creamy white border around the outside of the leaf. 'Dawson's White' and 'Langtrees' are newer cultivars with a similar variegation pattern.

Brunnera macrophylla

Buddleia
Butterfly Bush
LOGANIACEAE

Buddleia species are a group of hardy and tender trees and shrubs. They produce flowers in upright panicles or pendulous clusters. Flower color can be white, yellow, pink, red, purple, and blue. These upright, open plants work well in mixed shrub borders. Plants should be grown in full sun and a well-drained soil. Fall-blooming plants should be pruned in the spring. As the common name suggests, these plants are very attractive to butterflies and have become the background planting for the increasingly popular butterfly gardens. The genus name commemorates the sixteenth-century English botanist Reverend Adam Buddle.

Propagation: Plants are multiplied easily by softwood stem cuttings taken in early summer.

Representative species and cultivars: The approximately 100 species of *Buddleia* (synonym *Buddleja*) are native to Asia, Africa, and North and South America. Several are cultivated, but only two have bluish flowers.

Buddleia davidii is the hardiest species in the genus, tolerating winter temperatures to −10°F (−23°C). Native to China and Japan, it is a deciduous shrub that grows to about 10 feet (3 m) tall and produces fragrant blooms in the late summer and fall. Flower color is lilac-purple, but some cultivars have been selected for blue flower color as well as red and white. 'Black Knight' is a popular cultivar with purple-blue flowers that contrast nicely with the gray green foliage. 'Ellen's Blue' has deep blue flowers and silvery green foliage. 'Empire Blue' has violet-blue flowers with an orange center. 'Nanho Indigo' (synonyms 'Nanho Blue', 'Petite Indigo') is smaller than the species and has lavender-blue flowers; it reaches only 5 feet (1.5 m) tall. *Buddleia* 'Lochinch', a hybrid of *B. davidii* and *B. fallowiana,* produces violet-blue flowers against silver-green foliage on plants that reach 6 to 8 feet (2 to 2.4 m) tall.

Buddleia nivea is also a native of China. It is a marginally hardy, deciduous shrub growing to 10 feet (3 m) tall. It blooms in late summer and has lilac blue flowers.

Buglossoides
BORAGINACEAE

Buglossoides is a small group of herbaceous and woody perennials in the borage family. The flowers are tubular and similar to *Lithodora* flowers. They appear in early summer and can be yellow, purple, or blue. Plants are used in the rock garden or perennial bed. They prefer full sun to part shade and a well-drained, alkaline soil. The genus name is Greek for "like bugloss" (see *Anchusa*).

Propagation: Plants can be propagated by seed, division, and stem cut-

Buglossoides purpureocaeruleum

tings. Because they spread naturally from rhizomes, plants are easily propagated by division of the rooted rhizome pieces.

Representative species and cultivars: The 15 species of *Buglossoides* are native to Asia, Africa, and Europe. Many species were part of the genus *Lithospermum* before moving to *Buglossoides* and can still be listed under *Lithospermum* or *Lithodora* in catalogs. *Buglossoides purpureocaeruleum* (synonym *Lithospermum purpureocaeruleum*) is the most commonly grown species. Native to western Europe, it produces a 2-foot (60-cm) tall mass of foliage and flowers. The flowers appear in late spring and are unique because they open purple and fade to a gentian blue.

Camassia
Camas, Quamash
LILIACEAE

Camassia species deserves wider use in perennial gardens or for naturalizing in woodland settings. They are used more extensively in Europe than in the United States where they are native. These long-lived bulbs are easy to establish. They prefer well-drained soil in full sun or light shade. Plants bloom in late spring, producing 3- to 4-foot (1- to 1.2-m) tall upright flower spikes containing many light blue or white star-shaped flowers. Like the foliage of many other spring bulbs, the foliage of these plants dies down as the bulbs go dormant in summer. The genus name comes from the Native American name "quamash." The bulbs were an important food for Native Americans, and territorial battles were fought over quamash fields. The Lewis and Clark expedition also depended on boiled bulbs for food during their journey west.

Propagation: Plants are multiplied by seed or, more commonly, bulb offsets. Offsets should be removed from the bulb while plants are dormant in summer.

Representative species and cultivars: The six species of *Camassia* are native to North America. Three species are available as choice ornamentals for the perennial or woodland garden.

Camassia leichtlinii 'Caerulea' (Leichtlin quamash)

Camassia cusickii (Cusick quamash) is an Oregon native. It produces pale to deep blue flowers in spring on 30-inch (75-cm) tall plants. 'Zwanenburg' produces a deeper blue flower and is grown in preference to the species.

Camassia leichtlinii (Leichtlin quamash) makes the best garden plant in the genus, because its flowers are larger and the plants support the large flower spikes without staking. It is native to Oregon and California and produces robust plants 4 feet (1.2 m) tall. Flower color can be blue, purple, white, or yellow. In natural sites, this species can reseed and form dense clusters of spring blooms. 'Caerulea' has a deeper blue flower color than the species. 'Semiplena' is an interesting double, although, white-flowering form.

Camassia quamash (common quamash) has a wider natural distribution in western North America and can produce the longest flower spikes of the cultivated *Camassia* species, reaching more than 12 inches (30 cm). Flower color is violet-blue. Common quamash makes a good cut flower. 'Orion' is a dark blue cultivar with large flower spikes.

Campanula
Bellflower, Harebell
CAMPANULACEAE

Bellflowers are a mainstay of the rock garden, perennial border, and alpine garden, where they add mainly blue accents. They are a diverse group of annual, biennial, and perennial species ranging in height from diminutive creeping plants to upright 4-foot (1.2-m) tall plants. Flowers can be shaped like tubes, stars, or bells and bloom from spring through summer. The predominant flower color is blue, but purple, pink, or white is possible. Bellflowers perform best in full sun or partial sun and prefer locations where night temperatures are cool. In general, bellflowers require a well-drained soil that is slightly alkaline. Many are short lived in the garden, where conditions are not ideal. Taller species require staking. The genus name is Latin for "little bell."

Propagation: Seed and division are the most common forms of propagation, but many bellflower species root easily from stem cuttings. Seed of biennial types should be sown in the summer for flowering the following year.

Representative species and cultivars: The nearly 300 species of *Campanula* are native to the Northern Hemisphere and abundantly represented in Europe. Where do you start in describing this diverse group of plants? Plant aficionados can (and do) spend years collecting these plants, especially those interested in rock garden or alpine plants. Many species and their cultivars are available from specialty nurseries. Any list of bellflowers would fall short of describing the genus. A few of the more common blue species are included here.

Campanula aucheri is a wonderful addition to the rock garden. Bright blue flowers are produced on low-growing plants. The species is an alpine native.

Campanula aucheri

Campanula carpatica (Carpathian harebell) is native to central Europe and blue forms are usually available as the cultivars 'Blue Clips' or 'Wedgewood Blue'. These clump-forming plants to 6 inches (15 cm) tall are covered with blue (or white) saucer-shaped or bell-shaped flowers.

Campanula cochleariifolia (spiral bellflower, fairies' thimbles) is a good representative of the small creeping plants suited for the rock garden. It is native to the mountains of Europe. The common name "fairies' thimbles" aptly describes this plant with flowers shaped like dainty bells. Cultivars have blue flowers that literally cover the entire plant. 'Miranda' has silver-blue flowers. 'Bavarica Blue' has dark blue flowers. 'Elizabeth Oliver' is an interesting double-flowering form with lavender-blue flowers.

Campanula isophylla (falling stars) is an Italian native. It produces soft blue or white star-shaped flowers on trailing plants. The Kristal hybrids are becoming popular for pot plants or window boxes because they are long flowering and produce compact, upright plants. 'Stella Blue' is a Kristal hybrid with many bright blue flowers.

Campanula lactiflora (milky bellflower) is an upright plant growing more than 3 feet (1 m) tall. Native to Turkey and the Caucasus, it produces flowers in summer. Flower color can be white, violet, or shades of blue. Tall plants often need staking. 'Pouffe' grows only 1 foot (15 cm) tall with lavender-blue flowers.

Campanula carpatica 'Blue Clips'
(Carpathian harebell)

Campanula latifolia (great bellflower) is a vigorous, upright plant similar to *C. lactiflora* but not as good in the garden. It is also native to Turkey and the Caucasus, as well as many parts of Europe. 'Gloaming' is a compact grower to only 2 feet (60 cm) tall; it has pale blue flowers.

Campanula medium (Canterbury bells) is an upright, biennial plant long cultivated in the formal border. Native to southern Europe, it produces single or semi-double (cup-in-cup) flowers on 3-foot (1-m) tall plants. Flower color can be white, pink, or shades of blue.

Campanula persicifolia (peachleaf bellflower) is an upright plant to 3 feet (1 m) tall, most of which is a terminal flower spike. It makes an excellent cut flower as well as garden plant. Native to eastern Europe, Russia, and Asia, it produces a lavender-blue flower. 'Blue Gardenia' and 'Grandiflora Coerulea' are blue cultivars. 'Telham Beauty', a choice plant for the garden or as a cut flower, produces powder blue flowers on tall plants. 'Pride of Exmouth' produces small, semi-double (cup-in-cup), blue flowers on 2-foot (60-cm) tall plants. 'Victoria' is another double-flowering cultivar. It produces silver-blue, double flowers on small 15-inch (45-cm) tall plants.

Campanula pyramidalis (chimney bellflower) is native to southern Europe. It is among the tallest bellflowers cultivated, growing to 4 feet (1.2 m) tall and usually requiring staking. The star-shaped flowers can be blue or white.

Campanula rotundifolia 'Olympica' (Scotch harebell)

Campanula rotundifolia (Scotch harebell) presents a more airy appearance than other commonly cultivated bellflowers. Small bright blue flowers nod above threadlike leaves on 1-foot (30-cm) tall plants. The species is native to North America. 'Olympica' is a common cultivar.

Caryopteris
Bluebeard
VERBENACEAE

Bluebeards are a group of woody or herbaceous perennials grown in mixed shrub borders or treated as cut back plants for the perennial bed. Half-hardy species can be treated as annuals and make excellent cut flowers. Unique blue or violet-blue flowers are produced along the terminal stems on new growth. The flowers are five-lobed with one petal larger and fringed, leading to the common name "bluebeard." The flowers contrast nicely with the gray green foliage. Appearing in late summer, the flowers continue into fall and provide needed blue flower color for the perennial garden. Plants prefer a well-drained soil in full sun. They bloom on new wood, so they can be pruned or cut back in the spring to form compact, rounded mounds. The genus name is Greek for "winged nut" and describes the fruit.

Propagation: Plants are multiplied by seed or, more commonly, softwood stem cuttings taken in early summer before the plants bloom.

Representative species and cultivars: The six species of *Caryopteris* are native to Asia, but the most commonly cultivated plants are of garden origin. They are choice garden plants and make excellent cut flowers.

Caryopteris ×*clandonensis* (blue mist), a hybrid between *C. incana* and *C. mongholica,* was selected in 1930 by Arthur Simmonds in his garden at West Clandon, England. The location of the garden is the inspiration for the hybrid's botanical name. Plants are hardy to −10°F (−23°C) and grow 3 to 4 feet (1 to 1.2 m) tall. The blue flowers contrast nicely with the gray green foliage. Blue mist has become a popular garden plant with the introduction of several cultivars. 'Arthur Simmonds', 'Blue Mist', 'Dark Knight', 'First Choice', 'Kew Blue', and 'Longwood Blue' have been selected for their superior blue flower color. 'Dark Knight' and 'First Choice' have the deepest blue flowers. 'Worcester Gold' has yellow foliage.

Caryopteris incana (common bluebeard) is also commonly cultivated and is similar to blue mist, but is reliably winter hardy only to 10°F (−12°C). In northern gardens, it is treated as an annual. Native to China and Japan, it produces small clusters of violet-blue flowers that encircle the upper stems of the plant in late summer. Plants can reach up to 4 feet (1.2 m) tall. The upright stems of common bluebeard make excellent cut flowers.

Caryopteris mongholica is not as commonly cultivated as are the previously described bluebeards. It is a parent of *C.* ×*clandonensis*, lending its winter hardiness to *C. incana*. Native to northern China and Mongolia, it reaches about 3 feet (1 m) tall and is similar in flower to *C.* ×*clandonensis*.

Caryopteris ×*clandonensis* (blue mist)

Caryopteris odorata is an interesting member of the genus because its flowers are more pink than blue and they appear in the spring rather than the late summer as is typical with the other species. Native to the Himalayan mountains and hardy to −20°F (−29°C), it makes a nice plant if you can find it in specialty catalogs. Like *C. mongholica*, it is not commonly cultivated.

Catananche
Cupid's Dart
ASTERACEAE

Catananche species are hardy, herbaceous perennials that produce dandelion-like flowers on erect flower stems. Plants can reach 2 feet (60 cm) tall and form dense mats of basal foliage. They bloom for a long period in the summer and are a lilac blue. Cupid's dart is useful in the perennial bed or mixed with annuals. Flowers also can be cut, and they retain their color when dried. Plants require full sun and prefer soil on the dry side. The genus name comes from the Greek word for "powerful incentive" and refers, as does the common name, to the traditional use of this plant in love potions.

Propagation: Seed propagation is the most common form of multiplication, but root cuttings should be used for cultivars.

Catananche caerulea (Cupid's dart)

Representative species and cultivars: The five species of *Catananche* are native to the Mediterranean region of southern Europe. Only *C. caerulea* (Cupid's dart) is commonly cultivated. Native to southern Europe, it produces single, flowering heads on long stems beginning in summer and lasting into fall. It is a useful garden plant and cut flower. Several cultivars have been selected for their flower color, some with white and bicolored flowers. 'Blue Giant' has a flower that is darker blue than the species, and 'Major' has lilac blue flowers with a dark center. 'Blue Cupidone' produces lavender-blue flowers with a dark violet center and blooms the first year from seed. 'Bicolor' and 'Star Gazer' have white outer ray flowers with dark violet inner centers. Cultivars can be difficult to find because growers usually propagate Cupid's dart from seed.

Ceanothus
California Lilac
RHAMNACEAE

Ceanothus is a group of woody shrubs and small trees that produce white or bright blue flower clusters in the spring, summer, or into fall depending on the species. They make excellent specimen plants or can be used as a complement in mixed shrub borders. They also can be used as a hedge or espaliered along a wall. The blue-flowering species are not winter hardy in northern gardens, but are very popular in milder climates particularly in California, the Pacific Northwest, and Europe. All the species prefer full sun and a fertile, well-drained soil that is slightly acidic. The evergreen types should be pruned after flowering and the deciduous types in spring. The genus name is the old Greek word for a plant in the buckthorn family.

Propagation: Plants are multiplied by seed or stem cuttings. Because *Ceanothus* species hybridize easily, novel combinations are raised from seed for evaluation. Otherwise, cultivars are rooted as stem cuttings in early summer for deciduous types and in late summer for evergreen types.

Representative species and cultivars: All 55 species of *Ceanothus* are native to North America with many native to the milder areas of the West Coast. Many members of this large group of showy plants are found in cultivation, including several species and natural hybrids whose similarity makes identification of the plants difficult. *Ceanothus* hybrids are more often planted than the species. Some are of garden origin, and their parentage is unknown. Selected species and some of the popular hybrids are described here.

Ceanothus arboreus is a large plant sometimes reaching 20 feet (6 m) tall. 'Trewithen Blue' has large blue, fragrant flower heads.

Ceanothus 'Blue Mound' and 'Blue Cushion' are similar, producing mounded plants to 3 to 4 feet (1 to 1.2 m) tall. They have dense, dark foliage covered with dark blue flowers in spring.

Ceanothus 'Burkwoodii' is also an evergreen shrub to 6 feet (2 m) tall but has become popular because it blooms in the late summer and fall.

Ceanothus 'Concha', a hybrid between *C. impressus* and *C. papillosus*, is an evergreen shrub to 10 feet (3 m) tall. It produces dense clusters of reddish flower buds that open into deep blue flowers.

Ceanothus cyaneus (California blue brush) is a large shrub with showy blue clusters of flowers. Native to the West Coast of North America, it grows to 20 feet (6 m) tall and is very similar to *C. thyrsiflorus*.

Ceanothus 'Dark Star' grows 5 to 6 feet (1.5 to 1.8 m) tall with deep blue flowers produced in late spring. One reference suggests that it is a deer-proof shrub.

Ceanothus dentatus is a smaller evergreen shrub only reaching 4 feet (1.2 m) tall. It blooms in spring.

Ceanothus 'Edinburgh' is a dense-leaved, evergreen selection with blue flowers forming in spring into early summer. It grows to 10 feet (3 m) tall.

Ceanothus 'Gloire de Versailles' produces its blue flowers in summer and grows to 5 feet (1.5 m) tall. It is a little hardier than other blue-flowering types, surviving winter temperatures of 0°F (−18°C). Isn't it interesting to see so many European names for these North American plants?

Ceanothus gloriosus (Point Reyes ceanothus) is an interesting member of this genus because it grows as a low-spreading ground cover, reaching only 1 to 2 feet (30 to 60 cm) tall. Flower color is lavender-blue.

Ceanothus 'Concha', Hatfield House, Hertfordshire, England

Ceanothus ×lobbianus

Ceanothus 'Italian Skies' is a very good mound-growing selection with deep blue flowers appearing in spring. Plants eventually reach 5 feet (1.5 m) tall.

Ceanothus 'Julia Phelps' produces cobalt blue flowers on rounded 6-foot (2-m) tall shrubs. This evergreen is fairly well adapted to cultural conditions.

Ceanothus ×lobbianus, a hybrid of *C. dentatus,* has bright blue flowers. It is evergreen and blooms in spring.

Ceanothus 'Pin Cushion' is an evergreen shrub that produces light blue flowers on 6-foot (2-m) tall mounded plants.

Ceanothus prostratus is similar to *C. gloriosus* and has lavender-blue flowers.

Ceanothus thyrsiflorus (blue brush) is another large shrub with showy blue clusters of flowers. Like *C. cyaneus,* it is native to the West Coast of North America and grows to 20 feet (6 m) tall.

Ceanothus ×veitchianus, a hybrid between *C. griseus* and *C. rigidus,* is an evergreen, spreading shrub to 10 feet (3 m) tall. It produces deep blue flowers in spring.

Ceanothus 'Victoria' is a fast-growing shrub to 9 feet (2.7 m) tall. It is a popular cultivar because the plants are completely covered with deep blue flowers in late spring.

Centaurea
Cornflower, Knapweed
ASTERACEAE

Centaurea is a group of herbaceous plants suitable for the annual or perennial bed, depending on the species. Cornflowers are variable, growing from 1 to 4 feet (30 cm to 1.2 m) tall and producing yellow, pink, violet, or blue flowers. Some make good fresh and dried cut flowers. All prefer full sun and well-drained soil. The genus name is Greek for "centaur" and alludes to Chiron, the centaur of Greek mythology who taught the healing properties of plants.

Propagation: Plants are multiplied by seed or division. Seed sown for spring-planted bedding plants is the most common form of propagation. Perennial types can be divided while dormant.

Centaurea cyanus (bachelor's button)

Representative species and cultivars: This large genus contains 450 to 500 species native to Europe, North and South America, and Australia. Of the many species cultivated as ornamentals, two are notable for their blue flower color.

Centaurea cyanus (bachelor's button) is an annual species grown as a cut flower and is popular as part of wildflower mixtures common in seed catalogs. 'Blue Boy', 'Blue Midget', and 'Jubilee Gem' are compact blue selections, growing about 1 foot (30 cm) tall. The Florence series and Polka Dot mixture have 15-inch (38-cm) tall plants with lavender, pink, red, and white flowers. 'Florence Blue' is the blue representative from the Florence series.

Centaurea montana (mountain bluet) is a perennial species, producing 2-inch (5-cm) blue flowers in early summer on compact 1.5-foot (40-cm) tall plants. 'Grandiflora' is a larger-flowering type. White and pink forms are available.

Ceratostigma
Leadwort
PLUMBAGINACEAE

Ceratostigma species produce one of the bluest flowers for the perennial garden and are either 1-foot (30-cm) tall creeping ground covers or 3-foot (1-m) tall shrubs. Plants grow in full sun or light shade and may need winter protection in northern gardens. Blossoms appear in late summer into fall, and the blue saucer-shaped flowers contrast with the effective reddish brown sepals that persist after the petals fade. Plants prefer a moist, well-drained soil and are at home in the mixed perennial bed, used as a ground cover, or in the rock garden. The genus name is Greek for "horned stigma." The common name "leadwort" comes from the former inclusion of these plants in the genus *Plumbago,* which is Greek for "lead" and suggests the plant's use against lead poisoning.

Propagation: Plants are easily propagated from stem cuttings taken in late spring or early summer. Division is also an option.

Representative species and cultivars: The eight species of *Ceratostigma* are native to Asia and Africa. They originally were assigned to the genus *Plumbago* and the even older genus *Valoradia*. Two species are commonly available.

Ceratostigma plumbaginoides (synonym *Plumbago larpentiae*) is the only leadwort that is fully winter hardy. It creeps freely from underground rhizomes, making an excellent ground cover. A native of western China, it produces blue flowers in summer through fall. It is a superior perennial used in the front of the border or as a ground cover.

Ceratostigma willmottianum (Chinese plumbago) is not fully winter hardy, only surviving winter temperatures of 0°F (−18°C), but where winters are mild, it makes an excellent small shrub to about 3 feet (1 m) tall. It provides an outstanding blue-flowering background for the perennial border and, like *C. plumbaginoides*, blooms from summer through fall. Native to China, this species should be better known by U.S. gardeners. It was introduced from China in 1908 by the famous plant collector Ernest ("Chinese") Wilson, who sent seed

Ceratostigma plumbaginoides

to Ellen Willmott in Essex, England. The plants she raised from seed became the source of this plant for English gardeners.

Chionodoxa
Glory-of-the-snow
LILIACEAE

Chionodoxa is a group of small bulbous plants similar to *Scilla* species. It differs from *Scilla* in that its flower petals are separated and held upright compared with the more pendulous, bell-like flowers of *Scilla*. Several blooms appear on upright spikes in early spring. Each flower has six tepals that are clear blue with a light center. Plants make excellent additions to the rock garden or naturalized among ground covers. They are easy to grow and, if left undisturbed, colonize large patches of the garden. I can't imagine gardening without the cheerful blossoms of

Chionodoxa luciliae 'Gigantea'

Chionodoxa heralding the start of the growing season. Dormant bulbs can be planted in groups in fall. Like most bulbs, they do best in a well-drained soil. Plants prefer full sun or light shade. The genus name is Greek for "glory of the snow" and alludes to the early blooming of the plants, often pushing through late spring snows.

Propagation: Bulb offsets are used by commercial growers, but plants self-sow in the garden.

Representative species and cultivars: Of the six species of *Chionodoxa* native to Greece and Turkey, two are available in the trade. They are similar in flower, but by far the more common species is *C. luciliae*.

Chionodoxa luciliae produces 6-inch (15-cm) tall plants with light blue flowers. It is very winter hardy and native to Turkey. 'Gigantea' is a slightly larger plant with larger flowers. 'Pink Giant' is a pink form (but may actually be a selection of *C. forbessii*, which closely resembles *C. luciliae* and is often sold as such).

Chionodoxa sardensis is native to Greece and is similar to *C. luciliae*. This lesser-known glory-of-the-snow has a more uniform blue petal color. 'Deep Blue' is the usual cultivar.

×*Chionoscilla allenii* is a hybrid between *Chionodoxa* and *Scilla,* showing how similar these two genera are. It has an interesting mixture of traits. Flowers are more star-shaped, like those of *Chionodoxa,* but smaller. They are pale to deep blue in color and produced in abundance on 6- to 8-inch (15- to 20-cm) tall plants.

Cichorium
Chicory
ASTERACEAE

Chicory is the garden vegetable grown as the blanched salad green Belgium endive and as the red-leaved radicchio. The root of chicory is also used as a coffee substitute. It is not cultivated commonly as an ornamental and has escaped to become a pest in some locations of North America. Plants produce pale blue dandelion-like flowers in the late summer and fall. They prefer full sun and a fertile, well-drained soil. The genus name is old Latin for "chicory."

Propagation: Plants are multiplied by seed.

Representative species and cultivars: The eight species of *Cichorium* are native to Asia, Europe, and Africa. *Cichorium intybus* is the salad vegetable chic-

Cichorium intybus (chicory)

ory. It is not commonly planted as an ornamental, but has escaped to become a common field weed in Europe and most of North America.

Clematis
Clematis, Virgin's Bower
RANUNCULACEAE

Clematis is familiar to most gardeners. This group of mostly woody vines produces large star-shaped flowers in pink, white, lavender, blue, or bicolors. The showy pigmented parts of these flowers are actually sepals rather than petals. Most species require a support to climb, but several non-climbing herbaceous types make excellent perennials. All flower best in full sun in a well-drained soil with good fertility and organic matter. If pruning is necessary, spring bloomers can be pruned just after blossoms fade, while summer bloomers can be pruned in the spring because they bloom on new wood. The genus name is Greek for "climbing branch."

Propagation: Plants are multiplied by seed, stem cuttings, layering, and sometimes grafting.

Representative species and cultivars: *Clematis* is a large genus of approximately 250 species. Most climbing varieties sold in commerce are hybrids; however, some of the best blue-flowering plants occur on the smaller-flowering herbaceous perennial types.

Clematis alpina, as the name implies, is from mountainous areas of Europe. It is a climbing type that produces blue flowers with white centers in summer. The feathery seedpods are also ornamental. 'Pamela Jackman' is the most common cultivar with deep blue flowers.

Clematis crispa is native to the southeastern United States and produces lavender-blue, bell-shaped flowers in late summer. It is a deciduous climber with moderate vigor. It tolerates full sun or light shade and is worth searching for in specialty catalogs.

Clematis heracleifolia (tube clematis) is native to China and Korea and produces 2-foot (60-cm) tall non-climbing plants that bloom in late summer. They are welcome additions to the perennial border. 'Cote d'Azur' has light blue flowers, and 'Wyevale Blue' is a deeper blue than the species.

Clematis integrifolia (solitary clematis) makes an excellent herbaceous perennial and produces nodding blue flowers in early summer on compact 3-foot (1-m) tall non-climbing plants. It is native to central Europe (possibly a hybrid). 'Boughton Blue" has bright blue flowers with recurved petals. 'Hendersonii' was selected for bluer flower color. 'Durandii' produces large, textured flowers that are indigo blue.

Clematis macropetala (downy clematis) is a vigorous climber with 4-inch (10-cm) semi-double flowers. It blooms in spring and early summer. Native to Russia and China, it (and its cultivars) deserves wider popularity with U.S. gardeners. 'Blue Bird' was selected in Canada to be more winter hardy, surviving winter temperatures of −30°F (−34°C). 'Jan Lindmark' has mauve-blue flowers. 'Maidwall Hall' is a later-

Clematis integrifolia 'Boughton Blue' (solitary clematis)

blooming selection with dark blue flowers. Pink and white forms exist also.

Clematis hybrids contain numerous climbing cultivars with large blue flowers. Representative climbing hybrids include 'Beauty of Worcester', a blue-flowering double form; 'Elsa Spath', with deep lavender-blue flowers; 'General Sikorski', with large violet-blue flowers; 'Lasurstern', with wavy lavender-blue flowers; 'Mrs. Cholmondeley', with lavender-blue flowers; 'Romona', with lavender-blue flowers and dark stamens; and 'Perle d'Azur', with wonderful, azure blue flowers.

Clerodendrum

Glory Bower

VERBENACEAE

Clerodendrum is a diverse group of mostly tropical or subtropical woody vines, shrubs, and trees. The vines are most familiar to gardeners and are often seen in greenhouse conservatories. They are aggressive plants that usually need pruning or training to keep them in bounds. In frost-free gardens they are used as vines or landscape shrubs. *Clerodendrum trichotomum* is hardy where winter temperatures only reach 0°F (−18°C).

Clerodendrum ugandense
(blue glory bower)

Plants are usually noticed when the showy dark blue berries appear in the fall, and visitors to the garden are surprised to learn that these plants belong to the genus *Clerodendrum*. Plants need full sun or light shade and a well-drained soil. Indoor displays are best in a large container that allows the plants to develop. The genus name is Greek for "chance tree," but its connection to the plant is unclear.

Propagation: Plants are multiplied by seed or, more commonly, softwood stem cuttings.

Representative species and cultivars: *Clerodendrum* (synonym *Clerodendron*) is a large genus of approximately 400 species. Most are tropical, but some can be grown outdoors in northern gardens. Only one species is commonly cultivated for its blue flower color. *Clerodendrum ugandense* (blue glory bower) is a large shrub native to tropical Africa. It grows 5 to 8 feet (1.5 to 2.5 m) tall and produces dainty bicolored blue and white flowers that resemble small butterflies. It is suitable for a container patio plant or greenhouse specimen and blooms in late summer. Blue glory bower justifiably has become more widely available in the 1990s. *Clerodendrum myricoides* is similar to *C. ugandense* but is not as commonly cultivated.

Clitoria
Butterfly Pea
FABACEAE

Clitoria is a group of mostly tropical herbaceous and woody perennials. The most familiar plants in this genus are the vines that are used as annuals outdoors or as climbers in greenhouse conservatories. The flowers are somewhat pealike and tucked among the foliage. Plants require support and do well in full sun or light shade. They should have a fertile, well-drained soil or medium. The genus name refers to the resemblance of the flower to a clitoris.

Propagation: Plants are multiplied by seed.

Representative species and cultivars: Of the approximate 40 species of *Clitoria*, only *C. ternatea* (butterfly pea) from tropical Asia is usually cultivated. It is a vigorous vine, producing deep blue flowers. White and double forms are available. Butterfly pea can be used to great advantage as an outdoor container plant to provide a backdrop for lower-growing annuals.

Cochliostema
COMMELINACEAE

Cochliostema is a group of herbaceous perennial epiphytes that are similar to bromeliads in appearance until they flower. Then they appear more closely related to *Tradescantia* species. Flowers are produced in clusters from the axils of the leaves. The three petals are blue-violet and fringed with hairs. They alternate with the narrower sepals that show between the petals as the flowers unfold from the bud. Plants are tropical and, except in warm climates, are best suited for use in greenhouse displays. They prefer bright light and can be container-grown in a light medium suited for orchids. The genus name is Greek for "spiral stamen" and refers to the twisted anthers.

Propagation: Plants are multiplied by seed or offshoots. The easiest method of propagation is to remove the offshoots.

Representative species and cultivars: *Cochliostema* consists of only two species, both native to Brazil and Ecuador. They are unique members of

Cochliostema odoratissimum

the dayflower family because they have modified their structure to be epiphytic. Only one species is found in cultivation. *Cochliostema odoratissimum* (synonym *C. jacobianum*) produces a rosette of leaves and clusters of fragrant, violet-blue flowers in the leaf axils. In a greenhouse collection of epiphytic plants, it catches the viewer's eye because it so resembles a bromeliad, but the attractive flowers suggest a different genus. Here is a wonderful example of species from divergent backgrounds evolving a similar mechanism to exploit an environmental niche.

Codonopsis
Asia Bell
CAMPANULACEAE

Codonopsis species are herbaceous perennials in the bellflower family. Plants produce dainty, nodding, light blue flowers that are bell-shaped. Plant height is 2 to 3 feet (60 cm to 1 m), although plants sprawl along the ground. They are suited for the mixed perennial bed but are not as showy as most *Campanula* species. They do well in full sun or light shade in a well-drained, deep soil. Stems, leaves, and flowers have a strong, unpleasant odor. The genus name is Greek for "resembling bells."

Propagation: Plants are multiplied most commonly by seed, but also by stem cuttings.

Representative species and cultivars: The approximately 30 species of *Codonopsis* are native to Asia. Although these species have never risen to prominence as "must have" annual or perennial garden plants, their bell-shaped flowers make them interesting for the gardener who wants something a little different. Only one species is commonly available from garden catalogs; however, I found one specialty catalog that listed 11 species and an assortment suggesting that gardeners would want them all.

Codonopsis clematidea (Asia bell) is the only species in this genus commonly seen in gardens. Native to central Asia, it has pale blue flowers with yellow or black markings on the inner part of the flower. Plants can reach up to 3 feet (1 m) tall, but need support. They are not reliably winter hardy in northern gardens.

Codonopsis convolvulacea is not as commonly cultivated as *C. clematidea*, but produces violet-blue, hanging

Codonopsis clematidea (Asia bell)

bell-shaped flowers on 2-foot (60-cm) tall plants. It is native to the western mountains of China. 'George Forrest' has blue flowers with a purple-red basal spot.

Coleus

LAMIACEAE

Coleus is composed of familiar bedding plants grown for their various foliage colors and shapes. Most plants are shade loving, but newer cultivars can tolerate full sun. The foliage can exhibit fantastic mixtures of reds, greens, yellows, and oranges. Some cultivars have fringed, wavy leaf margins, while others have narrow cut leaves. *Coleus* is included here because most of its cultivars produce terminal spikes of blue or white flowers. The flowers are small and secondary to the foliage for ornamental characters, but they can add interest to a shady garden. In most cases, these plants are pruned to prevent flowering, so many gardeners do not see the tiny blue, two-lipped flowers. Plants prefer a lightly shaded area with a rich garden soil. They do not compete well with shallow-rooted trees like maples. To promote large leaves and lush growth, plants should be fertilized regularly, and to promote a bushy habit, plants should be pinched. They also can be used in the greenhouse conservatory and can be trained to an interesting topiary standard. The genus name comes from the Greek word for "sheath" and refers to the way the bottoms of the anthers are arranged together.

Propagation: Plants are multiplied most commonly by seed, but several newer cultivars are propagated vegetatively from stem cuttings.

Representative species and cultivars: *Coleus* is a genus of about 60 species of mostly evergreen perennials from Asia and Africa. Unfortunately, it has been proposed to change the genus name to *Solenostemon*. Only one species is extensively cultivated. *Coleus blumei* (synonym *Solenostemon scutellarioides*) is grown as an annual bedding plant, but is actually a tender perennial. Numerous cultivars are offered commercially that have been selected for their foliage characteristics and basal branching habit. Common series include Carefree, Dragon, Sabres, Rainbow, and Wizard.

Collinsia
Blue-eyed Mary
SCROPHULARIACEAE

Collinsia is a genus of herbaceous annuals that produce flowers on upright stems. Flower color can be pink, white, violet, blue, or bicolored. Plants can reach between 1 and 3 feet (30 cm and 1 m) tall and bloom in spring or summer. They are suited for naturalized woodland gardens or in annual flower beds. They do well in partial shade, but do not perform well in hot, humid climates. These interesting plants deserve more attention from discriminating breeders. The genus name commemorates the seventeenth-century Pennsylvania botanist Zaccheus Collins.

Propagation: Plants are multiplied most commonly by seed and bloom the following spring.

Collinsia verna (blue-eyed Mary)

Representative species and cultivars: The approximately 20 species of *Collinsia* are native to North America. Few are cultivated, but their showy flowers, range of colors, and possible use as cut flowers suggest that they may be more popular in the future.

Collinsia grandiflora (blue lips) is native to the Pacific Northwest. The flowers have light purple upper petals and blue-purple lower petals. Plants grow to 1 foot (30 cm) tall.

Collinsia verna (blue-eyed Mary) is native to moist woodlands of the northeastern United States. The flowers have white upper petals and bright blue lower petals. This species can colonize large areas, blooming for several weeks in spring. It is most effective naturalized along the edges of woodlands and, as it is such a beautiful plant in nature, it is surprising that it has never been exploited for garden cultivation.

Commelina
Dayflower
COMMELINACEAE

Commelina produces small, bright blue flowers similar to *Tradescantia* flowers but with three petals, one of which is smaller than the other two. Plants are herbaceous annuals or perennials and grow from jointed, trailing, or upright stems. Some plants grow from underground tubers and can be overwintered just like dahlias. The perennial dayflowers are wonderful additions to the summer-flowering border. They grow naturally in light shade or full sun in any moist soil. The genus name commemorates three Dutch brothers from the seventeenth century: two of them (Johann and Kaspar Commelin) became botanists, while the third did not. Their career choices are somehow related to the two petals of the flowers being large, while the third is smaller.

Propagation: Plants are multiplied by seed, division, or stem cuttings.

Representative species and cultivars: This large genus contains more than 100 species native to Asia, Africa, and the Americas. They are not commonly cultivated in the United States, but where I have seen them in Europe, they make effective contributions to the perennial border.

Commelina coelestis (blue spiderwort) is a tender, tuberous-rooted perennial native to Mexico. It forms upright plants 3 feet (1 m) tall with bright blue flowers and is the most commonly cultivated species. Plants bloom from summer into fall and must be lifted and overwintered or treated as annuals.

Commelina communis is not cultivated often, but has escaped to become a common roadside weed in the United States. Its pedestrian appearance should not deter gardeners from trying other fine members of this genus in the garden.

Commelina coelestis (blue spiderwort)

Commelina communis

Commelina tuberosa, like *C. coelestis,* is a tender, tuberous-rooted Mexican perennial with bright blue flowers. It forms upright plants that are shorter than blue spiderworts, only reaching 10 inches (25 cm) tall. It, too, must be lifted and overwintered if not treated like an annual.

Convolvulus
Dwarf Morning Glory
CONVOLVULACEAE

Convolvulus is a group of tender annual and perennial plants, many of which grow as twining vines. Flowers have the fused petals that are typical of morning glory, and can be yellow, white, pink, and blue in color. Depending on the species, the plants are effective on trellises, as bedding plants, or in hanging baskets. They do best in full sun in a well-drained soil or medium. They are noted for growing well on poor sites as long as the ground is not wet. The genus name is Latin for "twining."

Propagation: Plants are multiplied by seed, stem cuttings, or division. Seed is the most common form of propagation and may benefit from a hot water treatment or scarification to allow water uptake. Perennial plants can be divided.

Representative species and cultivars: *Convolvulus* is a large genus of approximately 250 species native to temperate and subtropical regions throughout the world. Several are serious agricultural weeds, but others are well-behaved garden plants with blue flowers.

Convolvulus sabatius (synonym *C. mauritanicus*) produces pale lavender-blue flowers on trailing stems. It is native to southern Europe and northern Africa. Plants in bloom are covered with flowers. This display occurs from summer into fall in the outdoor garden, while greenhouse plants can be forced for a spring display. They are well-suited for hanging baskets or as rambling rock garden plants.

Convolvulus tricolor is native to Greece and northern Africa. 'Royal Ensign' is more commonly available than the species. It is an annual,

Convolvulus sabatius

Convolvulus tricolor 'Royal Ensign

non-vining type that has become popular as a bedding plant. It produces large blue flowers with a yellow throat on compact 1-foot (30-cm) tall plants. The Flagship mix is a newer strain that contains plants with lavender, pink, red, and blue flowers.

Corydalis
FUMARIACEAE

Corydalis species are herbaceous annuals or perennials growing from underground rhizomes or tubers. They are small plants less than 2 feet (60 cm) tall. Flower color can be white, yellow, pink, or blue. The foliage can be fernlike and resembles the foliage of a close relative, bleeding heart (*Dicentra*). The flowers are distinctive with a long corolla tube terminating in a single spur. Most species bloom in spring. They are well-suited to rock gardens, naturalized in woodland settings, or mixed with other perennials. Plants do well in light shade in a moist, well-drained soil. The genus name is Greek for "lark."

Propagation: Plants are multiplied by seed or division of dormant plants. Division is the most common method of propagation for the perennial types that may form from rhizomes or small bulbs.

Representative species and cultivars: The more than 300 species of *Corydalis* are native to temperate regions throughout North America, Asia, and Europe, but only a few are cultivated. Most gardeners associate *Corydalis* with the yellow-flowering *C. lutea;* however, there are some lovely species with red, white, or sky blue flowers.

Corydalis cashmeriana is less common than *C. flexulosa,* but is also blue
flowering. It is a diminutive plant to about 6 inches (15 cm) tall. This
Himalayan native is suited for rock gardens.

Corydalis elata is from western China and produces dark blue flowers
above clumps of yellow-green foliage. Plants reach 15 inches (40 cm)
tall and prefer light shade.

Corydalis flexulosa is a Chinese native that is popular in Europe, but only
beginning to become available in the United States. It produces won-
derful, electric blue flowers that cover the fernlike foliage in spring.
Plants grow to about 1 foot (30 cm) tall and are useful in the rock
garden, perennial bed, or combined with bulbs. Deadheading (or
removing) spent blooms may induce additional flowering. 'Blue
Panda' has bright gentian blue flowers and extended bloom time.
'China Blue' has true-blue flowers that are darker than 'Blue Panda'.
'Pere David' produces turquoise-blue blossoms on spreading plants.
'Purple Leaf' has purple-blue flowers, but is early flowering and has
a purple area on the center of each leaf.

Corydalis flexulosa

Corydalis fumariifolia is a tuberous-rooted perennial from China and
Japan. It grows to 6 inches (15 cm) tall and produces blue flowers in
late spring.

Crocus
IRIDACEAE

What garden would be complete without crocus? These small bulbous
plants develop from corms that replace themselves each year. Plants
grow to 7 inches (18 cm) tall and produce cup-shaped flowers in early
spring or fall. Flower color can be white, yellow, lavender, or blue. Crocuses are excellent for naturalizing, for mixing with herbaceous perennials, or for use in the rock garden. They also can be forced and grown
in containers for indoor decoration. Crocuses prefer full sun or partial
shade in a well-drained, organic soil. The genus name comes from the
Greek word for "saffron," a spice and yellow dye made from the stamens of *Crocus sativus*.

Propagation: Plants are propagated from offsets (cormels) of the corms.
Crocuses also can spread naturally from seeds.

Representative species and cultivars: The 75 species of *Crocus* are native
to the Mediterranean region and Asia. Many are grown as ornamentals, but only a few have bluish flowers.

Crocus biflorus (Scotch crocus) is an early spring blooming species that
produces two flowers per plant, thus the species name "bi-florus."
Flower color can be lilac blue or white. Although, the common name
suggests otherwise, this species is native to central Europe.
Crocus chrysanthus (golden crocus) is the diminutive crocus that blooms
in such profusion in early spring. It should be planted in large
patches for best effect. It is a wonderful harbinger of spring and, if
the first wave of flowers is damaged by cold weather, the plants continue to bloom on additional flower stems. Although the flowers are
smaller than those of the Dutch hybrids, they tolerate the extremes

Crocus chrysanthus 'Blue Bird' (golden crocus)

of spring weather better. Flower color of the parent species is bright yellow, but hybrids of *C. chrysanthus* and *C. biflorus* have additional colors and lovely bicolors. 'Blue Bird' is pale blue with a white edging on the petals. 'Blue Pearl' has white flowers with blue markings on the outer tepals. 'Sky Blue' has a light blue flower. 'Snow Bunting' has a white flower with violet-blue markings on the outside of the tepals.

Crocus kotschyanus (synonym *C. zonatus*) is a fall-blooming crocus that produces a pale lilac-colored flower. Its variety, *C. kotschyanus* var. *leucopharynx*, has a lilac blue flower. This species is not grown as commonly as *C. speciosus*, but can extend the blooming period for fall crocuses into October.

Crocus pulchellus is another autumn-blooming crocus. It produces pale flowers with blue veins and an orange-yellow throat. Native to Yugoslavia and Turkey, it is similar in habit to *C. speciosus*.

Crocus speciosus (showy crocus) represents the fall-blooming crocuses and should not be confused with the similar *Colchicum* species that bloom at the same time. Although these plants appear alike to most gardeners, the *Colchicum* species belong to a different family (Liliaceae) and can be distinguished by having six anthers rather than the three characteristic of *Crocus*. Showy crocus is an easily grown, early flowering fall crocus. It is a delight to see patches of light blue peaking from beneath trees or shrubs beginning to show fall color. Plants self-sow from seed and can colonize large areas in a favorable environment. 'Cassiope' has bright blue flowers with a tinge of yellow at the base.

Crocus vernus is the species most responsible for the large-flowering Dutch hybrids. The species was the first ornamental crocus introduced into northern Europe from the Middle East in the late sixteenth century. It was distributed throughout northern Europe by Charles Lecluse (Carolus Clusius), who later, as professor of botany at the University of Leyden, helped popularize the tulip and lay the foundation for the bulb trade in The Netherlands. Dutch hybrid crocuses are later flowering than most of the species and have very large, showy flowers. Flower color is usually white to shades of purple. No true blues are known. 'Early Perfection' has violet-blue flowers, and 'Queen of the Blues' has lilac blue flowers.

Cynara
Cardoon
ASTERACEAE

For gardeners looking for a bold feature in the garden, cardoon fits the bill. It is a large thistlelike plant that always attracts attention. Growing to 6 feet (1.8 m) tall in fertile garden soil, it is topped by rounded flower heads with prominent, pointed basal scales (bracts). Many small lavender-blue flowers appear from the center of the bracts. The foliage is divided into leaflets that terminate in a spine. The plant is imposing and not for every garden. It is suited for use as an accent in mixed annual and perennial gardens and as a good dried cut flower. It also can be a late season feature in the vegetable garden. The young shoots can be blanched like celery. Plants need full sun and a fertile, well-drained soil. The genus name comes from the Greek word for "doglike" and refers to the flower bracts that resemble a dog's tooth.

Propagation: Plants are usually multiplied by seed, but they also can be propagated by division or root cuttings.

Representative species and cultivars: The 10 species of *Cynara* are native to the Mediterranean region into Africa. *Cynara cardunculus* is the only species in this genus grown as an ornamental, while *C. scolymus* (artichoke) is reserved for the vegetable garden. *Cynara cardunculus* (cardoon) is native to the Mediterranean area and is an imposing garden plant. It reaches 5 feet

Cynara cardunculus (cardoon)

(1.5 m) tall with numerous purple-blue terminal flowers from late summer into fall. 'Cardy' is a bluer selection grown as a cut flower.

Cynoglossum
Hound's Tongue
BORAGINACEAE

Cynoglossum is a lesser-known but very ornamental member of the borage family. Its members are herbaceous annuals, biennials, and perennials that produce deep blue flowers on terminal spikes in the spring. The flower stem uncoils to show tubular, funnel-shaped flowers. Plants grow to 2 feet (60 cm) tall and are suited for mixed annual or perennial gardens. Preferring full sun to light shade in a moist, well-drained soil, these plants can be short lived where summers are hot. The genus name is derived from the Greek word for "dog's tongue" and, with the common name, refers to the shape and texture of the basal leaves.

Propagation: Plants are multiplied by seed or division.

Representative species and cultivars: The approximately 50 species of *Cynoglossum* are distributed in most temperate regions. Several species are cultivated, but can be difficult to find in the United States.

Cynoglossum amabile (Chinese forget-me-not) is a biennial species from Asia with white, pink, or blue flowers. Plants grow 1 to 2 feet (30 to 60 cm) tall and are covered with many small flowers on a branched flower stalk in the spring. 'Firmament' is a compact blue selection.
Cynoglossum grande can reach 3 feet (1 m) tall and makes a better perennial for the garden than *C. virginaticum*. It is native to the Pacific coast where it is occasionally cultivated.
Cynoglossum nervosum (hairy hound's tongue) is a perennial species from the Himalayan mountains. Its deep gentian blue flowers appear in the spring on 2-foot (60-cm) tall plants. The plants are beautiful in bloom with a similar aspect to the better-known *Anchusa* species,

but with a darker blue flower color. Where summer night temperatures are cool, this species makes an excellent perennial plant.

Cynoglossum officinale is another biennial species native to Europe and Asia. Plants form a rosette of leaves the first year and then bolt to produce a long-flowering stem with dark purple-blue flowers. Plants are 2.5 feet (75 cm) tall in bloom.

Cynoglossum virginaticum is a North American perennial that is sometimes cultivated. It grows to 2.5 feet (75 cm) tall and produces blue "forget-me-not" flowers in spring.

Cynoglossum wallichii comes from Asia and is a biennial species with blue flowers. It can reach 3 feet (1 m) tall and is infrequent in cultivation.

Cynoglossum zeylanicum is an upright biennial species, growing up to 3 feet (1 m) tall. It is native to India and sometimes cultivated.

Cynoglossum nervosum (hairy hound's tongue)

Delphinium

Larkspur, Delphinium

RANUNCULACEAE

Many excellent *Delphinium* selections with blue flowers are available. The taller hybrids epitomize the formal perennial garden. Single or double flowers fill large upright spikes and can grow more than 6 feet (1.8 m) tall. Flower color can be white, pink, shades of purple, or blue. These plants are so showy that they look good under most conditions, but in the accomplished gardener's hands they respond to ideal handling to become spectacular. Most delphiniums are herbaceous perennials or biennials, but short-lived types sometimes are handled as annuals. They provide excellent late spring and summer blooms for the perennial bed and make good fresh or dried cut flowers. Several species can be naturalized in woodland gardens. Most species flower best in full sun in a fertile, well-drained soil with a slightly alkaline pH. The best plants grow where summer night temperatures are cool and can be short lived in hotter southern gardens. The gardens of northern Europe have excellent climatic conditions for delphiniums and are the benchmark for quality plants. Taller species and cultivars require staking. Allowing only four to seven stems to develop on taller delphiniums will ensure large flowering spikes. The genus name derives from the Greek word for "dolphinlike" and refers to the flower shape.

Propagation: Plants are multiplied by seed, division, and in some cases stem cuttings of early spring growth. Seed propagation, even of the cultivars, is the most common form of propagation, and seed may benefit from several weeks of chilling stratification before sowing.

Representative species and cultivars: This large genus of very popular garden plants contains more than 200 species native to northern temperate regions. One reference lists more than 80 species that have been in cultivation at some time. Many of these have blue flowers, but only a few are cultivated today even by the most avid gardeners, namely, *Delphinium elatum, D. grandiflorum, D. tatsienense,* and *D. tricorne.* Several of these species are parents of the more generally planted hybrids, but they also can make useful additions to the perennial garden, especially the cultivars of *D. grandiflorum*. The hybrids can be placed into two groups usually called the Belladonna and Elatum hybrids. These are of mixed origin, but undoubtedly *D. elatum* and *D. cheilanthum* from Siberia, *D. tatsienense* from China, and *D. grandiflorum* from Siberia and China are among the parents.

The Belladonna hybrids (*Delphinium ×belladonna*) first arose in Europe from a chance seedling around 1880. These plants are usually less than 3 feet (1 m) tall and produce open, branched flowering stems that contain many colorful, single flowers with a long spur. Colors include white and shades of blue. These are among the easiest delphiniums to grow especially in warmer climates. The Belladonna hybrids include 'Bellamossum', dark blue flowers; 'Blue Bees', wands of beautiful, light blue flowers; 'Blue Shadows', single, violet-blue flowers; 'Cliveden Beauty', large, light blue flowers; and the Connecticut Yankee series, large, light and dark blue flowers on long-lived, compact plants.

Delphinium elatum is native to Asia, China, and Siberia and was the first cultivated delphinium introduced into European gardens, although it is no longer commonly cultivated. It is very similar in stature to the hybrid delphiniums, but its flower spikes have fewer flowers. Also, individual flowers are spurred in this species.

The Elatum hybrids (*Delphinium ela-tum*) can reach 6 feet (1.8 m) tall and are characterized by large, dense flower spikes up to 3 feet (1 m) tall. Individual flowers are not spurred; rather the inner portion of the flower contains small petals (called "bees") that usually have a contrast-

Delphinium elatum

ing light or dark color. These hybrids are available in single, semi-double, or fully double flowers that can be white, pink, shades of purple, or shades of blue. Plants are usually grouped by height as follows: small—under 4 feet (1.2 m) tall, medium—4 to 6 feet (1.2 to 1.8 m) tall, and large—more than 6 feet (1.8 m) tall. The Elatum hybrids can be further subdivided into the English and Pacific hybrids.

The English hybrids are the most spectacular in the Elatum group. They are considered perennials and are multiplied vegetatively by division or basal stem cuttings. They are also the most particular about cultural requirements. As their name suggests, they were bred in Europe and have their origins in the nineteenth century. They proved difficult to grow in the United States, leading to the introduction of the U.S.-bred Pacific hybrids in the early twentieth century. The English hybrids are represented by the following: 'Alice Artindale', fully double, blue flowers tinged with pink, on a medium tall plant; Blackmore and Langdon hybrids, small sky blue flowers on tall plants; 'Blue Dawn', pale blue flowers on a medium tall plant; 'Blue Nile', dark semi-double flowers with a white center, on a medium tall plant; 'Blue Tit', purple-blue flowers with a dark center on a medium tall plant; 'Can-Can', fully double, light blue flowers on a medium tall plant; 'Crown Jewel', semi-double pink-blue flowers with a brown center, on a small plant; 'Faust', ultramarine-blue flowers with an indigo center, on a tall plant; 'Loch Leven', light blue flowers on a compact plant; and 'Skyline', late-flowering sky blue flowers on a medium tall plant.

The Pacific hybrids proved easier to grow in North America than the English hybrids; however, they are short lived and grown in the garden as annuals or biennials. They are also reasonably true from seed, making them easier to propagate. Modern delphinium cultivars have come to be dominated by the descendants of this group. The Pacific hybrids are subdivided into several series. The Clear Springs series includes early flowering plants that grow to 3 feet (1 m) tall and have deeply colored flowers with white centers. 'Light Blue Shades', 'Mid-blue', and 'Blue Springs' belong here. The Magic Fountain series consists of compact plants less than 3 feet (1 m) tall. Blue selections include 'Dark Blue', with a white or dark center; 'Heavenly Blue', light blue with a white center; and 'Sky Blue', with a white center. The Mid-Century hybrid series are plants between 4 and 5 feet (1.2 and 1.5 m) tall with sturdy stems. They are more mildew resistant. 'Moody Blues' is pale blue, and 'Ultra Violet' is a dark violet-blue. The Pacific Giant Court series is the most popular of the taller delphiniums. Blue selections include 'Black Knight', dark violet-blue with a white center; 'Blue Bird', clear mid-blue with a white center; 'Blue Dawn', a newer hybrid with bright dark blue flowers and a white center; 'Blue Jay', medium blue with a dark center; 'King Arthur', violet-blue with a white center; 'Round Table' mixed, a tall plant in various shades of blue with a white or dark center; 'Stand Up' mixed, compact plants that are said to not need staking and that have light to dark blue flowers with white centers; and 'Summer Skies', a popular light blue with a white eye.

Delphinium grandiflorum (Chinese larkspur; synonym *D. chinensis*) holds its own as a garden plant with the hybrid delphiniums. Its appear-

Delphinium grandiflorum 'Blue Butterfly' (Chinese larkspur)

ance differs from that of the hybrids as it produces distinctly spurred flowers on loose, airy flower stems. The plants are less than 2 feet (60 cm) tall and usually do not require staking. 'Blue Butterfly' (synonym 'Butterfly Compactum') is the most common cultivar and has a unique aquamarine-blue flower. 'Blue Dwarf' has a dark blue flower. 'Blue Mirror' has electric blue flowers with reduced spurs on compact plants. 'Sky Blue' has light blue flowers.

Delphinium tatsienense is a native of western China that resembles the Belladonna hybrids in stature and floral characteristics. Flowers are bright blue and spurred. Plants are short lived in the garden.

Delphinium tricorne (dwarf larkspur) is not commonly available except from specialty native plant nurseries. It is the common larkspur growing in woodlands of the northeastern United States. Useful for naturalizing in woodland settings, it has spurred flowers that appear in shades of blue and occasionally white. Plants are about 1 foot (30 cm) tall.

Dichorisandra
Blue Ginger
COMMELINACEAE

Dichorisandra species are tropical, evergreen or deciduous herbaceous perennials that vary in height from 1 to 15 feet (0.3 to 4 m). The upright spikes contain many small, three-petaled flowers. Flower color is violet-blue to blue with contrasting yellow stamens. In frost-free gardens, blue gingers are used as landscape plants for sites with partial shade and a well-drained but moist, fertile soil. They are also common in greenhouse conservatories where the bright floral display contrasts nicely with other tropical monocots. The genus name comes from the Greek for "twice, to part an anther" and refers to the fact that the anthers open in two places.

Propagation: Plants are multiplied by seed, cuttings, or division. They are easy to propagate from stem cuttings taken any time of year or by basal divisions.

Representative species and cultivars: *Dichorisandra* has about 35 species native to Central and South America. The most commonly cultivated species are *D. reginae* and *D. thyrsiflora*.

Dichorisandra reginae (queen's spiderwort; synonym *Tradescantia reginae*) is a Peruvian native grown mostly for its foliage that is dark green with zigzags of silver streaks on the upper surface and purple coloration on the underside of the leaf. Plants reach 12 inches (30 cm) tall and produce violet-blue flowers in upright spikes.

Dichorisandra thyrsiflora (blue ginger) is a native of Brazil. Its upright canes can reach 10 feet (3 m) in height. Stems contain whorls of leaves that terminate in 6-inch (15-cm) tall spikes of electric, violet-blue flowers with contrasting yellow centers.

Dichorisandra thyrsiflora (blue ginger)

Duranta
Sky Flower
VERBENACEAE

Duranta species include tropical woody trees and shrubs grown as landscape plants in frost-free gardens or as greenhouse specimens in containers. Sky flower can be grown as a specimen plant or pruned to form a hedge. Plants produce small blue, purple, or white flowers in hanging groups that lead to attractive orange-yellow berries. These easy-to-grow plants prefer full sun and are drought tolerant. When grown in the greenhouse, vigorous plants need restrictive pruning to keep them in bounds. Pot them in a well-drained medium and reduce watering during the winter. The genus name commemorates Castor Durantes, a sixteenth-century Italian botanist and physician.

Propagation: Plants are multiplied by seed, stem cuttings, or air layering. They are easy to propagate from stem cuttings taken in the summer, and bottom heat improves rooting.

Representative species and cultivars: *Duranta* has about 35 species native to Central and South America. The most commonly cultivated species is *D. repens* (sky flower, Brazilian sky flower; synonym *D. plumieri*). A small tree to 20 feet (6 m) tall, it produces hanging clusters (racemes) of blue, lilac blue, or white flowers in the summer leading to small, round, orange-yellow fruit. Plants can be trained into a small topiary standard and respond well in hanging baskets. 'Alba' is a white-flowering selection and 'Grandiflora' is a free-flowering form with lilac blue flowers.

Echinops
Globe Thistle
ASTERACEAE

Globe thistle is a very descriptive name for this genus of plants that produce a buttonlike group of bristly flowers. Each flower is pale to deep blue, protruding through stiff silvery bracts. Plants range from 3 to more than 6 feet (1 to 1.8 m) tall with thistlelike, prickly leaves that look more menacing than they really are. These sun-loving plants work well in a mixed perennial bed for summer bloom or as long-lasting cut flowers. They are easy to grow in any well-drained soil. The genus name comes from the Greek word for "like a hedgehog."

Propagation: Plants are multiplied by seed, division, or root cuttings. Species are propagated by seed that requires light to germinate. Cultivars are propagated by division of dormant plants or, more commonly, as root cuttings taken in the winter.

Representative species and cultivars: *Echinops* contains approximately 100 species native to Europe, Asia, and Africa. Several similar perennial species are cultivated for their flower color and for the texture they bring to the garden. Unfortunately, nomenclature in the cultivated members of this genus can be confusing. Some species are cross-listed or misrepresented in some catalogs.

Echinops bannaticus is native to southern Europe. It is a compact, 3-foot (1-m) tall plant with attractive light blue flowers, but several cultivars have dark silver-blue flowers. 'Blue Glow' has dark blue flowers and makes an excellent fresh or dried cut flower. 'Taplow Blue' produces bright blue flowers. It is sometimes incorrectly listed as a cultivar of *E. ritro*.

Echinops exaltus (Russian globe thistle) is a Siberian native that grows to 5 feet (1.5 m) tall. It is similar to (and often sold as) *E. ritro* and *E. spha-*

Echinops exaltus (Russian globe thistle)

erocephalus. All three species have thistlelike foliage and globe-shaped flower heads, but Russian globe thistle does not have hairs on the leaf surfaces.

Echinops ritro is a compact grower, usually less than 3 feet (1 m) tall. Native to southern Europe and central Asia, it has spiny, deeply cut leaves. The leaf underside is coated with white hairs. Flower color is bright blue. 'Veitch's Blue' with its deep blue flowers may be the most popular globe thistle because it produces a large quantity of flowers.

Echinops sphaerocephalus is native from central Europe into Russia. It is one of the tall-growing globe thistles, reaching up to 7 feet (2.1 m). The underside of the leaf is coated with white hairs. This species makes a bold statement as a backdrop for smaller perennials in a mixed border. Flower color is blue-gray and the flower heads are large.

Echium
Viper's Bugloss
BORAGINACEAE

I first became familiar with *Echium* as an interesting roadside weed. I was delighted to find that several species of *Echium* are used as specimen plants in greenhouse conservatories or as bedding plants in warmer climates. They can be annuals, biennials, or woody shrubs. In most species, the foliage is hairy and the flowers are produced on pyramidal spikes of many individual flowers. The flower buds can be red and open to form bright blue flowers often with protruding anthers. In some cases, flowers retain their red color. Plants are suited for use as focal points in perennial beds where the climate is mild, or as dramatic specimen shrubs in greenhouse conservatories. They benefit from full sun and a well-drained medium or soil. Plants that are overfertilized can become leggy. The genus name comes from the Greek word for "like a viper" and refers to the shape of the seeds.

Propagation: Seed propagation is common for the annual species, and stem cuttings are common for the shrubby perennial species.

Representative species and cultivars: The approximately 40 species of *Echium* are native to the Canary Islands and the Mediterranean region. All have blue or red flowers. The species with large pyramidal flower spikes are most ornamental.

Echium candicans (synonym *E. fastuosum*), *E. pininana* (tower of jewels), and *E. wildpretii* are representative of the shrubby forms of *Echium* that are grown as greenhouse specimens or outdoors in frost-free environments. They can reach between 3 and 10 feet (1 and 3 m) tall and are similar in flower, producing large, pyramidal groups of flowers that can reach several feet long. They are short-lived perennials or biennials. *Echium candicans* is the lowest growing of these species and is suitable as a traditional perennial where the climate is warm.

Echium ×hybridum, a hybrid of *E. candicans* and *E. pininana,* produces a bold spire of blue flowers. It is grown as a summer-blooming perennial in mild climates like southern California.

Echium vulgare (blue devil) is a European species grown as an annual bedding plant. This 2-foot (60-cm) tall plant has flowers in the axils of the flowering stem. 'Blue Bedder' is a blue-flowered selection with a pink tint.

Echium candicans

Eryngium
Sea Holly
APIACEAE

Sea hollies are a bold group of herbaceous annuals and perennials that produce rounded, bluish flower heads above prominent silvery bracts with prickly edges. Most of the perennial species grown in gardens are less than 3 feet (1 m) tall. They are summer bloomers used in mixed perennial beds to provide an interesting textural aspect. They are also at home in an informal meadow wildflower garden. Flower stems make excellent fresh and dried cut flowers. Plants need full sun and a well-drained soil, but tolerate a wide variety of conditions. *Eryngium* is an old name applied to this plant in herbals.

Propagation: Plants are multiplied by seed, division, and root cuttings. Seed should be sown as soon as it ripens so that is does not develop dormancy conditions that need chilling stratification to germinate. Division is the most reliable form of propagation.

Representative species and cultivars: These unique members of the carrot family are native to many temperate and dry regions. More than 200 species belong in this genus. Several perennial species are available to gardeners.

Eryngium alpinum (alpine sea holly) is native to mountains in Europe and grows to 2 feet (60 cm) tall. It may be the best sea holly for the garden, because of its large flowers that are the deepest blue of all the species commonly cultivated. Clusters of flowers form upright cylinders and are held in the center of large, spiny bracts that are very interesting. Blue cultivars deserve wider distribution in the United States. 'Amethyst' produces violet-blue flowers. 'Blue Star' has large, dark blue flowers that make excellent, long-lived cut flowers of commercial quality. 'Superbum' also produces large, blue flowers on vigorous plants.

Eryngium amethystinum (amethyst sea holly) is native in dry areas of the

Mediterranean. It grows less than 2 feet (60 cm) tall with steel blue flowers above bold, pointed bracts.

Eryngium bourgatii (Mediterranean sea holly) is more common in European gardens than in the United States. Its gray foliage has prominent white main veins that give it a unique appearance. The steel blue flowers, borne on small 1.5-foot (24-cm) tall plants, are held in rounded clusters that are produced in abundance on branched flower stems. 'Oxford Blue' has darker blue flowers.

Eryngium giganteum (Miss Willmott's ghost) is a short-lived perennial or biennial native to the Caucasus and Iran. Plants grow to 2 feet (60 cm) tall and produce flowers. The common name alludes to this plant's character in the garden. Large, white, and spiny bracts beneath the flowers are its unique garden feature. 'Silver Ghost' has even whiter, silvery bracts.

Eryngium planum (flat sea holly) is native to Europe and is common in gardens. It grows to 3 feet (1 m) tall and produces small flower heads that are numerous on branched flower stems. 'Blue Diamond' and 'Blue Dwarf' are smaller than the species, only reaching 1 foot (30 cm) tall. 'Blue Cap' has a deeper blue flower color. 'Blue Ribbon' produces double flowers. 'Fluela' has bluish stems holding blue flowers; it is a popular dried cut flower produced commercially.

Eryngium ×tripartitum is a clump-forming, drought-tolerant sea holly that produces many small violet-blue flowers on branched flower stems. Plants reach 3 feet (1 m) tall and work well in naturalized plantings that need little attention.

Eryngium alpinum 'Blue Star' (alpine sea holly)

Eryngium ×*zabelii* 'Donard Blue' produces large 3-inch (7-cm) cone-shaped flower heads with blue flowers on 2-foot (60-cm) tall plants. *Eryngium* ×*zabelii* is a hybrid between *E. alpina* and *E. bourgatii*.

Eustoma
Texas Bluebell
GENTIANACEAE

Eustoma is still better known and more commonly sold under its more familiar name, which in the United States is *Lisianthus* and in Great Britain is *Lisianthius*. It is a group of herbaceous annuals and short-lived perennials. Breeding efforts have made it a very popular cut flower crop, because the large flowers have excellent vase life. The flowers are cup-shaped and held on upright stems. Flower color ranges from white to pink, purple, and blue. Several cultivars produce picotee flowers, with a ring of contrasting color at the tip of the petals. These plants are suitable for containers or greenhouse use. They also can be used as bedding plants, but wiry stems should be supported and combined with other plants for best effect. They prefer full sun in a moderately fertile, well-drained soil. The genus name is Greek for "beautiful countenance."

Propagation: Plants are multiplied by seed, which is easy to germinate. Seedlings, however, are slow to develop and need protection from strong sunlight and drying out until they are well rooted.

Representative species and cultivars: *Eustoma* contains three species native to North and South America. Only one species is extensively cultivated. *Eustoma grandiflorum* (Texas bluebell; synonym *Lisianthus russellianus*) has been refined by years of breeding to produce some excellent F_1 hybrid selections. Its common name is not commonly used. Several excellent series are now available that include flower colors in bright blue, mid-blue, lilac, pink, and white, and picotees combine white flowers with a blue or pink margin. Flowers are about 3 inches (8 cm) in diameter and held on stout, upright stems. Plants can reach 3 feet (1 m) tall. They make excellent cut flowers. Available F$_1$ hybrid series include Echo, Heidi, Lizzy, Mariachi, Mermaid, and Yodel. Echo and Mariachi hybrids produce fully double flowers. The Heidi and Lizzy series have uniform flower color and compact plants suited for containers or bedding plants. 'Blue Lisa' is a dwarf form only growing to 8 inches (20 cm) tall. The dwarf cultivars make excellent pot plants and are better suited for bedding out with other annuals than the taller selections.

Evolvulus
CONVOLVULACEAE

Evolvulus is a non-twining genus in the morning glory family. It consists of tender, herbaceous or woody perennials native mostly to South America. Flower color can be purple, blue, or white. Plants are useful as bedding plants or in hanging baskets. They flower best in full sun in a well-drained soil. The genus name comes from the Greek word for "to unroll." It is the opposite of *Convolvulus* and refers to the non-twining habit of the plants.

Evolvulus pilosus 'Blue Daze'

Propagation: Plants are multiplied by seed or stem cuttings. Cuttings are the most common method of production for commercial growers.

Representative species and cultivars: The approximately 100 species of *Evolvulus* are native to North and South America, but only *E. pilosus* (synonym *E. glomeratus*) from South America is commonly available. It has become popular as a bedding and hanging basket plant. It produces bright blue, saucer-shaped flowers on a trailing 1 foot (30 cm) tall plant. Flowers are attractive all summer long. *Evolvulus* makes an excellent blue accent and tolerates dry sites. 'Blue Daze' is the cultivar most available to gardeners. It has become such a useful garden plant that it makes one wonder how many other garden gems await introduction from this genus.

Exacum
Persian Violet
GENTIANACEAE

Exacum is a group of tender annuals and herbaceous perennials grown mostly as greenhouse pot plants. Flowers have five fused lavender-blue petals that contrast with the protruding yellow stamens. White-flowering forms are also available. Persian violets are popular as seasonal pot plants, but also make good bedding plants in light shade and a moist, well-drained soil. The genus name comes from the Greek word for "to drive out," possibly a reference for the plant's use to drive out poison.

Propagation: Plants are multiplied most commonly by seed, but stem cuttings root easily.

Representative species and cultivars: The approximately 25 species of *Exacum* are native to tropical areas. *Exacum affine,* the most commonly grown species, produces a compact, branched plant to 1 foot (30 cm) tall. It is topped with lavender-blue flowers that look like they belong in the nightshade family (Solanaceae) rather than the gentian family

(Gentianaceae). This species is grown as a seasonal pot plant. 'Tiddly Winks' is a cultivar selected for pot culture. Other blue selections include 'Blue Gem' and 'Blue Midget'.

Felicia
Blue Marguerite, Blue Daisy
ASTERACEAE

Felicia species are tender annuals, and herbaceous or woody perennials used as summer-blooming bedding plants, hanging baskets, and container plants. Flowers are typically daisylike with the outer ray flowers usually blue and the smaller center flowers yellow—an interesting and unique contrasting color combination for blue flowers. Plants need full sun and a well-drained soil or medium. Occasional pinching makes them well branched and increases flowering. The genus name commemorates Mr. Felix, a nineteenth-century German.

Propagation: Plants are multiplied by seed or stem cuttings. Annual types are produced from seed, while perennial types can be rooted from stem cuttings any time of year.

Representative species and cultivars: The genus *Felicia* is native to Africa and consists of more than 60 species. It is closely related to and resembles *Aster*. The number of *Felicia* species that are becoming popular as ornamentals continues to increase. These species are most useful as bedding plants or in hanging baskets.

Felicia amelloides (blue marguerite; synonyms *F. capensis, Agathaea coelestis*) comes from South Africa and was the first cultivated *Felicia* species. It is treated as an annual and attains a height of about 2 feet (60 cm) as a bedding plant. It is excellent in hanging baskets. The outer ray florets are a bright azure blue contrasting with a yellow center. 'Astrid Thomas' is a compact selection with vivid blue flowers. 'Read's Blue' is a compact cultivar, and 'Santa Anita' has larger flowers. 'Variegata' is a variegated leaf selection.

Felicia amoena (synonym *Aster pappei*) and especially the cultivar 'Variegata' have become widely used plants for hanging baskets and containers. The blue flowers with yellow centers contrasting against the green and white foliage are interesting if not ornamental. This species is native to South Africa.

Felicia bergeriana (kingfisher daisy) has flowers similar to those of blue marguerite on smaller plants less than 1 foot (30 cm) tall. It has a larger area of central, yellow disk flowers and is best treated as an annual bedding plant. It is also a South African native.

Felicia heterophylla is a popular bedding plant from South Africa. Raised from seed, it becomes a low-growing plant about 1.5 feet (45 cm) tall. 'Spring Merchen' is a free-flowering selection with blue or purple-blue flowers. 'The Blues' has pale blue flowers.

Felicia amelloides (blue marguerite)

Gentiana
Gentian
GENTIANACEAE

Gentiana species are herbaceous annual and perennial plants synonymous with blue flowers. Even the name gentian brings to mind a shade of blue. This diverse group of plants produces flowers that bloom in spring, summer, or fall. The flower color is predominantly shades of blue, but white and yellow flowers are also seen. Most flowers are tubular, trumpet-shaped or bell-shaped, and some have fringed petal tips. They can grow as diminutive 6-inch (15-cm) plants, while some species can reach 3 feet (1 m) tall. They are well suited for the rock garden or alpine dish garden, but some have found homes in the perennial bed. Some species also can be naturalized in wildflower plantings. In general, gentians grow best in full sun or light shade in a well-drained soil. They perform well in climates with cool night temperatures. Consult a good reference on gentian, as some species require a more alkaline soil pH, while others must be given a more acidic, moist soil. Because they can be difficult to grow, gentians are not common garden plants in most regions of the United States; however, some species are easier to grow and are becoming more popular. The genus name commemorates Gentius, a king of Illyria who expounded the medical properties of some gentian.

Propagation: Plants are multiplied mainly by seed that may require chilling stratification to relieve dormancy. Perennial species can be divided in early spring.

Representative species and cultivars: *Gentiana* is a large genus of more than 350 species. Most gentians are native to alpine environments, but they occur in many cool temperate environments throughout the world; many are native to mountainous areas of North America. The genus is a collector's delight. Many species are available from specialty nurseries, and their diminutive size allows for much diversity in a small space. A few of the more easily grown and attainable gentians are listed here, but avid gardeners in the alpine or rock garden plant genre will find this collection too brief.

Gentiana acaulis (trumpet gentian; synonyms *G. excisa, G. kochiana*) is a wonderful mat-forming plant less than 6 inches (15 cm) tall with dark blue trumpet-shaped flowers. It is a perennial native to the Alps. Plants can be easy to grow, but may not flower well unless conditions are right. 'Helzmannii' is a rich blue, free-flowering form. Coelestina is a strain with large flowers.

Gentiana andrewsii (closed gentian, bottle gentian) is among the easier species to grow and flower. Native to moist meadows in northern North America, it produces oblong flowers that rarely open at the tip (hence the common name "closed gentian"). Flowering occurs in the fall on upright plants between 1 and 2 feet (30 and 60 cm) tall with a cluster of flowers at the tip.

Gentiana asclepiadea (willow gentian) has become more available to U.S. gardeners. It is a European species that produces blue flowers along the arching stems in the leaf axils rather than as terminal clusters. This lovely perennial plant blooms in late summer and reaches 2 feet (60 cm) tall. It is a gentian you might like to try if you have felt gentians were too difficult to grow. 'Alba' is a white form, 'Nymans' has large flowers on arching stems, and 'Rosea' is a pink-purple form.

Gentiana clusii is similar to *G. acaulis* with large blue flowers. Plants grow only 4 inches (10 cm) tall and tolerate alkaline soil. The species is native to the European Alps.

Gentiana cruciata (cross gentian) is among the easier gentians to grow. It is a very winter hardy species from the mountains of central Europe. The dark blue bell-shaped flowers appear in late summer on 12-inch (30-cm) tall plants.

Gentiana gracilipes is a summer-blooming species from northwestern China. It produces trumpet-shaped

Gentiana andrewsii (closed gentian)

flowers on trailing stems that arch upward at the tips. Flower color is lavender-blue, and plants only reach about 6 inches (15 cm) tall. This species tolerates partial shade.

Gentiana septemfida (crested gentian) is another fall-blooming species from the Caucasus. It produces numerous flowers in terminal clusters on arching 1-foot (30-cm) long stems. The flowers are a bright blue with a light throat. A form of this species, *G. septemfida* var. *lagodechiana,* is often sold because it is larger flowering. Among the easier gentians to grow, *G. septemfida* is a good starter plant for aspiring alpine gardeners. *Genti-*

Gentiana septemfida var. *lagodechiana* (crested gentian)

Gentiana verna (star gentian)

ana ×*hascombensis* (*G. septemfida* × *G. septemfida* var. *lagodechiana*) is similar to *G. septemfida*, but worth a try as possibly a more vigorous selection.

Gentiana sino-ornata produces dark blue trumpet-flowers with a white throat. Native to China and Tibet, it blooms in the fall on diminutive 3-inch (8-cm) tall plants.

Gentiana triflora is an Asian native found from Russia to Japan. This upright-growing plant to 2 feet (60 cm) tall produces axillary clusters of tubular-shaped violet-blue flowers in late summer. A white form is available.

Gentiana verna (star gentian) is a spring-blooming gentian that produces *Phlox*-like blossoms on small plants less than 2 inches (6 cm) tall. Native to northern Europe, these plants are covered with bright flowers in the spring. Alpine and rock garden aficionados must have this species in their collections.

Geranium
Cranesbill
GERANIACEAE

Geranium is very familiar to gardeners with perennial beds. This large genus contains several excellent garden plants. All cultivated plants have palmately lobed leaves. Most grow to less than 3 feet (1 m) tall and have a mounded habit. The saucer-shaped flowers appear in shades of blue, lavender, purple, pink, or white. Some *Geranium* species make long-flowering plants for the perennial bed, while others are more at home in woodland wildflower gardens. They prefer full sun or light shade in a moist, well-drained soil. Overfertilization can stretch plants, making them less tidy in the garden. Plants should be divided every few years to keep them in shape as the centers become more open. The genus name comes from the Greek word for "crane" and refers to the beaklike shape of the fruit that extends from the center of the fertilized flower.

Propagation: Plants are multiplied by seed, division, stem cuttings, and root cuttings, depending on the species or need to maintain a cultivar.

Representative species and cultivars: This large genus has more than 300 annual and perennial species native to temperate areas throughout the world. Several species have blue flowers, but these only scratch the surface of the many excellent geranium selections for the garden. Hybrids have been developed with blue flowers.

Geranium erianthum is a hardy perennial native to Russia, Japan, and Canada. Plants are less than 2 feet (60 cm) tall and bloom in summer. Violet-blue flowers are held above the foliage in branched, open stems.

Geranium himalayense creeps slowly from rhizomes to form large mats of foliage remaining less than 2 feet (60 cm) tall. It tolerates a good amount of shade and, as the name implies, the species is native to the Himalayan mountains. Plants are free-flowering, and the flower color is violet to mid-blue. 'Alpinum' has large blue flowers with violet towards the center. 'Baby Blue' produces large lavender-blue flowers. 'Irish Blue' shows a more consistent pale blue flower color. 'Gravetye' has large deep blue flowers with deeply cut leaves. 'Plenum' (synonym 'Birch Double') is a lavender-blue double-flowering form with extended blooming time.

Geranium ibericum produces lavender-blue, upward-facing flowers on 2-foot (60-cm) tall plants. It is similar to *G. platypetalum* and native to the same region in the Caucasus, Turkey, and Iran.

Geranium 'Johnson's Blue', a hybrid between *G. himalayense* and *G. pratense,* both with violet-blue flowers, is a very good garden plant, blooming for an extended period in summer. Flowers top 1.5-foot (45-cm) tall plants and can appear as bright blue under the right growing conditions.

Geranium 'Nimbus', a hybrid of *G. collinum* and *G. clarkei* 'Kashmir Purple', is a long-flowering selection with lavender-blue flowers and handsome foliage. Plants remain less than 2.5 feet (75 cm) tall on slightly trailing stems.

Geranium 'Philippe Vapelle', a hybrid between G. *renardii* and G. *platy-petalum,* has dark violet-blue flowers on mounded plants to about 1 foot (30 cm) tall.

Geranium platypetalum finds its way to gardens from the Caucasus and the Middle East. Deep violet-blue flowers are produced on mounded plants with hairy foliage. The petals on these flowers are notched at the top and a paler color towards the center. Plants do well in full sun or partial shade. 'Georgia Blue', a selection from the Republic of Georgia on the Black Sea, has larger flowers with overlapping petals.

Geranium pratense is native from Europe into China and produces flowers in early to mid-summer on mounded plants that can reach 3 feet (1 m) tall. Flower color is variable from white to violet and blue, and can have longitudinal stripes along the petals. 'Mrs. Kendall Clark' produces soft blue flowers with streaks of pink. 'Plenum Caeruleum'

Geranium 'Johnson's Blue'

is a semi-double with lavender-blue flowers, while 'Plenum Violaceum' is a semi-double with violet-blue flowers. 'Striatum' (synonym 'Bicolor') has white petals with violet-blue streaks. The Victor Reiter strain provides additional garden interest, because the new foliage emerges purple in the spring before fading to purple-green for the summer.

Geranium sylvaticum (wood cranesbill) produces violet flowers in spring on 2.5-foot (75-cm) tall plants. It combines well with early flowering bulbs.

Geranium sylvatica 'Amy Doncaster' (wood cranesbill)

Native to Europe, it has selections with pink, lavender, lilac, or blue flower color. 'Amy Doncaster' is an excellent blue-flowering selection with a white center. 'Mayflower' is superior to the species and produces a violet-blue flower with a white center.

Geranium wallichianum produces lilac or purple flowers in late summer on 1-foot (30-cm) tall plants. The species is native to Afghanistan and India. 'Buxton's Blue' may have the bluest flower of all the geranium selections: sky blue outer petals with a light center.

Gladiolus
IRIDACEAE

Gladiolus species are herbaceous perennials developing from corms. They are prized for their colorful sprays of flowers held above narrow, sword-shaped leaves. Each flower consists of six tepals that occur in a rainbow of colors, including shades of blue. In some cases, the lower three tepals are pigmented differently from the top and two side-wing tepals or they can have a distinctive light-colored "eye." The tepals of some cultivars have wavy or frilled edges. Plants can mix well with hardy perennials, but their main use is as a cut flower. They bloom for only a short period in the summer, which can be extended by planting corms at various intervals into early summer to ensure cut flowers throughout the season. Plants require full sun in a moderately fertile, well-drained soil. They should not be overfertilized, and they need to be irrigated in a timely fashion for quality blooms. Plants may require staking in some situations. Gladiolus does not tolerate cold winters, and corms should be lifted in the fall and overwintered dry in a well-ventilated area. The genus name comes from the Greek word for "sword-like" and refers to the shape of the leaves.

Propagation: Plants are multiplied by offshoots (cormels) of the main corm. Corms are interesting plant structures and renew themselves each season. Only the largest corms should be saved for overwintering to ensure the best flowering plants each year. New hybrids are raised from seed that takes 2 or 3 years to reach a flowering size.

Representative species and cultivars: *Gladiolus* is a relatively large genus of 180 species, but only a few are grown in gardens. They are native to the Mediterranean area and Africa, especially South Africa. Plants were introduced into Europe by John Tradescant Sr. in 1620. Tradescant was the royal gardener to King Charles I and collected plants along the coast of Africa on a ship commissioned to hunt pirates! Rabid interest in "glads" did not occur until the mid-nineteenth century, when the famous plant developers Victor Lemoine in France and L. B. Van Houtte in Belgium began to introduce hybrid glads. In the late nineteenth century, North American breeders like Luther Burbank and H. H. Graf made hybrid glads commercial successes on this side of the Atlantic. Today, gladiolus is known mostly as the myriad of hybrids grown in gardens and used as cut flowers. The modern-day hybrids only vaguely resemble the species from which they arose. Crosses of existing plants can yield fantastic results for color and flower form, which has led to a loyal following of amateur breeders and thousands of registered *Gladiolus* cultivars. Several of these cultivars produce flowers with varying shades of blue. A limited listing of these include 'Blue

Bird', 'Blue Conqueror', 'Blue Delight', 'Blue Frost', 'Blue Heaven', 'Blue Isle', 'Her Majesty', 'Madonna', and 'Wind Song'.

Gladiolus liliaceus was collected from the Transvaal in South Africa by noted plant explorer Collingwood Ingram. This curious glad became popular in the early twentieth century as the "brown Africander," because it had a brown flower that turned blue at night and then back to brown the following morning.

Globularia
Globe Daisy
GLOBULARIACEAE

Globularia species are perennials that are almost unknown to most gardeners, but prized by alpine and rock gardeners. They form mats of evergreen foliage from which arise blue or lavender-blue flower heads reminiscent of daisies in late spring and summer. They plants are charming when viewed up close and are well suited for alpine container production or for the rock garden. They prefer full sun and a light, well-drained soil or medium that is slightly alkaline. Plants are winter hardy to about −20°F (−29°C) and are intolerant of wet conditions during the winter. The genus name comes from the Greek words for "small round head" and describes the flowers.

Propagation: Plants are multiplied by seed or cuttings. Offset crowns can be separated from the main plant and rooted in early summer.

Representative species and cultivars: *Globularia* is a genus of approximately 20 species native to the rocky slopes of mountains in the Mediterranean region. It is a rock garden favorite, especially in European gardens.

Globularia cordifolia produces lavender flower heads, just above the creeping evergreen foliage. It is a native of central Europe and Turkey.

Globularia meridionalis (synonym *G. pygmaea*) is a quick-spreading plant
  with lavender-blue to purple flowers with a white center. It is an
  alpine native.

Globularia repens (synonym *G. nana*) forms woody mats of foliage with
  gray blue buttons of flowers. It is native to the Pyrenees and Alps.

Globularia trichosantha is a Balkan native that produces cushions of
  bright blue flowers on 8-inch (20-cm) tall stems above creeping
  plants.

Hebe
SCROPHULARIACEAE

Hebe species are evergreen woody perennials with flower spikes similar
in appearance to *Veronica* and at one time were included in the genus
Veronica. They are tender plants popular as landscape shrubs or mixed
in the perennial garden where winters are mild such as California, the
Pacific Northwest, and parts of Europe. Plants range between 2 and 6
feet (0.2 and 1.8 m) tall and produce spikes with white, lavender, purple,
or blue flowers. Plants are easy to grow in full sun with a well-drained
soil that is mulched to retain moisture. They only need pruning for
height control as they naturally retain a full appearance. The genus
name comes from the Greek word for "youth."

Propagation: Plants are multiplied by seed or stem cuttings. Cultivars
are propagated reliably by terminal stem cuttings taken in late summer.

Representative species and cultivars: Most of the approximately 100
species of *Hebe* are native to New Zealand, Australia, and New Guinea.
Flower color is generally white, pink, purple, or shades of blue.

Hebe elliptica (synonym *H. decussata*) is native to New Zealand and parts
  of South America. It is usually a large shrub to 6 feet (1.8 m) tall
  with short flower spikes containing white or blue fragrant blossoms.

Hebe ×*franciscana* 'Blue Gem' is a selection of the hybrid between *H. ellip-tica* and *H. speciosa*. It produces a showier plant with bluer flowers than either of the parent species and forms a rounded shrub to about 4 feet (1.2 m) tall.

Hebe speciosa is a rounded shrub to about 4 feet (1.2 m) tall. It is native to New Zealand. 'Alicia Amherst' is an excellent garden plant that produces a deep purple-blue flower spike. This cultivar may be of hybrid origin.

Hedyotis
Bluets, Quaker Ladies
RUBIACEAE

Depending on the reference consulted, the genus *Hedyotis* contains mostly tropical and subtropical herbaceous and woody perennials, or it exclusively contains the small bluets native to North America that were formerly in the genus *Houstonia* but are now included with the other species of *Hedyotis*. My first experience with bluets was walking along a hiking trail in Maryland and stopping suddenly because the path before me had turned blue. Bluets can grow in colonies that carpet large areas. They are diminutive plants only reaching 4 inches (10 cm) in height, but they bunch together to lift numerous flowers on thin flower stems. Each flower has four blue petals with a pale yellow center. Bluets appear in spring and early summer and are suited for use in the rock garden, woodland edges, or informal perennial beds. They grow well in light shade in a well-drained, moist soil that is slightly acidic. In a good environment, they can quickly spread by self-sowing. The genus name is Greek for "being charming," which certainly describes bluets.

Propagation: Plants are multiplied by seed or division. Seed germinates easily, and plants spread naturally by self-sowing in the garden.

Representative species and cultivars: The approximately 50 species of *Hedyotis* are native to North America, but only a few are cultivated.

Hedyotis caerulea (bluets; synonym *Houstonia caerulea*) is the most commonly cultivated species in the genus. It is not a staple in most garden centers, but can be found in catalogs specializing in native wildflowers and is worth the hunt, because it is a delightful perennial that brightens the spring garden. It is native to moist areas in eastern North America. Plants in flower can reach 8 inches (20 cm) tall. The flowers are the typical cross-shaped blue blossoms with a yellow eye. These are a garden delight because they can grow in mass to attract attention from a distance and then reward viewers when seen close up.

Hedyotis michauxii (creeping bluets; synonym *Houstonia serpyllifolia*) is less commonly cultivated than *H. caerulea*. Native to moist mountain areas in eastern North America, it is very similar to *H. caerulea*, but grows as a prostrate plant that roots as the stems creep along the ground. It is not as winter hardy as *H. caerulea*.

Hedyotis caerulea (bluets)

Heliophila
BRASSICACEAE

Heliophila is among the few members of the mustard family with blue flowers. It consists of annuals and herbaceous perennials that have white, pink, yellow, or blue flowers with the four-petal, crosslike shape typical of the family. The few members of the genus in cultivation are treated as annuals. They are useful in annual or mixed perennial beds. Plants perform best in full sun in a well-drained soil. In areas where the summers are hot and humid, these plants only provide early season color. They also can be grown as greenhouse pot plants. The genus name comes from the Greek word for "sun lover."

Propagation: Plants are multiplied by seed.

Representative species and cultivars: *Heliophila* is a South African genus of approximately 75 species, none of which are common in cultivation. Two species have bright blue flowers: *H. leptophylla* and *H. coronopifolia*. Similar in appearance, these two wiry plants are between 1 and 3 feet (30 cm and 1 m) tall and make seasonal container plants. Flower color is true blue with a contrasting yellow center. *Heliophila coronopifolia* 'Atlantis' is a blue selection. The dried seed pods of *H. leptophylla* are used in floral arrangements.

Hepatica
RANUNCULACEAE

Hepatica species are herbaceous perennials native to wooded areas. They are useful for planting in rock gardens and woodland plantings. Similar to other species in this family, *Hepatica* species have flowers whose showy part consists of five to seven sepals rather than petals. Flowers appear in spring and can be white, pink, or pale blue. Plants prefer partial shade and an organic, well-drained soil. The genus name comes from the Greek word for "liver" and refers to the shape of the leaves and its inferred use as an herbal medication.

Propagation: Plants are multiplied by seed or, more commonly, division of the crown.

Representative species and cultivars: The approximately 10 species of *Hepatica* are native to North America, Europe, and Asia. They are similar in appearance to *Anemone* species and useful as rock garden or woodland plants.

Hepatica acutiloba (common hepatica) is seen in wooded areas throughout northeastern North America. It is a herbaceous perennial with trilobed leaves that can persist throughout the winter. Plants form compact mounds to about 4 inches (10 cm) tall. The flowers appear in early spring before the foliage is fully expanded. Flower color is variable and can be white, pink, or pale blue. Double-flowering selections are known.

Hepatica americana is another woodland species that grows in North America from Florida to Canada along the east coast. It resembles the European hepatica *H. nobilis* so closely that some botanists consider them to be one species (*H. nobilis*) with botanical varieties in Japan (*H. nobilis* var. *japonica*) and North America (*H. nobilis* var. *americana*). The Japanese form is more compact than the American or European versions. All can have flowers that are white, pink, or blue.

Hepatica nobilis is the European counterpart of *H. acutiloba* and is similar to it in growth habit and flower form. It differs in having leaf lobes that are rounded rather than pointed as in *H. acutiloba,* and the undersides of the leaves are tinged purple. Double-flowering selections are available.

Hepatica transsilvanica is native to central Europe and is possibly the showiest of the hepaticas. It produces a larger flower with more sepals than the other *Hepatica* species described. Flower color can be blue, white, or pink as in the other species. Good blue selections can be propagated by division.

Hibiscus

Hibiscus, Marsh Mallow, Rose of Sharon
MALVACEAE

Hibiscus species are tender or hardy, herbaceous and woody plants noted for their large, saucer-shaped flowers. They lend a tropical flare to the garden. Flowers have five often overlapping petals that can be white, pink, red, yellow, or blue. Depending on the species, the flowers range from 3 to 10 inches (7.5 to 25 cm) in diameter. The center of the flower has a prominent display of anthers and style sometimes protruding several inches from the petals. Some species are grown for their colored, deeply cut leaves. *Hibiscus,* depending on the species, is useful in the perennial border (*H. moscheutos*), mixed shrub border (*H. syriacus*), or as a container plant for patios or greenhouse displays (*H. rosa-sinensis*). Plants prefer full sun and a moist, well-drained soil. They perform better where the soil is slightly alkaline. *Hibiscus* is the old Latin name for "marsh mallow."

Propagation: Plants are multiplied by seed, division, or cuttings. Herbaceous perennial species are commonly propagated by seed or division. Seeds with a hard coat benefit from a hot water treatment prior to sowing. Woody perennials are propagated from softwood stem cuttings.

Representative species and cultivars: *Hibiscus* is a large and diverse genus of approximately 200 species native to temperate and tropical areas throughout the world. Among the cultivated species, blue flower color is not common, but does occur in cultivars of *H. syriacus*. *Hibiscus syriacus* (rose of Sharon) is a very popular woody shrub for garden landscapes and grows to approximately 10 feet (3 m) tall. It produces large, colorful flowers continuously from midsummer into fall. Individual flowers do not last long, but they are replaced by other flowers in the same leaf axil. Flower color can be white, pink, rose, or blue. Often the center of the flower has a contrasting coloration such as a red center for a white bloom. 'Blue Bird' produces bright blue flowers that are 3 inches (7.5 cm) in diameter.

Hyacinthoides
Bluebell
LILIACEAE

Bluebells are perennial plants that replace themselves each year by bulb offsets. They are similar in appearance to *Scilla* species and at one time were classified as members of that genus as well as the genus *Endymion*. The plants bloom in spring with numerous 1-foot (30-cm) tall flower stalks above straplike foliage. Each stalk contains nodding, bell-shaped flowers in blue, white, or pink. In the moist shady garden, bluebells spread rapidly from bulb offsets and seeds. They are useful naturalized in a woodland garden or in mixed bulb plantings. Bluebells flower after most tulips are finished. The genus name *Hyacinthoides* means "like hyacinth." *Endymion* is a name derived from Greek mythology.

Propagation: Plants seed themselves naturally in the garden, but are usually propagated as bulb offsets.

Representative species and cultivars: The four *Hyacinthoides* species were separated from *Scilla* mainly because the bulbous plants are replaced each year rather than being perennial as in *Scilla*. *Hyacinthoides* species also lack the tunic (papery) cover found in *Scilla* bulbs.

Hyacinthoides hispanicus (Spanish bluebell; synonyms *Scilla campanulata, S. hispanica, Endymion hispanicus*) is native to Spain, Portugal, and northern Africa. It produces stiffly upright flower spikes containing numerous bell-like white, pink, or blue flowers. Plants reach 1 foot (30 cm) tall in bloom. 'Blue Giant', 'Blue Queen', 'Blue Sky', and 'Excelsior' are named blue cultivars.

Hyacinthoides non-scriptus (English bluebell; synonyms *Scilla non-scriptus, S. nutans, Endymion non-scriptus*) is common to woodland areas in Great Britain and Europe. Its flower spike is curved and less formal than that of Spanish bluebell and does not contain as many individual flowers per spike. It naturalizes readily in moist shady areas. Unlike Spanish bluebell, English bluebell has a pleasant fragrance and is often used as a cut flower.

Hyacinthoides hispanicus (Spanish bluebell)

Hyacinthus
Hyacinth
LILIACEAE

Hyacinths are familiar garden plants that grow from large bulbs. They produce a large truss of very fragrant blue, white, or pink flowers in the spring on plants reaching about 1 foot (30 cm) tall when in flower. Plants present a stiff formal appearance and are best used in formal flower beds or as forced pot plants to take advantage of the fragrance. A small group also can give a spring-flowering focal point to less formal plantings. In many parts of the country, hyacinths do not multiply naturally, and flower performance declines over several years. In these cases, plants are treated as annuals for spring interest only. Bulbs are planted about 6 inches (15 cm) deep in the fall for flowering the following spring. Hyacinths do well in full sun in a well-drained soil. Plants for forcing need a chilling pretreatment before being brought into flower. A special bulb treatment that removes the basal plate of the bulb results in the production of numerous side bulbs, which in turn results in a plant with numerous flower stems rather than the more common single-flowering stem. These multistemmed plants are usually sold as "multiflora hyacinths" and make good pot plants with a less formal appearance. The genus name *Hyacinthus* commemorates a youth from Greek mythology who was killed by a jealous Zephyrus because of his attachment to Apollo. After the boy's death, Apollo turned the boy into the plant we know as *Hyacinthus*.

Propagation: Bulbs are slow to produce offsets, so they are propagated commercially by bulb cuttage or tissue culture.

Representative species and cultivars: Taxonomists have reorganized this genus and moved all previous species of *Hyacinthus* into allied genera except *H. orientalis,* which is native to the Mediterranean region. Modern hybrid hyacinths have changed significantly from the species. The many cultivars occur in a variety of colors including blue, and some have double flowers. Two forms of hybrid hyacinths are known.

The Dutch hyacinths are the easily recognized, large-flowering types and include 'Amethyst', with violet-blue, strongly scented flowers; 'Blue Jacket', the darkest (navy) blue-flowering cultivar; 'Blue Magic', with deep violet-blue flowers and a white center; 'Delft Blue', with large flower spikes and a softer, lilac blue flower color; and 'Ostara', with single violet-blue flowers. The second group, the Roman hyacinths, are sometimes listed as *H. orientalis* var. *albulus* and developed from plants native to southern France. Rather than a stiff, dense spike of flowers, the Roman hybrids produce only 7 to 10 flowers per spike, but three or four spikes per bulb. Plants present a less formal appearance and are useful for forcing.

A small plant formerly listed as belonging to the genus *Hyacinthus* has blue flowers. *Brimeura amethystina* (synonym *Hyacinthus amethystinus*) is the alpine hyacinth native to the Pyrenees mountains. Plants are

Hyacinthus orientalis 'Delft Blue'

8 inches (20 cm) tall with nodding, bell-shaped flowers on loose, arched flower stems. They closely resemble a smaller version of English bluebell (*Hyacinthoides non-scriptus*).

Hydrangea
SAXIFRAGACEAE

Hydrangea is a group of woody perennials including shrubs, small trees, and vines. It contains many fine ornamental plants. The flowers appear in flat or pyramidal clusters and may be grouped by size. The large flowers are sterile with "petal-like" sepals that represent the showy pigmented (or white) part of the flower. The small flowers are fertile with reproductive parts and are less showy, although they also can be pigmented. Flower heads can have either all sterile flowers or clusters of sterile outer flowers with fertile inner flowers. Members of this latter group are called "lacecaps," while the fully sterile flower heads are called "mopheads" or sometimes "hortensia." Lacecaps are not as formal or top heavy as the fully sterile forms. Flower color is white, pink, or blue. Plants prefer full sun or light shade, but some species do well in deeper shade. Most prefer a moist, well-drained soil. *Hydrangea* makes excellent landscape plants for summer or fall flower displays and is used as fresh and dried cut flowers. *Hydrangea macrophylla* was once a very popular seasonal pot plant for winter forcing at Easter and Mother's Day. With increased interest in pot plants in the United States, *H. macrophylla* has made a comeback. The genus name is Greek for "water vessel" and refers to the shape of the fruit.

Propagation: Plants are multiplied usually from stem cuttings taken in early summer.

Representative species and cultivars: The approximately 100 species of *Hydrangea* are native to Asia and North and South America. Several species have blue flowers, but gardeners should not overlook the excellent white-flowering forms.

Hydrangea aspera is not as well known as many other *Hydrangea* species, but it is a worthy landscape plant for milder climates where winter temperatures do not go below 0°F (−18°C). It is a large, deciduous shrub growing to 10 feet (3 m) tall. Plants are native to parts of eastern Asia into China and several subspecies by region are recognized. Flattened flower heads appear in late summer with blue fertile florets surrounded by white or pink sterile florets. *Hydrangea aspera* subsp. *villosa* (synonym *H. villosa*) is native to Tibet and China. It is a large shrub or tree with leaves that are feltlike especially when they first emerge.

Hydrangea macrophylla (florist's hydrangea; synonyms *H. hortensis*, *H.* 'Otaksa') was developed in Japan as a horticultural variety and was introduced into England by Sir Joseph Banks in 1790. It produces both fully double and lacecap forms in white, pink, and blue. This plant is noted for its ability to change flower color based on the pH

Hydrangea macrophylla 'Blaumeise' (florist's hydrangea)

of the soil. The change is actually related to the availability of aluminum in the soil, which is associated with the pH. Plants in an acid soil (pH around 5) have blue flowers, while those grown at a higher pH (close to 7) have pink blooms. Many good cultivars are available for outdoor landscaping and forcing, including some that are not pH sensitive. Among the blue cultivars are 'Blaumeise' (synonym 'Teller Blue'), with large lacecap flower heads; 'Blue Bonnet', a pink or blue mophead; 'Blue Danube', a small plant with deep blue mophead flowers; 'Bodensee', a small plant with pink or blue lacecap flowers; 'Domotoi', a large mophead with pink or lilac blue flowers and frilled florets; 'Mariesii', a popular pink or blue lacecap; 'Mariesii Variegata', a form of 'Mariesii' with a variegated leaf; 'Merritt Supreme', a popular mophead for greenhouse forcing; 'Nikko Blue', a large blue mophead that is a popular landscape plant; 'Nachtigall'

Hydrangea macrophylla 'Uzi' (florist's hydrangea)

(Nightingale), another Teller hybrid with indigo blue, lacecap flowers; and 'Uzi', with reduced, cup-shaped sterile flowers.

Hydrangea serrata was at one time considered a subspecies of *H. macrophylla* and is still listed as such in some catalogs. The plants are similar, but *H. macrophylla* is native to Japan, while *H. serrata* is native to the Korean peninsula. Blue cultivars include 'Blue Bird', a lacecap with blue inner, fertile florets surrounded by purple-blue sterile florets; 'Blue Billow', a winter-hardy lacecap; 'Blue Deckle', a light blue lacecap; 'Izu No Hana', a pink or blue lacecap depending on soil pH, with fully double florets surrounding blue inner florets; and 'Preziosa', with white sterile flowers that turn pink or blue depending on soil pH.

Hyssopus
Hyssop
LAMIACEAE

Hyssopus is a group of herbaceous or woody perennial plants. Only *H. officinalis* is represented in the garden, but it has been cultivated since ancient times. Hyssop is grown in traditional herb gardens as a specimen plant or trained into a hedge. Flower color is purple-blue, and flowers have the typical two lips associated with members of the mint family. Plants prefer full sun and a well-drained, slightly alkaline soil. Hyssop is considered the "holy herb," because it was used in Biblical times to purify sacred places. There is some dispute whether the hyssop referenced in the Bible is the same plant with this name today. Regardless, *H. officinalis* has assumed this role. The earliest herbals ascribed medicinal properties for hyssop. It was used for a wide range of ailments, including rheumatism, jaundice, soothing toothaches, and even killing lice. Today, it is still used to flavor teas and cough lozenges. The oil has been used in the perfume industry, and hyssop also has been used to flavor liqueurs. The genus name is derived from the original Greek name *azob*, meaning "holy herb," and is said to have been applied to this plant by Hippocrates.

Propagation: Plants are multiplied by seed or stem cuttings. Seed propagation is easy, and plants self-sow naturally in the garden. Hyssop has become naturalized in parts of Europe and the United States. Stem cuttings taken in early summer root easily.

Representative species and cultivars: *Hyssopus* is a genus of five species from Siberia into the Mediterranean region. *Hyssopus officinalis* is the only species that is commonly cultivated. Native to southern Europe, it is winter hardy except in northern extremes. It grows to about 2 feet (60 cm) tall and is most often used in herb gardens, but also can be used in the perennial border. The violet-blue flowers are attractive to butterflies and can be taken as cut flowers. Selections of the species have white, rose, or blue flowers and come reasonably true from seed.

Iochroma
SOLANACEAE

Iochroma species are tropical woody plants with tubular flowers that appear in blue, purple, red, yellow, or white. They make good landscape plants in frost-free growing regions and are suited for container or ground bed use in greenhouse conservatories. They are easy to grow in a well-drained soil or potting medium in full sun or light shade. These are not cool weather plants. The genus name comes from the Greek word for "violet color" and refers to the flower color in some species.

Propagation: Plants are multiplied by seed or stem cuttings.

Representative species and cultivars: The approximately 25 species of *Iochroma* are native to South America. The most commonly available species is *I. cyanea* (synonym *I. tubulosa*), a large shrub from Ecuador and Peru with pendulous, tubular flowers that hang in clusters beside silvery foliage. Plants can reach 10 feet (3 m) tall and respond well to pruning. The flower color is dark purple or lavender-blue. The species is easy to grow and attractive in flower. It has become a staple for most greenhouse conservatories.

Ipheion
Spring Starflower
LILIACEAE

Ipheion produces star-shaped flowers on small 6-inch (15-cm) tall plants that have a true bulb. The taxonomy of this genus has been confused, and species now assigned to it were previously listed as belonging to *Brodiaea, Triteleia,* and *Milla.* Flower color ranges from nearly white to blue. Plants are best used in the rock garden or in the front of mixed perennial or shrub beds. They also can be used as greenhouse container plants. They develop best in a light, well-drained soil in full sun and may not be winter hardy in severe climates. Every 3 or 4 years the bulbs need to be lifted and separated to keep them flowering well. The origin of the genus name is unknown.

Propagation: Plants are multiplied by seed or, more commonly, by separation of bulb offsets.

Ipheion uniflorum (starflower)

Representative species and cultivars: The approximately 10 species of *Ipheion* are native to Central and South America. *Ipheion uniflorum* (starflower) is the only species commonly planted. It produces one (rarely two) white or light blue flowers per flowering stem in early spring. Each bulb, however, produces many flower stems. These plants are excellent in the rock garden or in containers for seasonal interest. 'Rolf Fiedler' has electric, mid-blue flowers. 'Wisley Blue' is offered in catalogs more often than the species because it produces larger flowers with more consistent blue. *Ipheion uniflorum* var. *violacea* (synonym *I. violacea*) produces a light blue flower.

Ipomoea
Morning Glory
CONVOLVULACEAE

Ipomoea is a diverse genus of tropical annual and perennial plants. They can be twining vines, herbaceous plants, woody shrubs, or even trees. Most have the characteristic morning glory flower that is funnel-shaped, opening with a large face. Flower color can be blue, purple, pink, red, or white. The most commonly cultivated plants are the summer-blooming, twining vines used to cover trellises or fences. Selections of *I. batatas* with dark purple foliage have become popular also and are being grown as bedding plants or ground covers in full sun in a well-drained soil. They can be direct seeded in the garden and with good fertility will cover large structures by the end of the summer. The genus name is Greek for "resembling a worm" and refers to the plants' resemblance to *Convolvulus* (bindweed), which was once referred to as "worm."

Propagation: Plants are multiplied by seed or stem cuttings. Seed should be soaked in water for several days prior to planting; any seed that does not swell should be "nicked" with a sharp knife to allow water to enter the seed.

Representative species and cultivars: *Ipomoea* is a large genus comprising as many as 500 species. They are all tropical plants. The numerous cultivated species include the economically important sweet potato (*I. batatas*). Several vining types have blue flowers.

Ipomoea indica (blue dawn flower) is less common than other morning glory species. It produces large purple-blue flowers on vigorous vines.

Ipomoea nil is similar to *I. tricolor*, and many catalogs sell both as morning glory without differentiating between the two species.

Ipomoea tricolor (common morning glory) is very common in American gardens. Native to Central and South America, it was introduced to Western gardens from seeds brought back to Spain from Cortez's conquest of Mexico. Its sky blue flowers quickly enchanted Europeans and became a feature in many artworks as well as gardens. This vigorous vine can grow to 20 feet (6 m) in a single season. The flowers are large, 3 to 4 inches (7 to 10 cm) across, and can completely cover the foliage when in full bloom. 'Blue Stars' has a unique lavender-blue blossom with irregular, white streaks running from the center of the flower to the petal tips. 'Heavenly Blue' is the most popular blue cultivar. Its large blossoms become lighter blue toward the center of the flower. Mt. Fuji is a group of star-patterned selections in a mixture of colors including deep blue and sky blue. 'Praecox' has large sky blue flowers.

Ipomoea tricolor 'Praecox'
(common morning glory)

Iris

Iris, Fleur-de-lis

IRIDACEAE

Iris is among the oldest recorded groups of ornamental plants. These species grow from either a fleshy rhizome or a bulb. The flowers are familiar to almost all gardeners. They are made from three showy sepals that form the lower, usually spreading part of the flower and are called the "falls," and three showy petals that form the upright top or "standard" part of the flower. Many color combinations are found in *Iris* including mixtures of white, red, blue, and yellow. Plants vary in height from 6 inches to 2.5 feet (15 to 75 cm). Depending on the species, irises bloom in spring or summer, and some may rebloom in the fall. Irises make excellent garden plants for formal or informal perennial beds. Smaller species are used in the rock garden. Others are more at home in or alongside a pond. Irises are good fresh cut flowers, and the seed pods can be used in dried arrangements. Many irises respond to normal growing conditions usually found in the garden, while others prefer a constantly moist soil or to be submerged in water. Plants bloom best in full sun or light shade. Bearded irises prefer an alkaline soil pH. Plants should be divided when they become crowded. The genus is named after the Greek goddess of the rainbow.

Propagation: Plants are multiplied by seed or, more commonly, division of the rhizome or from bulb offsets.

Representative species and cultivars: *Iris* is a large genus with more than 300 species native to temperate areas. About 20 species are commonly cultivated, but the number of hybrids and cultivars is overwhelming. Some catalogs list irises by the four subgenera into which the genus has been divided: *Nepalensis, Xiphium, Scorpiris* (Juno), and *Iris*. Subgenus *Nepalensis* contains only one species (*I. decora*), and it is unusual for the genus because it does not have a rhizome or bulb. Subgenus *Xiphium* has bulbs with annual roots and includes the Dutch, Spanish, and English types of *Iris*. Subgenus *Scorpiris* has bulbs with perennial roots. These are known as the Juno iris. The remaining irises grow from rhizomes and belong to subgenus *Iris*.

Iris cristata (crested iris) is wonderful small species native to moist woodlands in eastern North America. It produces a lilac blue flower with a yellow crest on the falls. Plants are about 1 foot (30 cm) tall and best used in naturalized settings or in the rock garden. 'Abbeys Violet' has violet-blue flowers.

Iris douglasiana may be worth growing simply because it commemorates David Douglas, a plant collector from Scotland who explored vast areas of western North America. It is a tender, West Coast native that produces wonderful blue or purple-blue flowers on 3-foot (1-m) tall plants. It tolerates shade and needs moisture.

Iris ensata (Japanese iris; synonym *I. kaempferi*) produces a 2.5-foot (75-cm) tall upright plant with large flowers to 10 inches (25 cm). Comprised mostly of recurved falls, the flowers are flat and can be less formal looking than the upright flowers of the more common bearded iris. Single and double flowers occur. Among the numerous cultivars are many with blue flowers. 'Activity', 'Favourite', and 'Nikko' are blue or blue-and-white cultivars. 'Variegata' has blue flowers and a green leaf with a white outer edge.

Iris gracilipes is another small woodland iris. Native to China and Japan, it grows from 6 to 10 inches (15 to 25 cm) and produces small blue flowers in late spring.

Iris laevigata is an Asian native growing to 3 feet (1 m tall). It produces blue flowers on plants that are at home in wet or pond gardens. 'Variegata' is a variegated leaf form.

Iris pallida is a European native most often grown as the variegated leaf forms, but it does have a pale blue flower. 'Argentea Variegata' has a white edge on green leaves and 'Variegata' has a yellow edge.

Iris prismatica is native from Canada into the Carolinas. In midsummer it produces lovely violet-blue flowers on 2-foot (60-cm) tall plants. It is another good choice for a North American native plant for wet, garden areas.

Iris reticulata (reticulated iris) is a popular early spring-blooming plant that grows from a bulb. It often blooms early enough to be dusted with late winter snows. Only 6 inches (15 cm) tall, it can spread quickly to form large patches. Most cultivars have blue flowers: 'Cantab', bright blue with a yellow patch on each petal; 'Clairette', sky blue standards and dark blue falls with white spots; and 'Harmony', sky blue standards with royal blue falls and golden markings. The similar iris with yellow flowers is *I. danfordiae*.

Iris sanguinea is a little-known Chinese native with flowers that vary from violet to deep intense blue. Plants are 3 feet (1 m) tall and bloom in early summer.

Iris setosa is the northernmost representative of the genus in North America. Plants are native to Alaska, but are also in Korea and Japan. They can grow from 6 inches to 3 feet (15 cm to 1 m) tall and produce blue falls and bristly standards. They are obviously winter hardy.

Iris sibirica (Siberian iris) is clump forming with thinner foliage and smaller flowers than bearded iris. It prefers a moist site but does well in normal garden soil. A mature clump of Siberian iris is an elegant sight in the garden. Some plants rebloom in fall. Siberian iris is less

Iris reticulata 'Harmony' (reticulated iris)

prone to disease and iris borers than bearded iris. Flower color can be combinations of blue, white, and yellow. Blue cultivars are numerous and a selected assortment that covers the color range include the following: 'Blue King', with nearly true blue flowers; 'Bonnie Blue', with light blue flowers; 'Caesar's Brother', a common cultivar with bright, violet-blue flowers and a short blooming time; 'Ego', with medium blue flowers; 'Flight of Butterflies', with small, bright blue flowers; 'Marilyn Holmes', with midnight blue flowers; 'Papillon', a late-blooming selection with light blue flowers; 'Perry's Blue', with sky blue flowers; and 'Silver Edge', a tetraploid with violet-blue flowers and a ruffled, silver edge. Chinese Siberian iris is a selection of tetraploid hybrids originating from China. They have good garden performance and larger flowers. 'Blue Water' has purple-blue flowers with white markings.

Iris siberica 'Bonnie Blue' (Siberian iris)

Iris verna (vernal iris) is similar to *I. crestata*. Both species are native to eastern North America and grow to less than 1 foot (30 cm) tall. Flowers are lilac blue. Vernal iris is a dwarf plant best used in the rock garden because it prefers a drier soil.

Iris versicolor (blue flag iris) is a North American native growing to 3 feet (1 m) tall with lavender-blue flowers. It is suited for naturalizing in wet sites.

Dutch, English, or **Spanish iris.** The hybrids of subgenus *Xiphium* are known as Dutch, English, or Spanish iris. Each group is distinctive in the time it blooms and its hybrid origin. Dutch iris blooms first followed in about 2 weeks by the Spanish, then the English iris. These hybrids grow from bulbs that should be planted 6 inches (15 cm) deep. The most commonly available group in the United States is the Dutch hybrids partly because they are more winter hardy. In general, they grow about 1 to 2 feet (30 to 60 cm) tall and bloom in late spring. These upright, formal looking plants are best grown in groups and make good cut flowers. Many color combinations are available. Blue-flowering Dutch irises include 'Blue Magic', with violet-blue flowers; 'Imperator', with indigo blue flowers; and 'Wedgewood', with clear blue flowers that are popular as cut flowers. Blue-flowering English cultivars are represented by 'Queen of the Blues', a popular selection with indigo blue standards and purple-blue falls.

Bearded irises are another group of *Iris* hybrids. They are the most popular irises available to gardeners. It is not possible in this brief format to do justice to the many fine bearded iris cultivars. One has only to visit a collection of iris in bloom to be overwhelmed with the diversity this group can offer. Plants are usually grouped as dwarf, intermediate, and tall bearded irises. Dwarf bearded irises are often sold under the name *I. pumila*, but actually are hybrids between *I. pumila* and other *Iris* species. They are less than 1.5 feet (45 cm) tall. Blue cultivars include 'Blue Echo', 'Blue Frost', and 'Little Sapphire'. Intermediate and tall bearded irises are often listed under *I. germanica*. They are between 2 and 3 feet (60 and 90 cm) tall with a great diversity in flower color combinations. Some hybridizations resulted in fertile tetraploids (having twice the number of chromosomes) that led to larger flower sizes. Some cultivars with blue and blue color combinations include 'Blue Staccato', 'Rain Cloud', 'Ruffled Ballet', and 'Sapphire Hills'.

Louisiana hybrids tend to spread freely in moist environments and bloom in midsummer. They are complex hybrids of at least five *Iris* species. They show moderate winter hardiness and perform better where the winter temperature does not go below 0°F (−18°C). Similar in flower to bearded iris, they are beardless and do very well in wet environments. They also do well on dry sites. Most selections have red or yellow flowers, but cultivars with blue flowers include 'Eolian', with ruffled blue and yellow flowers, and 'Sinfonietta', with blue flowers and yellow highlights.

Lathyrus
Sweet Pea
FABACEAE

Lathyrus species are a group of annual and perennial plants native to temperate regions from both hemispheres. Some are vigorous climbers, while others form short erect plants. They climb by means of tendrils. The flowers are typical for the pea family with the petals modified to form an upper banner, two side wings, and the last two petals fused to form the lower keel. Flower color can be white, pink, red, purple, yellow, or blue. Plants bloom in spring and early summer. Sweet pea can be used as a climbing plant, mixed with other perennials, or grown as a cut flower. Cut flowers can be produced outdoors or in a cool greenhouse. Fragrant sweet peas are a beautiful and nostalgic cut flower. In general, sweet peas do better in cool weather and can be very disappointing to gardeners in hot southern climates. They do very well in temperate climates with cool summer nights. Plants flower best in full sun or light shade in a fertile, well-drained soil. The genus name is an old Greek name for "pea."

Propagation: Plants are multiplied mainly by seed since sweet peas do not transplant easily. Seed should be planted in early spring to give plants time to develop during cooler weather. In milder climates, seed can be sown in the fall for early spring germination.

Representative species and cultivars: *Lathyrus* is a genus of approximately 130 species native to temperate regions in the Northern Hemisphere and to South America. Several species make good garden plants where the climate is appropriate. Blue is not a predominant color in this genus, but several cultivars have blue or purple-blue flowers.

Lathyrus nervosus (blue pea; synonym *L. magellanicus*) is native to South America and produces purple-blue flowers on vines that can reach 15 feet (4.6 m) long.

Lathyrus odoratus (common sweet pea) is prized for its attractive flowers and its pleasant fragrance. It is a vigorous climbing annual growing up to 10 feet (3 m) tall. It makes an excellent cut flower, and many selections of this species have been made both for flower color and fragrance. The species has an interesting history. It was discovered in Sicily by an Italian priest, Franciscus Cupani, in the late seventeenth century. Cupani wrote about sweet pea and distributed seeds because of the flower's remarkable fragrance. The blue and red flowers were nothing like the modern hybrids today. Sweet pea was one of the first flower crops intensively hybridized in Europe and became so popular in England that on its 200th anniversary exhibition in 1900 more than 260 selections were displayed. A major breakthrough in sweet pea breeding

Lathyrus odoratus Royal Family mix
(common sweet pea)

was the introduction of the Spencer hybrids in 1904 by Silas Cole. They had larger flowers and were appropriately dubbed "grandiflora sweet peas." Modern hybrids are usually available by series and these include Bijou, a bush type in a range of colors and with petals that have a wavy margin; Early Multiflora (synonym Mammoth) mix, with large flowers on tall stems for cutting; Explorer mix, a 2-foot (60-cm) tall bush type in a series of colors; Royal Family mix, heat-resistant plants with large flowers that are excellent when cut; and 'Snoopea'.

Lathyrus sativus is an annual sweet pea native to central Europe, North Africa, and Asia. It has rambling stems that reach about 3 feet (1 m) tall. This species is most often grown as a cover crop or for animal feed, but it has a nice pale blue flower. 'Azureum' has sky blue flowers.

Lathyrus vernus (spring vetchling) is a perennial species with violet, red, pink, or blue flowers. The term "vetchling" is used for a sweet pea that is non-climbing. Plants grow to about 2 feet (60 cm) tall and combine well in the mixed perennial bed. *Lathyrus vernus* var. *cyanus* has light blue flowers.

Laurentia

CAMPANULACEAE

Laurentia species are annual and herbaceous perennials growing between 1 and 2 feet (30 and 60 cm) tall. Flowers have five petals that are separate and are similar in appearance to *Lobelia* flowers. Flower color can be white, violet, or light blue. Plants bloom over a long period in the summer, making them good companions in the annual or perennial bed. They require full sun to light shade in a well-drained soil. The genus name commemorates the seventeenth-century Italian botanist M. Laurent.

Propagation: Plants are multiplied by seed or stem cuttings.

Representative species and cultivars: The approximately 25 species of *Laurentia* are well distributed in Australia, Africa, Europe, and the

Americas. They are not common garden plants, but the two species described here have become more widely available to gardeners. They are native to Australia or New Zealand.

Laurentia axillaris (synonym *Isotoma axillaris*) is a 1.5-foot (45-cm) tall annual covered with lavender-blue flowers. It is more widely distributed than *L. fluviatilis*. The selection 'Blue Stars' has a lighter blue flower color and blooms throughout the hot summer months.

Laurentia fluviatilis (synonym *Isotoma fluviatilis*) produces short, prostrate plants with star-shaped flowers that range in color from light blue to white. It works well in hanging baskets.

Lavandula
Lavender
LAMIACEAE

Lavenders are herbaceous and woody perennials noted for their use in the perfume industry. Oils from these plants are used commercially for the fragrance they impart to perfumes, soaps, and other toiletries. In addition to their use as herbs, lavender species make very good garden perennials. Their flowers can be used as dried cut flowers or in potpourris. Lavender plants have a stiff upright growth habit and the flowers occur in terminal spikes above the foliage. The small individual flowers are typical of the mint family. Flower color is usually lavender-blue or purple, and plants bloom over a long period in summer. Plants prefer full sun and a well-drained soil with a slightly alkaline pH. Over-fertilization can make plants lose their form. Large lavender plants do not transplant well. The genus name is Latin for "to wash."

Propagation: Plants are multiplied by stem cuttings or division. Stem cuttings taken in early summer are easily rooted.

Representative species and cultivars: The 28 species of *Lavandula* are mostly native to the Mediterranean area. Several species are grown for their fragrant oil and their ornamental value. The two most commonly available lavenders with blue flowers are described here.

Lavandula angustifolia (English lavender; synonym *L. officinalis*) is the most popular and useful species of lavender. It produces 3-foot (1-m) tall plants with grayish foliage topped with showy flower spikes. They are useful as edging plants or mixed with other perennials. This species is the one used most often for commercial oil production. 'Hidcote Blue' produces dark blue flowers on compact 12-inch (30-cm) tall plants. 'Lavender Lady' has lavender-blue flowers and

Lavandula angustifolia (English lavender),
Red Butte Arboretum, Salt Lake City, Utah

silvery green foliage; it blooms the first year from seed. Munstead strain is a larger plant to 16 inches (40 cm) tall with purple-blue flowers. Cultivars with pink, purple, or white flowers also can be found.

Lavandula latifolia (spike lavender; synonym *L. spica*) is a good garden plant, though it is smaller and more silvery-leaved than English lavender. The oil of spike lavender is inferior to English lavender and is used mostly to scent soaps. Flower color is a lavender-blue. Hybrids between *L. angustifolia* and *L. latifolia* are called lavandin (*L. ×intermedia*) and have a lavender-blue or violet flower color.

Limonium
Statice, Sea Lavender
PLUMBAGINACEAE

Limonium species are a diverse group of annual and perennial plants useful for the garden and for cut flowers. They produce basal leaves and either a single or branched flower stem. Individual flowers are small and papery, often with pigmented sepals. The combination provides an interesting floral feature. Flower color can be white, blue, pink, or yellow. The flowers are effective in the garden during summer. Several species are grown as commercial cut flowers. Plants require a well-drained soil and prosper in full sun or in partial shade. Perennial types do not transplant well once established and are best left alone without division. The genus name is a derivation of a Greek name applied to a plant growing in salt marshes.

Propagation: Annual types are multiplied by seed, while perennial species can be propagated by seed, division, or root cuttings.

Representative species and cultivars: The approximately 150 species of *Limonium* have a wide distribution in Europe, Africa, and North America. Some produce blue flowers and are probably most familiar to gardeners as cut flowers.

Limonium gmelinii (Siberian statice) is a less commonly grown species from Europe. It is a 1- to 2-foot (30- to 60-cm) tall perennial with unbranched flowering spikes. The flowers are lilac blue with reddish sepals.

Limonium latifolia (sea lavender) is the most common blue-flowering perennial statice. Plants are almost 3 feet (1 m) tall when in flower. The flowers are produced on branched flowering stems that provide an airy cloud above the foliage. Sea lavender can be used as a cut flower similar to baby's breath (*Gypsophilla paniculata*). 'Blue Cloud' and 'Blue Diamond' are bluer than the species.

Limonium perezii is a tender perennial usually treated as an annual. Dark blue flowers with a white center are produced on 3- to 4-foot (1- to 1.2-m) tall plants.

Limonium sinuatum (statice) is the species used most often as a commercial fresh or dried cut flower. The stiff flower stems produce papery flowers made up of pigmented petals against whitish sepals. Flower color is varied and includes blue. Cultivars are usually offered as series containing individuals with white, yellow, pink, salmon, and blue flowers. The Excellent series is tolerant to warm temperatures and available in blue and light blue among other colors. The Forever mix produces a range of colors on large-flowering spikes. The Fortress series has good long stems for cut flowers and is available in blue and heavenly blue among other colors. The Otis series has good quality plants in separate colors including light blue and dark blue. It was selected for plant size and suitability of greenhouse or outdoor production. The Pacific series yields good uniformity with large flowering spikes and is the standard for cut flowers. It is available as a mix or in individual colors including heavenly blue and midnight blue. The most commonly seen blue statice is probably 'Heavenly Blue' from this series. The Petite Bouquet mix, consisting of dwarf plants in a full range of colors, is suitable for bedding out. The Soiree series has a full range of colors on early blooming plants.

Lindelofia
BORAGINACEAE

Lindelofia is a hardy perennial genus with plants that resemble hound's tongue (*Cynoglossum* spp.). It is more common in European gardens than it is in American. The blue flowers are in the typical "forget-me-not" shape common to members of the borage family. Plants bloom in spring the second year after seeding and are best used in the rock garden or mixed perennial bed. They do well in full sun but must have a well-drained soil. Winter protection may be required in colder climates. The genus name commemorates Friedreich von Lindelof, a patron of botanists in nineteenth-century Germany.

Propagation: Plants are multiplied by seed or division.

Representative species and cultivars: *Lindelofia* consists of 10 species native to Asia. Only one species is commonly cultivated. *Lindelofia longiflora* is native to the Himalayan mountains and grows to less than 2 feet (60 cm) tall. Flower color can be variable when plants are produced from seed. Some plants produce bright blue flowers, but others are shades of purple-blue. Plants with good blue color can be retained by division for a more uniform planting.

Linum
Flax
LINACEAE

Linum usitatissiumum has been cultivated as a commercial source of fiber for making linen for centuries. Mummies from ancient Egypt were wrapped in linens made from flax, which probably is the oldest cultivated plant that was not used as a food source. Prior to wood pulp being used for paper manufacturing, flax was the fiber of choice from the Middle Ages into the nineteenth century for making paper. The genus *Linum* also contains annual and perennials that make excellent garden plants. They are usually less than 3 feet (1 m) tall and produce saucer-shaped yellow, white, red, or blue flowers. Individual flowers do not last long on the plant, but they are produced continuously to make this a long-blooming summer plant. They work well in the rock garden, mixed annual and perennial beds, or as part of wildflower mixes. Flaxes are easy to grow. They prefer full sun and must have a well-drained soil. Plants are usually short-lived perennials, but reseed in the garden. *Linum* is the old Latin name for "flax."

Propagation: Plants are multiplied most commonly by seed, but can be divided, and stem cuttings root easily.

Representative species and cultivars: *Linum* is a large genus containing more than 200 species native to most temperate regions of the world. The perennial flax species have some of the finest blue flower color available to the gardener, but the species with red or yellow flowers are charming also.

Linum narbonense (narborne flax) is a European native growing to about 2 feet (60 cm) tall. This long-blooming perennial has blue flowers with a white center. Winter protection is required in colder climates.

Linum narbonense (narborne flax)

'Heavenly Blue' has bright blue flowers and a more compact habit than the species.

Linum perenne (perennial flax) is the most commonly cultivated flax for the garden. It is native to Europe and parts of western North America. Plants grow to 1.5 feet (45 cm) tall and are covered with blue or white flowers that bloom from spring through summer. Several botanical varieties are available, making the nomenclature confusing. *Linum perenne* subsp. *alpinum* (synonym *L. alpinum*) is similar to the species but smaller at 1 foot (30 cm) tall and has wiry stems and smaller leaves. *Linum perenne* subsp. *lewisii* (synonym *L. lewisii*) is the blue flax native to the Rocky Mountains in North America. *Linum perenne* var. *nanum* is another short version of the species at about 1 foot (30 cm) tall. It is available primarily as the deep blue cultivar 'Saphyr' (synonyms 'Blau Saphir', 'Blue Sapphire', 'Nanum Saphyr', 'Nanum Sapphire').

Linum perenne (perennial flax)

Lithodora
BORAGINACEAE

Lithodora species were previously in the genus *Lithospermum,* which included blue-flowering species now assigned to *Lithodora, Buglossoides,* or *Moltkia.* At present the genus *Lithodora* consists of woody shrubs usually used in the perennial garden. Flowers have five spreading petals attached at the base, giving them a star-shaped appearance. Plants bloom in the summer. The cultivated forms of *Lithodora* are less than 2 feet (60 cm) tall. They prefer full sun with a well-drained, moist soil and do not tolerate climates that are too hot or too cold. Plants are marginally hardy in northern areas, but do not tolerate the hot summers of the southeastern United States. They do well in cooler regions of the Pacific Northwest and in northern Europe. The genus name is Greek for "rock skin" and refers to the hard, polished surface of the seeds.

Propagation: Plants are multiplied by seed or cuttings. Seed may require scarification of the outer coat to allow water uptake. Stem cuttings taken after the plants have flowered root easily and are the usual propagation method for the cultivars.

Representative species and cultivars: The seven species of *Lithodora* are native to southern Europe into Greece and Turkey. They represent some of the brightest and deepest blue flowers available to gardeners; however, they are tender evergreens and do not tolerate cold winter temperatures.

Lithodora diffusa (synonym *Lithospermum diffusa*) is the most commonly cultivated species. Native to Spain and Portugal, it is a low-growing prostrate, evergreen shrub that is popular in mild climates. It is an excellent rock garden or ground cover plant. Unlike other species of *Lithodora,* it requires an acid soil to do well. It has become a popular plant in Europe, with several cultivars named for flower color. 'Heavenly Blue' has a deeper blue flower color than the species, and 'Star'

Lithodora diffusa 'Heavenly Blue'

has a white edge that outlines attractive blue flowers. 'Grace Ward' is
a trailing plant prized for creeping over stones or for containers.

Lithodora oleifolia may be the most winter hardy of the available species.
It can tolerate 10°F (−12°C) and is native to the Pyrenees. It has a
more tubular flower than *L. diffusa*. The flower buds are pink before
opening to a pale blue. Plants creep by underground stolons.

Lithodora zahnii is a small, upright, evergreen shrub native to Greece.
The 1-foot (30-cm) tall plants are topped with sky blue flowers in
late summer.

Lobelia
Lobelia, Cardinal Flower, Indian Tobacco
CAMPANULACEAE

Lobelia contains several annual and perennial plants familiar to almost
every gardener. They produce a very distinctive flower that is modified
to have an upper lip split into two narrow lobes and a lower lip split

into three lobes. Flower colors found in the species are usually bright red or blue, but newer hybrids give a wider range of colors. The annual types are used as bedding plants and as trailing features in containers or for hanging baskets. The perennial types can be used in mixed annual and perennial beds or naturalized in a woodland garden. The perennials require a moist, organic soil for best performance and light shade. They can be short lived in the garden. Annuals do well in full sun or light shade in a well-drained soil or potting medium. The numerous hybrids between perennial species of *Lobelia* do well in light shade and moist, well-drained soil. They are not as hardy as the species and do better where summers are cool. The genus name commemorates seventeenth-century herbalist Matthias L'Obel who tried to organize plants into a cataloging system before Carl Linnaeus developed the current system.

Propagation: Plants are multiplied by seed or division. Seed propagation is most common for most annual and perennial species. Seed germinates best in the light, and the perennial species and hybrids benefit from 2 weeks of chilling prior to sowing.

Representative species and cultivars: In *Lobelia* are more than 300 species of mostly herbaceous plants native to North and South America, Europe, Africa, and Australia. Popular annual and perennial species are grown as ornamentals. The most recognizable is *L. cardinalis* (cardinal flower), which grows naturally in moist woodland areas of North America. It produces a bright red flower, but also has been used as a hybrid parent to provide plants with a range of colors. Blue-flowering species include the popular annual *L. erinus* and the perennial *L. siphilitica*.

Lobelia erinus (trailing lobelia) is a trailing annual species used extensively as a bedding plant. It is also used in containers, window boxes, and hanging baskets. Individual flowers are also popular as dried pressed flowers. Flower colors are blue and shades of blue. In good environments, these plants can bloom all summer and into the fall. Seed companies offer numerous selections of this species. These can be divided into two basic types: those that are trailing and best for baskets or containers, and those that are more upright and thus more suited as bedding plants. Selected blue cultivars include 'Blue Moon', a heat-tolerant, blue bedding plant; 'Crystal Palace', the long-time standard for dark blue flowers and bronze foliage; and 'Sapphire', a bright blue trailing type with a small white eye. Newer F_1 hybrids are available in several series. The Fountains series is a heavy blooming, trailing type in a range of colors including light blue. The Palace series is similar to the standard 'Crystal Palace' but blooms earlier and has blue flowers and bronze foliage, blue flowers with a white center, and royal blue flowers. The Regatta series is a trailing type similar to the Fountains series but earlier to flower. It is available as blue splash (large portion of flower center is white), midnight blue, and sky blue. The Riviera series is a group of dwarf plants that offers a range of individuals with blue flowers including blue eyes, blue splash, marine blue, and sky blue. *Lobelia tenuior* and *L. gracilis* are two Australian natives with blue flowers that are very similar to trailing lobelia, but are not currently available commonly.

Lobelia siphilitica (giant blue lobelia)

Lobelia siphilitica (giant blue lobelia) is a North American native found in moist, woodland areas. It produces a bright blue flower on plants 2 to 3 feet (0.6 to 1 m) tall. The flowers are on erect spikes. This lobelia is a wonderful perennial for an informal garden. It can be short lived and should be divided or replaced every 3 to 4 years. 'Blue Peter' is a vigorous blue selection.

Lobelia ×*speciosa* is a hybrid of *L. cardinalis*, *L. siphilitica*, and *L.* ×*hybrida*. The crosses are tetraploids that result in robust plants with large flowers.

Flower color can be pink, red, or blue. Plants are more winter hardy than the popular *L. ×hybrida* selections like 'Queen Victoria'. The nomenclature can be confusing in these hybrids. Catalogs may list them under *L. ×speciosa* or simply as the Complement series. 'Complement Blue' has a violet-blue flower, but most of these selections are shades of pink and red.

Lupinus
Lupine
FABACEAE

Lupines are members of the pea family. Erect spikes contain many pealike flowers that range in color from white and yellow to red, blue, and mixed colors. Plants bloom in spring and summer. Taller species and hybrids are useful additions to the perennial bed, while smaller species are often naturalized as wildflowers. Lupines also can be taken as cut flowers. Plants prefer full sun and a well-drained soil. The most popular garden hybrids do best where the summers are cool; otherwise they are short lived. The genus name is derived from the Latin word for "wolf" and evidently comes from an erroneous belief that the plants destroyed the soil where they were planted.

Propagation: Plants are multiplied mainly by seed, which benefits from scarification of the outer coat to allow water uptake. Some species also may benefit from cool stratification at 41°F (5°C) for several weeks before planting.

Representative species and cultivars: *Lupinus* is a large genus of approximately 200 species, mostly from North America, but also Europe, Africa, and South America. Most garden lupines are hybrids derived from *L. polyphyllus* and several other *Lupinus* species, particularly *L. arboreus, L. mutabilis,* and *L. nanus.* They became known as the Russell hybrids after George Russell, their chief hybridizer from Yorkshire, England, in the 1930s. These and other hybrids are properly classified as *L. ×regalis,* although they are often listed in catalogs as *L. polyphyllus* or *L. hy-*

bridus. The original Russell hybrids, which have been reselected for improved flowering and plant performance, are offered in series usually as a mixture of colors including blue. Most common are the Carnival mix, improved for flower size and color; the Gallery mix, a dwarf form only reaching 1.5 feet (45 cm) tall; the Minarette mix, another early blooming dwarf series; and 'Russell Hybrid Improved', a full-sized, 3-foot (1-m) tall plant with very large flowers. *Lupinus* species are not as available to gardeners as are the hybrids; however, several of them make good garden plants and others are grown for naturalizing as wildflowers.

Lupinus arboreus is common to open areas of California. It can be a tall plant reaching 6 feet (1.8 m). It usually has yellow flowers, but forms with purple or blue flowers are also produced.

Lupinus argenteus is from southwestern North American and has blue flowers and silvery foliage. Plants bloom in midsummer, but do not tolerate heavy wet soils. They can be grown in containers.

Lupinus texensis
(Texas bluebonnet)

Lupinus mutabilis is from South America and is another of the species that provides the background for the original Russell hybrids. It is an annual or short-lived perennial to about 3 feet (1 m) tall. Flower colors are a combination of pale blue keels, yellow wings, and blue standard petals.

Lupinus perennis is native from the East Coast of North America into the Plains states. It is the common prairie lupine growing to 2 feet (60 cm) tall and producing lavender-blue flowers.

Lupinus polyphyllus has very palmately compound leaves (up to 15 leaflets) as suggested by its name. It is native to moist, forested areas of the West Coast of North America and can produce plants up to 5 feet (1.5 m) tall. Flower color is violet-blue.

Lupinus texensis (Texas bluebonnet; synonym *L. subcarnosus*) has become synonymous with the Ladybird Johnson wildflower program that became so popular for roadside plantings of native species. Texas bluebonnet has become a popular part of wildflower mixes. This small 1-foot (30-cm) tall plant is best used in large mass plantings. Other less commonly planted wildflower species with blue flowers include *L. hartwegii* from Mexico and *L. nanus* from California.

Malva
Mallow
MALVACEAE

Malva species are a group of herbaceous annual and perennial plants that are not as well known as their larger-flowering relatives such as the *Hibiscus* species, although they are equally deserving of a place in the perennial or mixed annual and perennial border. These upright plants produce flowers in clusters in the leaf axils. Flowers are between 2 and 3 inches (5 and 7.5 cm) in diameter and have five petals each with a notch at the tip of the petal. Flower color can be white, pink, purple, or blue. Mallows are relatively easy to grow in full sun and a moist, well-drained soil. Taller plants may require staking. The genus name comes from the Greek word "to soften" and refers to the properties of the plant sap.

Propagation: Plants are multiplied by seed, which because of its hard coating needs scarification to allow water uptake. Seedlings volunteer in the garden.

Representative species and cultivars: *Malva* is a genus of approximately 30 species native to Europe, Africa, and Asia. The only commonly cultivated species are *M. alcea*, *M. moschata*, and *M. sylvestris*. Of these, only *M. sylvestris* has blue flowers. *Malva sylvestris* is a half-hardy perennial that can reach 4 feet (1.2 m) tall. It produces flowers from summer into fall. This variable species has selections with red, purple, or blue flowers. 'Primely Blue' is the most commonly available blue form, but is currently not grown widely in North America. It is shorter than the species, only 2 to 3 feet (2.5 to 1 m) tall, and produces wonderful pale blue flowers streaked with dark blue veins.

Meconopsis
Blue Poppy, Welsh Poppy
PAPAVERACEAE

No book about blue flowers would be complete without a description of blue poppy. *Meconopsis* is a classic example of the finicky species native to alpine regions of the Himalayan mountains: they only thrive in cool, moist summers and where the winters are relatively mild—the Pacific Northwest in North America and parts of northern Europe. In these places, blue poppy does well and can be a common perennial. I enjoy *Meconopsis* for the fabulous tales of the European plant collectors sent to western Asia to bring these plants back for cultivation. Notable are the memoirs of Ernest H. Wilson, who was sent by the Veitch nursery to collect the yellow-flowering *M. integrifolia,* and F. Kingdon Ward, who brought back a form of blue poppy *(M. betonicifolia* var. *baileyi)* that made such a stir during the Chelsea flower show in England. I recommend reading *Chinese Wilson, A Life of Ernest H. Wilson* by Roy Briggs and *Plant Hunting on the Edge of the World* by F. Kingdon Ward if you would like to gain a perspective on the challenges that were involved in introducing many of our common garden plants from Asia. *Meconopsis* species produce large poppy-shaped flowers with numerous conspicuous stamens in the center of the flower. Although the generic common name is "blue poppy," flower color can be yellow, orange, or white as well as blue. Plant height ranges from 1.5 to 8 feet (45 cm to 2.4 m) and the plants bloom in spring and early summer. In unsuitable environments, plants refuse to bloom and do not overwinter. Where summers are cool and winters mild, *Meconopsis* species are regal plants for the perennial bed or rock garden. The genus name is Greek for "poppylike."

Propagation: Plants are multiplied by seed, but some can be divided. Seed sown as soon as it is ripe produces seedlings that can be overwintered.

Representative species and cultivars: *Meconopsis* contains 45 species native to alpine regions of western Asia, except for the Welsh poppy (*M. cambrica*) that hails from western Europe. Numerous blue species of *Meconopsis* are used as ornamentals, but the species with red or yellow flowers should not be overlooked.

Meconopsis betonicifolia (Himalayan blue poppy) is the most recognizable of the blue-flowering species. As the common name implies, this poppy is native to Tibet and western China. Cultivated plants are from a collection made by F. Kingdon Ward (*M. betonicifolia* var. *baileyi*) that proved easier to grow than previous introductions into Europe. This 4-foot (1.2-m) tall perennial species produces a sky blue flower that is 2 inches (5 cm) in diameter.

Meconopsis grandis is smaller than *M. betonicifolia* with a flower color that is not as blue, but it is more winter hardy. Also native to the Himalayan mountains, it can be short lived especially in dry environments.

Meconopsis horridula is a wonderful small blue poppy that grows about 2 feet (60 cm) tall. It is unusual because all parts including the fruits are covered with spines. Native to Nepal, Tibet, and western China, this poppy is at home in the perennial bed, but is more common in rock gardens. It is a biennial species and dies after it flowers, so it must be reseeded for permanent plantings.

Meconopsis horridula

Meconopsis ×sheldonii

Meconopsis ×*sheldonii,* a hybrid between *M. grandis* and *M. betonicifolia,* has become a popular garden plant. It grows 3 to 4 feet (1 to 1.2 m) tall and has flowers that are usually larger and slightly down facing compared with those of *M. betonicifolia.* It can be an easier plant to grow and has bright, clear blue flowers. *Meconopsis* ×*sheldonii* 'Branklyn' is a deep blue selection named for a small, yet delightful garden in Scotland that features *Meconopsis.*

Meehania
Meehan's Mint
LAMIACEAE

Meehan's mints are creeping, herbaceous perennials that are not often seen in cultivation. They are found naturally in woodland areas. Trailing stems can reach 2 feet (60 cm) long during a growing season and spread to colonize an area 8 feet (1.7 m) in diameter. Plants produce a short whorl of two-lipped flowers typical of the mint family. Flowers appear in spring through early summer. Flower color is lavender-blue to lilac, and plants are attractive in bloom. They prefer a moist but well-drained organic soil and light shade. They are useful for naturalized woodland gardens and could be used as a ground cover for shady gardens. The genus name commemorates Thomas Meehan who lived in Philadelphia in the nineteenth century. Meehan was a botanist, writer, and statesman, and should be better known by U.S. gardeners. He authored an influential publication on gardening and was responsible for having Philadelphia set aside the homestead of John Bartram, the father of American botany, as the nation's oldest botanic garden.

Propagation: Plants are multiplied by seed, division, or cuttings. Because these species are stoloniferous in their growth habit, new plants are easily separated and divided.

Representative species and cultivars: *Meehania* is a small genus of six species native to North America and Asia. They are not common in cul-

Meehania cordata

tivation. The best garden candidate from North America is *M. cordata*. I first saw this plant blooming at the Mt. Cuba Center in Delaware. It has a pale lavender-blue flower color and was remarkable because it covered a large area in dappled, woodland shade. Mt. Cuba Center has been introducing superior selections of native North American plants, and Meehan's mint may be a future introduction from this station.

Mertensia
Bluebells
BORAGINACEAE

The genus *Mertensia* constitutes a group of herbaceous plants well suited for the perennial bed and rock garden, but they really are most at home in a naturalized woodland setting. Plants develop from tuberous roots and range in height from 6 inches to 2 feet (15 to 60 cm) tall. The tubular flowers appear as terminal clusters, and flower color is usually blue, but occasionally white. The flowers exhibit the interesting habit of the borage family in which pink buds turn to blue flowers, and they are early spring bloomers. Plants do well in partial shade and a moist, organic soil. The foliage disappears during the summer like that of spring-blooming bulbs, so these plants should be interplanted with ground covers or ferns that fill in the space left behind as the foliage recedes. The genus name commemorates the nineteenth-century German botanist Carl Mertens.

Propagation: The most common form of propagation is division of tuberous roots, but seed propagation is also used.

Representative species and cultivars: The approximately 50 species of *Mertensia* are native to northern climates. The most familiar and useful garden plant is Virginia bluebells (*M. virginiana*), but lesser-known species also can make excellent garden plants.

Mertensia asiatica (synonym *M. simplicissima*) is a small, trailing species native to Russia, Korea, and Japan. It produces pale blue flowers typical of the genus, but has the added attraction of powder blue foliage. It can be difficult to establish.

Mertensia ciliata is similar to *M. virginiana*, but with narrower leaves, and it is native to mountain river beds in western North America. Plants can reach 3 feet (1 m) tall on upright, arching stems.

Mertensia maritima is different from the typical woodland *Mertensia* species. It is a seaside plant, with a low spreading habit only 6 inches (15 cm) tall. The bluebell-shaped flowers appear above fleshy blue-green leaves. I was pleased to see that one of the larger, wholesale perennial nurseries in the United States has started to carry this species.

Mertensia pterocarpa (synonym *M. sibirica*) is a very winter hardy species native to Siberia and eastern Asia into Japan. Plants are less than 2 feet (60 cm) tall and produce loose clusters of blue flowers.

Mertensia virginiana (Virginia bluebells; synonym *M. pulmonariodes*) is native to northeastern North America, where it flourishes in open woodland settings. It can be used in the perennial bed for early season color, but is at its best in a woodland garden. In a good environ-

Mertensia virginiana
(Virginia bluebells)

ment, it self-sows from seed and forms large patches. In addition to blue forms, white and reddish forms of this species can be found.

Several *Mertensia* species are not as easy to grow as Virginia bluebells and are difficult to locate except from specialty nurseries. These are dwarf species less than 8 inches (20 cm tall) like *M. longiflora* from northwestern North America, and *M. primuloides* and *M. echioides* from the Himalayan mountains. They are usually grown only by rock or alpine garden enthusiasts willing to provide the special environments that they need.

Moltkia
BORAGINACEAE

The genus *Moltkia* constitutes a group of half-hardy, herbaceous and woody perennial plants. They are grown for the many tubular flowers effective in late spring and summer. Flowers are typical of the borage family, starting pink or purple in the bud and opening to blue. These plants are used for the rock garden or front of the perennial bed. They need full sun and a well-drained, alkaline soil. They should not be over-watered or kept in wet conditions in winter. The genus name commemorates Count Joachin Gadske Moltke, an eighteenth-century Danish patron of botany.

Propagation: Plants are multiplied by seed or stem cuttings.

Representative species and cultivars: The six species of *Moltkia* are native to Europe and Asia. Some species used to belong to the genera *Lithospermum* and *Lithodora*. *Moltkia* is considered the shrub borage.

Moltkia ×*intermedia* is a hybrid between *M. suffruticosa* and *M. petraea* with funnel-shaped flowers that appear in midsummer.

Moltkia petraea is the most commonly available moltkia. It is a dwarf shrub growing to 1.5 feet (45 cm) tall. Native to Greece, it has deep, intense blue flowers that occur in abundance in summer. Like other members of the genus, it is half-hardy, tolerating winter temperatures as low as 0°F (−18°C).

Moltkia suffruticosa (synonyms *Lithodora graminifolia, Lithospermum graminifolia*) is from Italy. It shows upright growth to about 1 foot (30 cm) tall and produces clusters of blue or purple-blue flowers in late spring into summer.

Muscari
Grape Hyacinth
LILIACEAE

Grape hyacinths are small bulbous plants that bloom in early spring. Clusters of small closed, bell-shaped flowers are produced on dense spikes held 8 to 10 inches (20 to 25 cm) above the foliage. The flowers are among the truest blue flowers for the garden, but also may be white. Grape hyacinths are used to best effect when planted in masses in a natural setting, but also mix well with other bulbs in a more formal garden. They are also useful in the rock garden, and they work well with ground covers like English ivy (*Hedera helix*) or lily turf (*Liriope*) that are able to cover the bare area left after grape hyacinth foliage goes dormant for the summer. The small bulbs of grape hyacinth should be planted in early fall to become established and start foliage growth. Plants do well in full sun to partial shade in a well-drained soil. The genus name is Latin for "musk" and refers to the odor in some species.

Propagation: Plants can be propagated by seed or, more commonly, by separation of bulb offsets. Commercial growers also may use bulb cuttage or tissue culture methods to rapidly increase new cultivars.

Representative species and cultivars: Approximately 50 species constitute the genus *Muscari,* which is native to Europe, Asia, and Africa. Several species and their cultivars are common garden plants, while others deserve increased use as ornamentals.

Muscari armeniacum is probably the most commonly planted form of grape hyacinth. It is the 6- to 8-inch (15- to 20-cm) tall plant familiar to anyone who gardens. Native from Turkey into the Caucasus, it has several cultivars selected for their flower color. These include 'Blue Spike', with double, blue flowers that are long lasting; 'Early Giant', with large, deep blue flowers and a white rim at the tip of the fused tepals; and 'Heavenly Blue', also with large, bright blue flowers.

Muscari aucheri is not as commonly grown as the other grape hyacinths, because the flower spike is not as large. It has sky blue flowers and

Muscari armeniacum

makes a good rock garden or container plant. It is native to Turkey. The species most often listed as *M. tubergenianum* (see below) is probably a selection of *M. aucheri*.

Muscari azurea (synonyms *Hyacinthus azurea, Hyacinthella azurea*) is less than 4 inches (10 cm) tall and similar to other grape hyacinths, but with more open blue flowers and obvious petal tips. It is native to Turkey.

Muscari botryoides is similar to *M. armeniacum,* and these two make up the bulk of the bulbs sold as grape hyacinth. Native to central and southern Europe, *M. botryoides* was the first grape hyacinth grown in Europe, cultivated as early as the sixteenth century. The species name is Greek for "bunches of grapes." Flowers are bright blue and fragrant. Several botanical forms of this species exist in various heights and flower color. *Muscari botryoides* var. *album* is the most common white form of grape hyacinth.

Muscari comosum (tassel grape hyacinth) is native to southern Europe, Turkey, and Iran. Its flowers are unique: the lower flowers on the spike are brownish, while the upper flowers are purple-blue and sterile, and held away from the main stalk on "tassels." The most commonly sold form of this species is *M. comosum* 'Monstrosum' (synonym *M. plumosa*), which produces a feathery flower spike of sterile lavender-blue flowers that are unusual. This cultivar is sold as a novelty plant and can become quite tall, reaching 1.5 feet (45 cm).

Muscari latifolium is a large grape hyacinth that is not as refined a garden plant as other grape hyacinths, but its large size can be effective in certain garden settings. Native to Asia, it produces dark indigo blue flowers. It is very distinct because it only sends up one straplike leaf per bulb.

Muscari neglectum (musk hyacinth) is native to Europe, Asia, and northern Africa. It bears dark blue flowers with a white rim around the tips of the tepals. The flowers have a distinctly musky fragrance. Plants develop foliage in the fall that overwinters. These plants increase rapidly in the garden.

Muscari paradoxum (synonym *Bellevalia pycnantha*) is native to Russia and central Europe into Turkey and Iran. In garden catalogs, look for this plant with the other grape hyacinths rather than under its newer placement in the genus *Bellevalia*. It produces very dense clusters of blackish blue flowers that open to show a yellowish rim on the flowers. Plants grow about 1 foot (30 cm) tall.

Muscari tubergenianum is a less common form native to Iran. It bears deep blue flowers at the bottom of the flower spike and pale blue sterile flowers at the top, creating a striking color contrast. This species deserves a wider distribution in gardens.

Myosotis
Forget-me-not
BORAGINACEAE

Forget-me-nots are annual and perennial plants familiar to most gardeners and readers of poetry. They produce bright blue flowers on a curled flower spike that opens sequentially. Each flower has five petals fused at the base but separated at the tips. A conspicuous light eye is in the center of the flower. Plants are useful in mixed annual and perennial beds or naturalized along a stream edge. Forget-me-nots also mix well with spring-flowering bulbs or scattered in the rock garden. They prefer light shade and a moist, well-drained soil. In many cases, flowering plants do not overwinter and must be replaced by seedling volunteers for continued bloom year after year. The genus name is Greek for "like a mouse ear" and refers to the shape of the leaves of some species. The common name, forget-me-not, is associated with Victorian Europe's practice of placing meanings on flowers. A bouquet sent by an admirer held flirtatious messages that varied depending on the flower species in the bouquet. In this case, forget-me-nots stood for fidelity and undying love.

Propagation: Seed is the most common form of propagation, but perennial types can be divided in spring. Seed needs light to germinate and prefers a cool soil temperature. Annual types can be sown in the garden or grown as bedding plants.

Representative species and cultivars: *Myosotis* consists of approximately 50 species, most of which are native to New Zealand but also found in Europe, North America, and Asia. Only a few species are available in cultivation. *Myosotis alpestris* and *M. sylvatica* are the two most commonly cultivated forget-me-nots. They differ only in minor aspects of the flower structure. True plants of *M. alpestris* persist in the garden longer than *M. sylvatica*; however, many plants sold as *M. alpestris* are mislabeled and are probably *M. sylvatica*.

Myosotis alpestris (alpine forget-me-not) is native to Europe and is a short-lived perennial. Plants form 8-inch (20-cm) tall clumps topped in the spring by bright blue flowers with a yellow center. Spring-sown plants do not bloom until the following spring. Cultivars listed in catalogs under *M. alpestris* are most likely *M. sylvatica* cultivars.

Myosotis scorpioides (synonym *M. palustris* in catalogs) is native to Europe and Asia and is a short-lived perennial. Its growth is more prostate than that of *M. sylvatica*, but the flower form and color are very similar. This species is useful in the front of the perennial border, but it also thrives in the moist conditions around a water feature. 'Bill Baker' has bright flowers with good foliage on creeping plants. 'Sapphire' is a blue-flowering compact form. The botanical form *M. scorpioides* var. *semperflorens* is a smaller plant with a longer blooming period into summer in good environments.

Myosotis sylvatica and its cultivars are the more frequently planted forget-me-nots. Also native to Europe, this species can grow to 1 foot (20 cm) tall. Selections are available with white, rose, or blue flowers. Blue cultivars include 'Blue Ball', a compact plant with azure blue flowers; 'Blue Bird', a large plant with bright blue flowers; 'Indigo Blue' and 'Ultramarine', with indigo blue flowers; and the popular Victoria series. 'Victoria Blue' is a uniform, compact plant with azure blue flowers; it and its pink-flowering counterpart 'Victoria Rose' make excellent complements to spring-flowering bulbs.

Myosotis sylvatica (forget-me-not)

Nemesia

SCROPHULARIACEAE

Nemesia species are colorful, low-growing plants used for annual displays. Their very interesting flowers beg for closer inspection. Like their counterparts in other members of this family, *Nemesia* flowers are two-lipped. The upper petals (lip) are divided into four lobes, while the lower lip has two lobes. Each lip can have contrasting colors, making for interesting bicolor combinations. The color range in these flowers includes yellow, white, pink, red, purple, violet, and blue. Plants are useful in mass as bedding plants or mixed with other summer annuals. They prefer full sun and a moist, well-drained soil that is slightly acidic. The genus name is from the old Greek name applied to this plant.

Propagation: Plants are multiplied by seed or stem cuttings. The usual form of propagation is by seed, which requires a relatively cool soil of 60°F (15°C) and darkness for germination.

Representative species and cultivars: *Nemesia* consists of around 50 species of annual and perennial plants from South Africa. Although still not common in garden centers, these plants are more available to gardeners thanks to recent breeding efforts. The garden public's enthusiasm for pastel colors suggests that *Nemesia* could get wider distribution in the future.

Nemesia caerulea (synonym *N. fruticans*) produces white, pink, or lavender-blue flowers on wiry stems reaching 2 feet (60 cm) tall. The lower lip of the flower has a yellow spot. Plants are used for bedding out, containers, or cut flowers. 'Joan Wilder' has consistent lavender-blue flowers.

Nemesia strumosa produces low-growing plants that flower at about 1 foot (30 cm) tall. Flowers are single or bicolored and come in a full range of colors including blue. This species is usually represented in the garden by one of the cultivars. 'Blue Gem' has all bright blue flowers. 'Blue and White' is a recent European Fleuroselect winner with bicolored, deep blue and white flowers. The Tapestry (synonym Pastel Tapestry) mix has pastel colors, including blue, on single or bi-colored flowers.

Nemophila
Baby Blue Eyes
HYDROPHYLLACEAE

Nemophila species are an interesting group of annuals that are unfamiliar to most gardeners. They produce rather fragile plants less than 2 feet (60 cm) tall. The flowers are similar to those of other members of the family; they are rounded or bell-shaped and appear in the summer. Flower color is white, purple, or blue. Some flowers have a bright spot at the end of each petal. Plants are useful to provide spring color, but do not tolerate summer heat. They can be incorporated in mixed annual and perennial gardens or as spring features in the rock garden. They do best in light shade in a moist, well-drained soil. The genus name is Greek for "to love a grove" and suggests the natural habitat of these plants.

Propagation: Plants are multiplied by seed that requires darkness to germinate.

Representative species and cultivars: The 13 species of *Nemophila* are native to North America. Two are available to gardeners.

Nemophila maculata is a Californian native that is similar to *N. menziesii*, but the flowers are white with a violet-blue spot at the end of each petal. Plants are annual and reach about 1 foot (30 cm) tall.

Nemophila menziesii (baby blue eyes; synonym *N. insignis*) is the most commonly available blue species. It grows to under 1 foot (30 cm) tall and produces blue flowers often with a pale center. 'Coelestis' has a white flower with a light blue edge to the petals. 'Pale Face' has a white flower with flecks of purple-blue spotting on the petals.

Nemophila menziesii (baby blue eyes)

'Penny Black' and 'Total Eclipse' have dark blackish blue flowers with a white edge.

Neomarica
Twelve Apostles
IRIDACEAE

Neomarica species are tender plants from South America that resemble *Iris* species. Like some irises, they grow from thick rhizomes. Flower color is usually blue, but also can be white or yellow. The three outer petals of the flower are larger than the inner petals and are wider at the tip than at the base. Where climates are warm, these plants can be used in perennial borders. In temperate regions, they are usually seen only in greenhouse displays. Plants prefer partial shade and an organic, well-drained soil. The common name is derived from the notion that the plant grows with 12 leaves (give or take one or two). The genus name means "new marica." The previous name for this species, *Marica*, is Greek for "to flag" and refers to the flowers that last only a short time.

Propagation: Plants are multiplied by seed or, more commonly, division of the fleshy rhizome.

Representative species and cultivars: *Neomarica* is a genus of 15 species native to Central and South America. They are not commonly available because the flowers, though ornamental, last only a short time.

Neomarica caerulea is a Brazilian native and is the most commonly seen plant in cultivation. It has bright blue flowers with white and yellow marking in the center of the flower.

Neomarica gracilis is similar to *N. caerulea* with blue and white flowers.

Nepeta
Catmint, Catnip
LAMIACEAE

This useful group of annuals and perennials is gaining renewed popularity with gardeners. Catmints form spreading plants between 1 and 3 feet (30 cm and 1 m) tall. The flowers are held above the foliage in upright flower spikes that contain many small yellow, white, lavender, or blue flowers typical of the mint family. These species are used in perennial beds as edging plants and can be taken as cut flowers. Catnip (*Nepeta cataria*) is grown in herb gardens and used as a flavoring or in sachets to excite cats. Plants prefer full sun (partial shade where summers are hot) in a well-drained garden soil. They are relatively easy to grow and should not be overfertilized or they will lose their shape. They can be short lived in climates with hot, humid summers. Divide plants when they become crowded. The genus name is probably from the old Tuscan city Nepete in northwestern Italy.

Propagation: Plants are multiplied by seed, division, or stem cuttings. Cultivars are propagated by division of dormant plants or by softwood stem cuttings taken in early summer.

Nepeta ×*faassenii*

Representative species and cultivars: *Nepeta* contains more than 250 species native to Europe, Asia, and Africa. Several blue-flowering species are among the best catnips for the garden.

Nepeta ×faassenii is a hybrid of *N. mussinii* and probably *N. nepetella*. It blooms in the spring with lavender-blue flowers held above 1.5-foot (45-cm) tall plants with silvery foliage. Plants are more erect than those of *N. mussinii* and flower for a longer period. Seed-grown plants are probably *N. mussinii* even though they are commonly listed as *N. ×faassenii*. Blue cultivars include 'Blue Dwarf', a compact grower; 'Blue Wonder', a heavier-blooming selection with larger foliage; and 'Dropmore', with lavender-blue flowers and gray green foliage. 'Six Hills Giant', a popular, vigorous hybrid to 3 feet (1 m) tall with lavender-blue flowers, can rebloom in late summer if cut back after spring flowers are gone. It is one of the better catnips for gardens, although its true heritage is unclear: it is sometimes listed as a cultivar of *N. ×faassenii*, but is just as often listed under *N. sibirica*.

Nepeta grandiflora is not as commonly available to U.S. gardeners, but can be useful because it blooms over a long period in the summer. It grows between 1.5 and 3 feet (45 cm and 1 m) tall, producing violet-blue flowers. It is native to the Caucasus. This species is often represented in the garden as the cultivar 'Dawn to Dusk', which grows to 1.5 feet (45 cm) and produces large spikes of lavender flowers from darker lavender-blue buds.

Nepeta mussinii (synonym *N. racemosa*) is native to Turkey, Iran, and the Caucasus. It produces violet-blue spikes of flowers in the summer on compact plants that are less than 2 feet (60 cm) tall. It is very similar to *N. ×faassenii* and plants sold in many nurseries as perennial catnip may belong to the hybrid or to the species. 'Little Tich' is designed for edging and only grows 6 inches (15 cm) tall. 'Superba' is a low-growing plant with extended bloom throughout the summer. 'Walkers Low' is a compact plant to about 18 inches (45 cm) tall; it also makes a good edging plant.

Nepeta nervosa has become more available to U.S. gardeners. It is a 1- to

2-foot (30- to 60-cm) tall, compact plant that blooms most of the summer. The dense flower spikes have light blue flowers. This species is not as attractive to cats, which can be a plus for catnips expected to perform in the garden. It is native to India.

Nepeta sibirica produces lavender-blue flowers arranged in a loose flower spike on large 4-foot (1-m) tall plants. It is native to Russia and eastern Asia. Plants bloom from midsummer into fall. 'Souvenir d'Andre Chaudron' (synonym 'Blue Beauty') is a smaller selection with medium blue flowers that last most of the summer.

Nepeta subsessilis is an excellent blue-flowering catnip that deserves wider distribution. Native to Japan, it produces bright blue flowers above rounded mounds of foliage. Plants grow about 3 feet (1 m) tall.

Nepeta tuberosa is an interesting catnip because it grows from a tuber. Native to Spain and Italy, it is not as winter hardy as the other catnips listed here. It grows to about 1.5 feet (45 cm) tall and produces lavender-blue flowers on upright spikes throughout the summer.

Nepeta yunnanensis is native to western China. It spreads by stolons to form dense mats of foliage reaching 2 feet (60 cm) tall. It produces blue flowers in abundance over a long period in the summer.

Nierembergia
Cup Flower
SOLANACEAE

Nierembergia species are annuals, perennials, and shrubs in the night-shade family. They are most commonly used in gardens as annuals for bedding plants or in rock gardens. The cup-shaped flower is similar to the flower of *Campanula*. Flower color can be white, purple, or purple-blue. Plants prefer full sun and a fertile, well-drained soil. The genus name commemorates Juan Nieremberg, a seventeenth-century professor at the University of Madrid.

Propagation: Plants are multiplied most commonly by seed, but stem cuttings root easily.

Nierembergia hippomanica var. *violacea*

Representative species and cultivars: This genus of 35 species is native to Mexico and South America. It was almost unknown by gardeners until the introduction of *Nierembergia hippomanica* var. *violacea* (synonym *N. caerulea*) 'Mont Blanc' as a 1993 All America Selections and European Fleuroselect Gold Medal winner. It produces a compact, self-branching plant to 8 inches (20) tall that is covered with cup-shaped, white flowers with a yellow center. 'Purple Robe' has a similar plant form with lavender-blue flowers. Like other members of the nightshade family, *Nierembergia* has flowers that are not "true blue" but have a purple tint.

Nigella
Love-in-a-mist, Devil-in-a-bush
RANUNCULACEAE

Nigella species are grown as bedding plants or for cut flowers. The inflated seed pods are used in dried flower arrangements. Plants are usually grown in mixed annual and perennial beds, because they only bloom for a few weeks in late summer. They produce bright blue, purple, yellow, or white flowers above threadlike leaves that form the "mist" around the flowers. Plants prefer full sun in any well-drained garden soil. They are easy to grow from transplants or seeds sown directly in the garden. Plants may require staking to remain upright. The genus name is Latin for "black" and refers to the color of the seeds. The seeds of some species are grown as the seasoning known as black cumin. The contradictory common names refer to the way the flowers are nestled into the feathery, threadlike leaves.

Nigella damascena 'Miss Jeykll' (love-in-a-mist)

Propagation: Plants are multiplied by seed that prefers cool germination conditions around 60°F (15°C). Seed is often sown directly in the garden in early spring, as plants can be difficult to transplant.

Representative species and cultivars: The 20 species of *Nigella* are native to Asia and the Mediterranean area. Species with blue flowers are *Nigella hispanica, N. integrifolia,* and *N. sativa* (black cumin), but they are not frequently available to gardeners and are not superior to *N. damascena,* which is the only species commonly grown by gardeners. *Nigella damascena* (love-in-a-mist) is an annual bedding plant with blue or less commonly white flowers. Native to southern Europe, it grows to about 2 feet (60 cm) tall. 'Miss Jeykll' is the most commonly grown form of this species with semi-double flowers. 'Persian Jewels' is similar with mixed colors of pink, white, and blue.

Nolana
Chilean Bellflower
NOLANACEAE

Nolana species are tender, herbaceous perennials usually grown in gardens as annuals. They have small petunia-like flowers that are purple or blue and produced in the leaf axils on spreading 1-foot (30-cm) tall plants. They can be used as bedding plants or in hanging baskets. Plants require full sun and do well in most well-drained garden soils. The genus name is Latin for "little bell" and refers to the shape of the flowers.

Propagation: Plants are multiplied by seed, but stem cuttings root easily. Germination can be erratic and limits the availability of garden transplants from garden centers. Seed is often sown directly in the garden in spring.

Representative species and cultivars: *Nolana* is a South American genus of about 20 species. They are not familiar garden plants, but at least one species is available from seed catalogs. *Nolana humifusa* produces flowers that are 2 inches (5 cm) in diameter on trailing stems. It does well as a bedding plant for the front of a border, but is recommended mostly for pots and hanging baskets. Flower color is a pale blue with a white center. 'Blue Bird' and 'Little Bells' have a deeper lilac blue color. Other less commonly available species with bluish flowers include *N. paradoxa* and *N. acuminata*.

Nymphaea
Water Lily
NYMPHAEACEAE

Water lilies are a group of submerged plants that grow from either a rhizome or tuber. There are hardy types that come from temperate regions including North America, and tropical types. Most blue-flowering forms are tropical or hybrid types. They are not winter hardy and must be overwintered in a sheltered location. Water lilies produce circular, floating foliage and multipetalled flowers that usually protrude above the water on a single flower stem. Colors range from white, pink, red, yellow, and blue. Hardy waterlily blooms last 3 to 4 days and open during the day. Tropical water lilies can be grouped into day-blooming and night-blooming types. Hardy forms can be naturalized in ponds. It has become very fashionable to have hardy, tropical or hybrid water lilies in backyard ponds. They are also features in many of the larger botanical garden conservatories. Culture is fairly easy. Plants are submerged in large tubs to the proper depth, about 18 inches (45 cm), depending on the species. They require at least 5 hours of sunlight for best bloom and should be fertilized regularly. The genus is named after the "water nymphs" of Greek mythology.

Propagation: Water lilies can be propagated by seed. Because hybrids do not come true from seed, they should be propagated by division of the rhizome or offsets from the tuber. Some species produce plantlets from the top of the leaves and these can be removed for propagation. Commercial growers propagate water lilies by tissue culture.

Nymphaea (water lily)

Representative species and cultivars: *Nymphaea* is native to temperate and tropical regions and constitutes about 50 species. Only the tropical water lilies and their hybrids show blue flower color.

Nymphaea caerulea (Egyptian blue lotus) is native to Africa. It is a day-blooming type with pale blue flowers and yellow stamens.

Nymphaea capensis (South African blue water lily) is a day-blooming type with fragrant, light blue flowers and dark yellow inner stamens. It is native to Africa and Madagascar.

Nymphaea gigantea is the Australian representative with blue flowers. It is a day bloomer and, as the name implies, has large flowers that are 6 inches (15 cm) in diameter.

Nymphaea stellata (Indian blue lotus) is also day blooming with bright blue flowers held high above the water. It is native to India.

Numerous hybrid water lilies have excellent blue flowers. These are all tropical, day-blooming types. Some of the more readily available selections include 'Blue Beauty', a heavy bloomer with fragrant, blue flowers held well above the water; 'Blue Triumph', with dark blue flowers and yellow stamens that are tipped with blue; 'Daubeniana' (synonym 'Daubenyana'), a cross between *N. caerulea* and *N. micrantha* with lavender-blue flowers and yellow stamens, forming plantlets on the tops of the leaves; 'Pamela', with long-blooming pale blue flowers; and 'Wood's Blue Goddess', with sky blue flowers and purple stamens.

Omphalodes
Navelwort, Creeping Forget-me-not, Blue-eyed Mary
BORAGINACEAE

Omphalodes species are herbaceous annual and perennial plants that are similar to *Myosotis* species. They are not as commonly available in the United States and can be distinguished from *Myosotis* species because they are usually creeping perennials rather than upright plants. They also lack the yellow center commonly found in *Myosotis* species. Flower color is white or bright blue, and flowers are usually produced on creeping stems in the spring. Plants prefer a moist, well-drained soil and partial shade. They are suited to the rock garden, but do best in a woodland setting where they can naturalize. The genus name is Greek for "resembling a navel" and refers to the shape of the seed.

Propagation: Plants are multiplied by seed or spring division. Seed can be sown in the garden and allowed to naturalize.

Representative species and cultivars: *Omphalodes* is native to Europe, Asia, and Mexico and constitutes about 30 species. All are recognizable for their resemblance to forget-me-not flowers. They are some of the best true-blue flowers for a shady garden; however, they are not as winter hardy as *Myosotis* species, only surviving winter temperatures to $-10°F$ ($-23°C$).

Omphalodes cappadocica (navelwort) is native to Turkey and produces bright azure blue flowers on plants that grow less than 1 foot (30 cm) tall. Each bright flower has a tiny white eye. 'Cherry Ingram' has larger flowers and compact growth compared with the species. 'Starry Eyes' also has large flowers that are near white with a central blue eye on each petal. 'Lilac Mist' is a mutant of 'Starry Eyes' with soft lilac flowers.

Omphalodes linifolia is an annual species and is very different from the other species listed here: it prefers full sun and a drier, well-drained soil. It is most often grown for its white flowers, but *O. linifolia* var. *caerulescens* is a blue-flowering form. Plants grow about 1 foot (30 cm) tall. The species is native to southwestern Europe.

Omphalodes luciliae is the miniature in this group, producing plants that only reach 4 inches (10 cm) tall. It is welcome in the rock garden or for the alpine collection. The flowers are held on loose flowering stems that grow away from a central rosette of gray leaves. Flower color is light to lavender-blue.

Omphalodes verna (blue-eyed Mary) and *O. cappadocica* are the most commonly available perennial species in the genus. *Omphalodes verna* should not be confused with *Collinsia verna*, which shares the same species and common name. This blue-eyed Mary refers to the appreciation of the plant by Marie Antoinette. It is a creeping plant reaching 10 inches (25 cm) tall and spreading by underground stems. It can be used as a ground cover for shady, woodland areas and is native to southern Europe. Flower color is bright azure blue, turning to pink as the flowers fade. 'Alba' is a white-flowering form. 'Grandiflora' has large, deep blue flowers and is thought to be more winter hardy than the species or *O. cappadocica*.

Otacanthus
Brazilian Snapdragon
SCROPHULARIACEAE

Otacanthus species are a group of tender, herbaceous perennials native to Brazil. All produce purple or blue flowers with a white spot at the tip of the petals on the lower lip. Flowers resemble those of snapdragon and appear in terminal clusters. These species are useful as bedding plants or container plants for greenhouse displays and make an excellent cut flower. They also may have economic value due to the secondary products made by the plants that have potential uses as essential oils or as insect pheromones. Plants prefer full sun and a moist, well-drained soil that is slightly acidic. They should be pinched to promote branching and additional flowering.

Otacanthus caeruleus
(Brazilian snapdragon)

Propagation: Plants are multiplied by seed or cuttings. Seed is easy to germinate, and stem cuttings can be rooted any time of year.

Representative species and cultivars: The six species of *Otacanthus* are native to Brazil. *Otacanthus caeruleus* (Brazilian snapdragon) is the only species available. It was introduced originally from Brazil into Europe in the mid-nineteenth century, where it was grown as a greenhouse pot plant. It was reintroduced into Australia in the 1980s and has shown promise as a garden and cut flower plant. It is currently available in North America and Europe and should become popular, because it has a long flowering period and a true, bright blue flower. Plants reach about 24 inches (60 cm) tall.

Oxypetalum
Oxypetalum, Blue Milkweed
ASCLEPIADACEAE

This interesting genus in the milkweed family contains tender, herbaceous and woody perennials native to South America. Flowers are produced in open, terminal clusters with five spreading petals. Flower color can be white, yellow, purple, or blue. Plants are recognizable as milkweeds from the shape of the seed pods. *Oxypetalum* is used in mixed annual and perennial beds and usually treated like an annual. Cut flowers are long lasting. Plants need full sun and do well in most well-drained garden soils. They can self-sow from seeds, which can be a nuisance for some gardeners. The genus name is Greek for "sharp petals."

Propagation: Plants are usually multiplied by seed, but perennial types can be rooted from stem cuttings.

Representative species and cultivars: The approximately 150 species of *Oxypetalum* are native to South America. Only *O. caeruleum* is commonly cultivated. Some taxonomists consider it to be significantly different from other *Oxypetalum* species and separate it into its own one-species genus called *Twee-*

Oxypetalum caeruleum

dia. *Oxypetalum caeruleum* (synonym *Tweedia caeruleum*) can reach 3 feet (1 m) tall. It produces powder blue flowers in loose, open clusters. Although this species was introduced in 1852, it has remained uncommon in American gardens until the introduction of 'Heaven Born'. This cultivar is gaining in popularity because the flower color mixes well with other pastel colors currently in fashion in many gardens. It is perennial in mild climates.

Parahebe
SCROPHULARIACEAE

Parahebe species are herbaceous and woody perennials suited for mixed perennial beds or rock gardens. In milder climates, they can be perennial, but may best be treated as annuals in other regions. Flowers have four or five petals, are more or less tubular, and appear in spring and summer. Flower color can be white, pink, or blue. Plants flower best in full sun in a well-drained soil. They prefer summers that are not hot and humid. The genus name is Greek for "near *Hebe*" and refers to the close botanical relationship between these species and those of the genus *Hebe*.

Propagation: Plants are multiplied by seed, stem cuttings, and division.

Representative species and cultivars: *Parahebe* is a genus of about 15 species native to New Zealand and Australia. Previously, these

Parahebe perfoliata

species had been listed in *Hebe* and *Veronica,* and thus may be offered under any of these genera in catalogs. The most commonly available blue forms are *P. canescens* and *P. perfoliata.*

Parahebe canescens is a creeping form that only reaches 4 inches (10 cm) tall. Native to New Zealand, it produces blue flowers in the summer that resemble *Veronica* flowers. It is suited for the rock garden.

Parahebe perfoliata is a taller plant growing to about 1.5 feet (45 cm) tall on sprawling stems. It is recognizable for its leaves without petioles that surround the stem and numerous flowers on an upright-flowering stem. The violet-blue flowers resemble *Veronica* flowers.

Passiflora
Passion Flower, Granadilla
PASSIFLORACEAE

Passiflora is a group of chiefly tropical woody vines, although several are native to North America. They are recognizable for the showy flowers produced in abundance along the climbing stems. Most gardeners have seen these flowers hanging from supports in greenhouse conservatories. The flowers are unique in composition: they are circular, usually with five indistinguishable sepals and petals that form the showy part of the flower. In front of these, is the fringed "corona," an outgrowth of the flower stem that can be pigmented. Large-flowering types produce flowers that are 4 inches (10 cm) across. Plants are most often grown indoors or in the greenhouse. With bright light and temperature control, passion flowers are relatively easy to grow and the major feat for the gardener with a small collection greenhouse is keeping the vines under control. The container needs to be large enough to support the plants, and the potting mix should be well drained but not allowed to dry out. Night temperatures should not go below 50°F (10°C). The genus name is Latin for "passion flower" and was selected because Spanish colonists in South America thought that various parts of the flower symbolized Christ's passion and crucifixion.

Propagation: Species are multiplied by seed, but cultivars are multiplied more commonly by stem cuttings or simple layering.

Representative species and cultivars: The approximately 400 species of *Passiflora* are native mostly to South America, but also appear in Asia, Australia, and North America. The edible fruit often used for juice comes from *P. edulis,* but other species also produce edible fruit. No species in this genus has truly blue flowers, but *P. caerulea* and its hybrids have blue bands in their coronas.

Passiflora ✕*alato-caerulea,* a hybrid of *P. alata* and *P. caerulea,* is free flowering and often recommended as the best passion flower for use as a houseplant. The large purple and white flowers have coronas that are purple at the base and blue in the middle with white tips.

Passiflora caerulea (blue passion flower) is a fast-growing species from South America that can climb more than 25 feet (7.5 m). The abundant, fragrant flowers have a blue corona against white petals. This species is more hardy than most passion flowers, surviving winter temperatures as low as −10°F (−23°C). 'Constance Elliot' has large flowers with a pale blue band on the corona.

Passiflora ✕*coriacea* is a hybrid between *P. incarnata* and *P. caerulea.* It has white flowers with reddish spots on the petals and sepals. The coronas are purple, white, and blue.

Passiflora quadrangularis (granadilla) is most often grown for its large, edible fruit, but the flowers are also large and showy. They are recurved and have a wavy corona banded with white and purple-blue. The species is native to Central and South America.

Passiflora caerulea
(blue passion flower)

Patersonia
IRIDACEAE

Patersonia species are herbaceous perennials developing from rhizomes. They produce very showy, three-petaled white, yellow, or purple-blue flowers on 2- to 3-foot (60-cm to 1-m) tall plants that bloom in spring or early summer, but only for a short time. Plants require full sun and a well-drained soil. Because these species are tender perennials, they must be lifted and overwintered in colder areas. They are interesting plants for mixed perennial gardens or as container plants for seasonal greenhouse displays. Their short flowering time limits their general usefulness as garden plants. The genus name commemorates Scottish botanist William Paterson, who collected in Australia.

Propagation: Plants are multiplied by seed or, more commonly, division. The usual form of propagation is division of the rhizome.

Representative species and cultivars: *Patersonia* contains about 20 species native to Australia and New Guinea. They are not common garden plants, but they are occasionally seen in warm climate gardens and as container plants in greenhouse displays. *Patersonia glauca* and *P. longiscapa* are similar species and the most commonly cultivated. Both produce attractive *Iris*-like flowers that are 1 inch (2.5 cm) in diameter and purple-blue in color. *Patersonia longiscapa* is the smaller of the two species, only reaching 1.5 feet (46 cm) tall.

Pentaglottis
Green Alkanet
BORAGINACEAE

Pentaglottis is a herbaceous perennial similar to *Anchusa*. The blue "forget-me-not" flowers appear in spring and early summer. Plants are best used in mixed perennial beds or naturalized in a moist area. They do best in partial to deep shade. They may self-sow and can become weedy.

Pentaglottis sempervirens

The genus name is Greek for "five tongued" and refers to the scales at the base of the flower.

Propagation: Plants are multiplied by seed or division.

Representative species and cultivars: *Pentaglottis sempervirens* (synonym *Anchusa sempervirens*) is the only species in this genus. Native to Europe, it produces a 2-foot (60-cm) tall plant with typical blue "forget-me-not" flowers in a coiled flower stem. In its native habitat, it can self-sow and colonize large areas where the environment is moist and shaded.

Perovskia
Russian Sage
LAMIACEAE

Perovskia species are herbaceous or woody perennials that have become very popular with gardeners. They are relatively large plants to 5 feet (1.5 m) tall with silvery foliage that mixes well with other garden perennials. They are topped with narrow flower spikes containing many small, light blue-purple or yellow flowers. Flowers appear in late summer and last into fall. Plants do well in full sun and must have a well-drained soil. They should be cut back to a few inches above the ground in winter or spring and pinched to encourage branching. The genus name commemorates a nineteenth-century Russian official, Vasili Perovski.

Propagation: Plants are multiplied by seed, division, and cuttings. Stem cuttings taken in summer before the plants have flowered are the most common method of propagation for commercial growers. Division of the crown while plants are dormant is also possible.

Perovskia atriplicifolia (Russian sage)

Representative species and cultivars: The nine species of *Perovskia* are native from the Middle East (Iran and Afghanistan) into the Himalayan region. The most commonly available species is *P. atriplicifolia,* but additional plants of apparent hybrid origin are also on the market.

Perovskia atriplicifolia (Russian sage) has become an indispensable component in the perennial garden. Native from Afghanistan into Tibet, it grows 4 to 5 feet (1.2 to 1.5 m) tall and combines well with other late season perennials including ornamental grasses. 'Filagran' has a finer textured leaf and 'Blue Mist' has lighter blue flowers. 'Longin' (possible a hybrid) is a more upright plant with lavender-blue flowers.

Perovskia 'Blue Spire', a hybrid probably between *P. atriplicifolia* and *P. abrotanoides,* is a widely available cultivar with more dissected leaves than the species.

Perovskia scrophulariifolia is native to central Asia. It is a more compact plant than *P. atriplicifolia* with smaller leaves and a deeper blue flower. Its growth habit is similar to that of Russian sage.

Petrea
Queen's Wreath
VERBENACEAE

Petrea species are tropical shrubs and woody vines. These vigorous vines grow on trellises or structural supports in greenhouse conservatories. They also make interesting container specimens when trained as a small tree standard. In tropical landscapes, they are grown as a climbing vine similar to *Wisteria*. Plants do not tolerate temperatures below 50°F (10°C). The flowers have five straplike petals and are produced in hanging clusters. Flower color is violet-blue. In conservatories, plants bloom profusely in winter through late spring. They prefer full sun and a well-drained soil or potting medium. Carl Linnaeus named the genus to commemorate Robert James (Lord Petre), an eighteenth-century English patron of botany, and plants were introduced to gardeners in 1834.

Propagation: Plants are multiplied by seed, stem cuttings, or layering. The most common form of propagation is by softwood stem cuttings taken after the plants have flowered.

Representative species and cultivars: The approximately 30 species of *Petrea* are native to Mexico and South America. *Petrea volubilis* (queen's wreath) is the only species commonly cultivated in North American and European greenhouses and gardens. It blooms in profusion in winter when grown in a greenhouse conservatory. Bright violet-blue flowers hang in clusters that can reach up to 12 inches (30 cm) long and are very eye-catching. *Petrea volubilis* 'Albiflora' is a white-flowering form. In tropical gardens, vines can reach up to 40 feet (12 m) long. In Brazil, children remove the flowers and fly them as little helicopters. The five petals are fused to a corolla tube, and they make an interesting aerodynamic display when spun like a top.

Petraea volubilis
(queen's wreath)

Petunia
SOLANACEAE

Petunia selections are very familiar to all gardeners and are among the most popular bedding plants. Most modern petunias are F_1 hybrids with greater garden performance than the species. They produce large flowers in many colors on erect or trailing stems. They have been separated into four sections on the basis of flower characters (grandiflora, floribunda, multiflora, and millifora). Within each section is a full range of colors from yellow, white, and pink to shades of purple and blue. There are also bicolors and double flowers. Bicolors are of two types: picotee or star. Picotee flowers show a solid inside color with a wide rim along the edge of the petals in a contrasting color. Star flowers have a stripe of contrasting color (often white) down the center of each petal giving a starburst effect. Petunias are commonly used in mixed or mass plantings of annuals or in hanging baskets. They require full sun and respond to good garden culture including fertilization and timely irrigation. The genus name is derived from *petun,* the Brazilian name for tobacco.

Propagation: Plants are multiplied most commonly by seed, but stem cuttings root easily.

Representative species and cultivars: All 40 species of *Petunia* are native to South America. They are tender perennials grown as annual plants in temperate gardens. Gardeners know *Petunia* from the many superior hybrids developed since the nineteenth century. *Petunia ×hybrida,* a group of hybrids, was derived primarily from crosses with *P. axillaris, P. integrifolia,* and *P. violacea,* and the first selections are credited to Isaac Buchanan, a New York hybridizer. Numerous cultivars have blue flowers. Like many other members of the nightshade family, blue petunias are often tinged with purple, but several clear blue cultivars are available. Cultivars change rather often in this competitive market for petunias. They are selected for flower color, size, garden performance, and how well they flower in the small packs for spring display in the garden center. A brief listing of current major series with blue flowers is included here by flower type.

Grandiflora petunias (large flowers): **Aladdin,** early flowering with a wavy, ruffled petal edge (available as 'Blue', 'Blue Ice' with darker petal veins, and 'Sky Blue'); **Cloud,** extra large flowers with ruffled petal edge; **Countdown,** very early to flower with good garden performance (available as 'Navy Blue' and 'Iridescent Blue'); **Daddy,** large, ruffled flowers with dark veins in the petals; **Danube,** the only fully double, blue flower; **Dreams,** compact, with lots of flowers that are disease tolerant ('Midnight' is dark violet-blue); **Eagle,** compact, branched plants for good garden performance; **Falcon,** early flowering and compact plants (available as 'Blue' and 'Mid-blue'); **Flash,** large flowers and good weather tolerance (available as 'Blue' and 'Picotee Blue'); 'Hulahoop', a blue and white picotee; **Super Magic,** an improved version of the older Magic petunia with vivid flower colors (available as 'Sky'); **Super Cascade,** an updated version of the popular Cascade petunias, known for good hanging basket performance; and **Ultra,** compact growth, early flowering, and good garden performance even in poor weather (available as 'Blue', 'Blue Star', 'Blue Vein', 'Sky Blue').

Floribunda petunias (medium-sized flowers): **Celebrity,** a former All America Selections winner with large flowers and more disease and weather resistance compared with most grandiflora types (available as 'Blue', 'Blue Ice' with darker veins, and 'Sky Blue'); and **Madness,** similar garden performance to Celebrity with vivid flower colors (available as 'Midnight' with dark blue flowers and 'Orchid' with lavender-blue).

Multiflora petunias (many smaller flowers): **Carpet,** among the most popular multifloras because of early flowering, compact branching, and heat tolerance (available as 'Blue', 'Blue Lace' with dark veins, 'Blue Star' bicolor, 'Sky Blue', and 'True Blue'); **Primetime,** a heavy-flowering, compact grower with great garden performance (available as 'Blue', 'Blue Star' bicolor, 'Light Blue', 'Mid-blue', and 'Blues' mix); **Joy,** compact free-flowering plants (available as 'Blue', 'Starlight' bicolor, and 'Sky'); and **Polo,** early flowering bright colors (available as 'Blue' and 'Blue Star' bicolor).

Milliflora petunias (dwarf, non-trailing plants): 'Fantasy Blue', the blue-flowering representative of a new class of petunias with a dwarf, bushy growth habit, abundant flowers that bloom sooner than other petunia types and hide the foliage.

Phacelia
California Bluebell
HYDROPHYLLACEAE

Phacelia species are annual and perennial plants producing tubular or saucer-shaped flowers with protruding stamens usually in late spring or summer. Flower color can be blue, white, purple, or yellow. These species are most often used as annuals or naturalized in woodland gardens. Winter-sown plants raised in the greenhouse also can be used to provide spring color associated with bulbs. Plants prefer full sun or light shade in a well-drained soil. They do not do well in hot, humid summers. Perennial types are difficult to establish, but work well in rock gardens. The genus name is Greek for "a cluster" and refers to the bunches of flowers in some species.

Propagation: Plants are multiplied by seed that is often sown in place in the garden.

Representative species and cultivars: The more than 150 species of *Phacelia* are native to North and South America. They are not common garden plants, but can be effective.

Phacelia campanularia (California bluebell) has the bluest flowers in the genus. It grows about 1 foot (30 cm) tall with clusters of bright blue tubular flowers. Native to California, this annual blooms in late spring and summer.

Phacelia grandiflora
(California bluebell)

Phacelia grandiflora (California bluebell) is similar to *P. campanularia,* but has lavender-blue flowers. Both species are the commonest forms found in gardens.

Phacelia purshii is not commonly cultivated, but is a widespread woodland wildflower in the middle United States. It is notable for its small light blue flowers with fringed petals.

Phacelia sericea is occasionally seen in gardens and has purple-blue flowers. Native to the Rocky Mountains, it reaches around 2 feet (60 cm) tall.

Phacelia tanacetifolia is the giant in this group, growing to 4 feet (1.2 m) tall. It is native from California into Mexico and has purple-blue flowers. It, too, is occasionally seen in gardens.

Phlox
Phlox, Moss Pink
POLEMONIACEAE

Phlox species are herbaceous annual and perennial plants of which several are very important garden plants. They can vary in form from small creeping plants to large upright plants to 4 feet (1.2 m) tall. Flowers are borne singly or in large pyramidal clusters. Flower color ranges from white to pink, yellow, red, purple, or blue. Some species bloom in spring, others in summer. These plants are indispensable members of formal or mixed perennial beds. The creeping types make good edging plants and are at home in the rock garden. Other species are better associated in the woodland garden. Plants prefer full sun or in some cases light shade. The soil should be well drained. Taller species require staking. The genus name is Greek for "a flame" and refers to the bright colors in some species.

Propagation: Plants are multiplied by seed, division, or root cuttings. Most creeping types are propagated by stem cuttings taken after the plants have flowered. Many taller cultivars are propagated by root cuttings removed from dormant plants and stuck in sand. Some commercial growers propagate some species by tissue culture.

Representative species and cultivars: Except for one Russian species, the approximately 70 species of *Phlox* are all native to North America. Numerous hybrid and garden forms exist. Only the perennial species have blue flowers.

Phlox divaricata (woodland phlox) is a 1-foot (30-cm) tall plant that creeps by surface rhizomes. Flowers are held on upright stems and appear in spring. Flower color is lavender-blue. Plants are effective in shaded woodland areas. This plant deserves to be better known. 'Blue Dreams' has lilac blue flowers in early spring. 'Clouds of Perfume' is a Dutch selection with very fragrant lavender-blue flowers. 'Dirgo Ice' is a common cultivar with light blue flowers. 'London Grove' has fragrant, blue flowers on mildew-resistant plants. The species is native to eastern North America. *Phlox divaricata* subsp. *laphamii* is from the western part of that range and has fragrant violet-blue flowers. *Phlox* 'Chatahochee', a hybrid between *P. divaricata* subsp. *laphamii* and *P. pilosa,* has lavender-blue flowers and a purple eye. It tolerates shady garden conditions.

Phlox divaricata (woodland phlox)

Phlox drummondii (annual phlox) is native to Texas and is grown either as a bedding plant or for containers. It does better in cool weather. Plants are well-branched and grow to less than 1 foot (30 cm) tall. Flowers cover the plant in late spring and occur as white, yellow, pink, red, rose, and lavender-blue. The Beauty mix consists of compact plants containing the full range of colors including blue. The Dolly mix contains an extended color blend with some plants having sky blue flowers. The Palona mix produces early flowers in all colors including light blue.

Phlox paniculata (garden phlox) is the tall phlox seen in so many perennial gardens. It originates from the eastern United States. Well-grown plants can reach 4 feet (1.2 m) tall and usually need some support. They are summer blooming, usually fragrant, and occur in numerous color combinations. Blue is not a common color in this species, but 'Blue Boy' comes close with its midseason display of lavender-blue flowers on a 3-foot (1-m) tall plant. 'Franz Schubert' has lilac blue flowers. 'Little Boy' grows only to 1.5 feet (45 cm) tall and has fragrant, purple-blue flowers with a white eye. 'Miss Kelley' is one of the truer blues for a garden phlox. Individual flowers are very large.

Phlox stolonifera (broadleaf creeping phlox) is another low-growing, shade-tolerant species that blooms in the spring. It works well with similar perennials or naturalized in a woodland area. It is acid loving and combines well with *Rhododendron* species. Native to the eastern United States, it is most often represented in gardens by its cultivars. The most popular of these is 'Blue Ridge' with lilac blue flowers, but other selections have white and pink colors.

Phlox subulata (moss pink) prefers a sunny location and can form large mats of mosslike, evergreen foliage in suitable locations. It is native to eastern and central United States. Flowers are among the first to appear in the spring. The many cultivars of moss pink occur in pink, white, near red, and blue. 'Blue Hills' and 'Emerald Blue' are the lavender-blue cultivars most often seen in gardens.

Phyteuma
Horned Rampion
CAMPANULACEAE

Phyteuma species are interesting members of the bellflower family with inflated, "horned" flowers arranged in rounded groups. The five slender petals are fused at the tips to form this characteristic feature. What they lack in attractiveness, they make up for in novelty. Flower color is blue or lavender, and blossoms appear in late spring and summer. These herbaceous perennials are used most commonly as rock garden or alpine container plants. Taller types can be used in the perennial bed. They prefer full sun, but do not tolerate hot, humid weather. The soil must be well drained. The genus name is Greek for "the plant," an old, but vague name for this genus. I wonder if it has anything to do with the fact that some *Phyteuma* species were used as aphrodisiacs?

Phyteuma comosum (horned rampion)

Propagation: Multiplication is by seed or division in spring. Seed may require chilling stratification prior to germination to relieve dormancy.

Representative species and cultivars: The approximately 40 species in this interesting genus are native to Europe and Asia. Many come from alpine environments. Those grown in gardens have blue, lavender-blue, or violet flowers. These plants seem made for the alpine container or trough garden, because their curious flowers beg for close inspection.

Phyteuma comosum has been moved by some botanists to its own genus containing only this species. Its new name is *Physolepis comosum*. A small, mounded plant native to the Alps, it is the finest horned rampion for alpine container culture. Flower color is variable, but is usually more lavender than blue. The tips of the flowers are a deeper color than the bulbous base of the flowers.

Phyteuma cordatum is confined to a limited growing range in the Alps. It produces pale blue horned flowers just 8 inches (20 cm) tall.

Phyteuma hemisphaericum is a small plant growing between 2 and 4 inches (5 and 10 cm) tall. Native to mountainous regions of Europe, it has deep blue flowers and rivals *P. comosum* as an alpine container plant.

Phyteuma orbiculare has violet-blue flowers that curve inwards. This European native grows between 6 and 18 inches (15 and 45 cm) tall.

Phyteuma scheuchzeri produces deep blue flower heads that are typical of horned rampion and held on stems that reach 1.5 feet (45 cm) tall. It is native to the European Alps and a worthy rock garden plant.

Phyteuma orbiculare

Platycodon
Balloon Flower
CAMPANULACEAE

Platycodon, a familiar garden plant, is a hardy, herbaceous perennial producing blue, white, or pink flowers in terminal clusters. The common name comes from the closed, inflated shape of the flower bud prior to its opening into a five-pointed, bell-shaped blossom. The flower resembles but is larger than most *Campanula* flowers and blooms for an extended period in the summer. Plants require full sun or partial shade in any well-drained garden soil. In a fertile soil, they may need staking. New shoot growth emerges in late spring, and care should be taken not to site new plants where balloon flowers will eventually emerge. Division is not necessary for many years. Plants often do not

Platycodon grandiflorus var. *mariesii* (balloon flower)

bloom until the second season after seeding. The genus name is Greek for "broad bell" and refers to the size of the flower.

Propagation: Multiplication is from seed or division. Seed germination improves with exposure to light, and even the double-flowering forms can be raised from seed.

Platycodon grandiflorus var. *mariesii*

Representative species and cultivars: *Platycodon* contains only one species, and it is native to Asia. *Platycodon grandiflorus* has had a place in perennial gardens for many years. Plants usually grow about 2.5 feet (75 cm) tall, but compact types are available that do not require staking. The flower can vary in color, size, and form: white (*P. grandiflorus* 'Albus'), pink (*P. grandiflorus* 'Roseus'), dwarf (*P. grandiflorus* var. *mariesii*), or semi-double (*P. grandiflorus* 'Japonicus'; *P. grandiflorus* 'Semi-plenum'). These are produced reasonably true to type from seed. The species usually produces purple-blue flowers, but most selected cultivars are bright blue. 'Fuji Blue' has large flowers that last a long time in the garden; it can be taken as a cut flower. 'Komachi' is also a good blue, but is interesting because the "balloons" usually stay closed and the flowers never open. Double flowers are found on 'Double Blue' and 'Hakone Blue'. 'Sentimental Blue' is an F_1 hybrid with an intense blue flower color on compact plants that can bloom the first year from seeds.

Plectranthus

Plectranthus, Swedish Ivy, Candle Plant

LAMIACEAE

Plectranthus is a large group of mostly tender, herbaceous and woody perennials. They are closely related to *Coleus* species and have similar uses and cultural requirements. The flowers are produced in upright spikes containing many small, two-lipped, tubular flowers. Flower color can be blue-violet, purple, or white. Some species produce bi-colored flowers or flowers with dark spots on the petals. The plants can be upright or trailing in habit. Several species, such as *P. australis,* known as Swedish ivy, are grown solely for their attractive foliage and their ability to tolerate low light conditions. Others are grown for their striking flowers and are used as bedding plants. Trailing forms are grown for hanging baskets. *Plectranthus* is more commonly seen in tropical gardens or conservatories, but could be used like *Coleus* in temperate gardens. Plants require light shade and benefit from pinching, which causes them to become full and bushy. They prefer a moist, well-drained soil with moderate fertility. The genus name is derived from the Greek word for "spur flower."

Propagation: Plants are multiplied by seed or stem cuttings. The most common form of propagation is a softwood stem cutting taken any time of year.

Representative species and cultivars: The more than 250 species of *Plectranthus* have a worldwide distribution, but occur mainly in Asia, Australia, and Africa. The genus is a member of the mint family with close ties to the genus *Coleus.* Previously, only those species with interesting foliage have been cultivated, but several species are now being grown for their flower display and others should be considered.

Plectranthus argentatus is an evergreen shrub from Australia grown for its trailing habit and its gray green leaves that have a wavy margin. The pale blue flowers are small but abundant on upright spikes that can reach 12 inches (30 cm) tall. Plants can reach 3 feet (1 m) tall.

Plectranthus coeruleus, native to dry areas of South Africa, is a trailing succulent that produces small blue-flowering spikes.

Plectranthus fruticosus is a bushlike plant growing to 4 feet (1.2 m) tall. Native to shady areas of South Africa, it produces blue-mauve flowers that are similar in form to flowers of *Coleus.*

Plectranthus hilliardiae has been popular as a bedding plant in cool conservatory displays. It produces large, terminal flower spikes for fall and winter displays. The tubular flowers are light purple with contrasting blue spots on the turned up "lips." Plants can reach 2 feet (60 cm) tall when in flower.

Plectranthus oertendahlii (candle plant) is a fairly common indoor plant grown mostly for its trailing habit and attractive leaves with a felt-like, hairy underside. The flowers are produced year-round in upright spikes and are white or light blue. This species is native to South Africa.

Plectranthus thyroides (synonym *Coleus thyroides*) is an upright, bushy plant native to Africa. It can reach 3 feet (1 m) tall and can be grown as a bedding plant or a greenhouse container plant. The flowers are bright blue.

Plumbago
Leadwort
PLUMBAGINACEAE

Plumbago species are tender, herbaceous and woody perennials, although a few are annuals. They produce red, white, or blue flowers in terminal clusters. Flower shape is similar to that of phlox with five petals fused at the base. Plants do not tolerate frost, but are perennial in mild climates. Otherwise, they are grown as greenhouse specimens, outdoor annuals for mixed annual and perennial beds, or as container plants that can be brought inside to overwinter. Plants prefer full sun in a well-drained soil or potting medium. While actively growing, leadwort should have moderate fertility for continued flowering. The genus name is from the Latin word for "lead," possibly for an old use in treating lead poisoning.

Propagation: Plants are multiplied by seed, stem cuttings, and root cuttings. The most common method of propagation is by softwood stem cuttings, and rooting is aided by bottom heat.

Representative species and cultivars: *Plumbago* is native to warmer regions including Asia, Africa, and South America. About 12 species be-

Plumbago auriculata (cape leadwort)

long to the genus, of which the most available are the red-flowering *P. indica* (synonym *P. rosea*) and the blue-flowering *P. auriculata.*

Plumbago auriculata (cape leadwort; synonym *P. capensis*) is native to South Africa and has sprawling, woody stems with numerous pale blue (sometimes white) flowers in terminal clusters. Its trailing habit and soft blue flower color combine nicely with an informal flower border. In the garden, flowers appear from summer until frost. Where the climate is mild, this species is perennial and can reach 10 feet (3 m) or more in height.

Plumbago caerulea is less familiar to gardeners than cape leadwort. It is an annual species native to Peru. This upright plant to 1.5 feet (45 cm) tall produces flower spikes with purple-blue flowers.

Polemonium
Jacob's Ladder, Greek Valerian
POLEMONIACEAE

Polemonium is a genus of herbaceous annual and perennial plants. Flowers are produced in loose, terminal clusters above the characteristic "Jacob's ladder" foliage that can give a fernlike character to some species. Individual flowers are shaped like tubes, bells, or saucers and occur in white, pink, yellow, purple, or blue. Blossoms appear in spring or summer. These species make excellent plants for the perennial bed or woodland garden, but can be short lived where summers are hot and humid. They are also used as cut flowers. Plants do well in full sun, but most prefer partial shade and a moist, well-drained soil. The genus name most likely commemorates Poleman, a Greek philosopher. A more romantic interpretation suggests that the name is from the Greek word for "war" and was applied to this genus because two ancient kings went to war over a dispute about it.

Propagation: Plants are multiplied by seed or division. Seed can take more than 20 days to germinate. Plants should be divided when they are dormant.

Representative species and cultivars: Most of the approximately 20 species of *Polemonium* are native to North America, but some also appear in Europe, Asia, and South America. They occur in moist woodlands or open alpine areas along stream beds.

Polemonium caeruleum (Jacob's ladder) is the most familiar garden plant in this genus. Native to Europe, Asia, and North America, it has several botanical varieties that are sometimes split into separate species: *P. caeruleum* var. *album* is a white form and *P. caeruleum* var. *himalayanum* is a larger plant with bright blue flowers. Plant height starts at 1 foot (30 cm) tall, but vigorous plants can reach 3 feet (1 m) tall. 'Brise d'Anjou' has a leaf with a creamy white margin and is attractive

Polemonium caeruleum 'Lace Tower' (Jacob's ladder)

Polemonium reptans 'Blue Pearl' (creeping polemonium)

for its foliage after the flowers fade. 'Lace Tower' is a wonderful selection with lacy, dissected leaves and cobalt blue flowers.

Polemonium cashmerianum is native to the mountains around Nepal. It produces lavender-blue flowers with a white center on 2-foot (60-cm) tall plants. This species has a long summer-blooming period.

Polemonium foliosissimum (leafy polemonium) is similar to *P. caeruleum* and produces an upright plant to about 2 feet (60 cm) tall. It is native to the western United States and has a purple-blue flower color.

Polemonium pulcherrimum (skunkleaf polemonium) is native to the mountains of northwestern North America, growing as a 1-foot (30-cm) tall plant with blue flowers and a yellow center. Flower color also can be white. This species makes worthy rock garden or alpine plants.

Polemonium reptans (creeping polemonium) is the common wildflower native to woodlands in eastern North America. It grows to about 1 foot (30 cm) tall and can naturalize in the proper setting with adequate moisture and light shade. 'Blue Pearl' is available more than the species and has a clear, light blue flower color. 'Lambrook Mauve' is a selection with lavender-mauve flowers from East Lambrook Manor in Somerset, England.

Polemonium viscosum (synonym *P. confertum*) is another Rocky Mountain native suited to the rock garden. It produces blue, funnel-shaped flowers on plants usually less than 1 foot (30 cm) tall.

Polygala
Milkwort
POLYGALACEAE

Milkworts are not common garden plants in North America. Cultivated more frequently in European gardens, they are a diverse group of annual, herbaceous and woody perennials. The flowers are wonderfully complex and at first glance resemble pea flowers. They differ because both the petals and sepals of milkwort flowers are pigmented. The five sepals form the lateral "wings" of the flower, while the five petals form the lower "keel" that is fringed at the tip. Flower color can be blue, pink, lavender, yellow, or white. The flowers present an attractive and gay appearance while in spring or summer bloom. Milkworts are primarily used in the rock or alpine garden, but also can be grown in cool greenhouse conservatories. The taller forms are suited for mixed annual and perennial borders. Plants prefer full sun or partial shade and a fairly rich, organic soil that is well drained. Hardy and tender forms of milkwort are used in the landscape. The genus name means "much milk" and, like the common name, refers to the milky juice produced by the roots and the suggestion that animals that graze on it have enhanced milk production.

Propagation: Plants are multiplied by seed, division, or stem cuttings. Species are usually propagated by seeds, while cultivars are divided or multiplied by cuttings. The seeds of hardy species should be sown in the fall or given chilling stratification. Softwood stem cuttings can be taken in the summer.

Representative species and cultivars: *Polygala* species are found throughout the world and number more than 500. They can be found in temperate and subtropical areas. *Polygala calcarea* (chalk polygala) is the species most often cultivated for its blue flowers. It is a creeping, evergreen plant reaching only 2 inches (5 cm) tall with a spread up to 8 inches (20 cm). This western European native is half-hardy and perennial where the temperatures do not go below 0°F (−18°C). Flower color is a true blue with the keel petals fringed with white. The small flowers cover the entire plant when in bloom during late spring and early summer. Plants are used in the rock garden or in containers for the alpine garden. As the species name indicates, this plant prefers a more alkaline soil. 'Bulley's Form' is a more vigorous plant than the species and produces a deeper blue flower. 'Lillet' flowers over a longer period than the species.

Pontederia
Pickerel Weed
PONTEDERIACEAE

Pontederia species grow beside or in shallow water. They are not floating plants; rather they root into the constantly wet soil. Blue or white flowers are produced in upright spikes and can be effective all summer into the fall. Plants prefer full sun, but tolerate partial shade. They are usually easy to grow in ponds where they are submerged to about 1 foot (30 cm) and should be fertilized once a month to encourage continued flowering. Plants have the nice feature of spreading slowly and not outgrowing a container in a single season or taking over a small pond. The genus name commemorates the eighteenth-century botanist Giulio Pontedera.

Propagation: Plants are multiplied by seed or, more commonly, division of creeping rhizome.

Representative species and cultivars: All five species of *Pontederia* native to North and South America grow around or in freshwater marshes. *Pontederia cordata* (pickerel weed) is the only commonly cultivated species. Its leaves reach about 2 feet (60 cm) above the water's surface. Plants native to the species's northern range have a more heart-shaped leaf, while those in South America tend to have a more lance-shaped leaf. The upright spikes of flowers are usually blue, but a white form is also available commercially. Plants are winter hardy and do not need to be removed from the pond once established, except to divide overgrown plants.

Primula
Primrose
PRIMULACEAE

Primula is a large and varied genus that has been divided by horticulturists into as many as 25 sections. The hybrid primulas that contain individuals with blue flowers come from section *Primula* also known as *Vernales*.

One can only be envious of gardeners from climates that have suitable conditions for growing primroses. These early spring blooming perennials thrive where summers are cooler, like northern Europe, Great Britain, New Zealand, and the Pacific Northwest in North America. Elsewhere, hot and humid summers limit the usefulness of these plants, making them short-lived perennials or forcing their use as annuals. Primulas produce a rosette of leaves from which the flower spike emerges. Individual flowers are tubular or saucer-shaped with distinct petals fused at the base. Often, the inner part of the petal is a different color from the outer part of the petal, forming a colorful "eye."

Besides the species, *Primula* is separated into several garden groups based on flowering type. Auricula types are evergreen hybrids developed from *P. auricula* and *P. hirsuta* with large, colorful, saucer-shaped flowers. Candelabra types have flower spikes with groups of flowers tiered along tall stems; they tend to be planted where soil is moist, like around ponds or streams. Juliana types are semi-evergreen, with flowers in rounded clusters or umbels; *Primula juliae* is the dominant species in the background of these hybrids. Acaulis and Polyanthus types have large, rounded clusters of flower heads and up to 20 large, individual flowers. They are grown as seasonal pot plants. They are similar in appearance, but Acaulis types generally have only one flower per flower stem, while Polyanthus types have multiple flowers per stem.

In general, primroses require partially shaded conditions, and most species must have a moist, organic soil with moderate fertility. Some, however, need full sun and a moist, well-drained soil. They are prized by collectors for rock gardens and alpine houses. They also can be used in less formal gardens along the edge of a moist woodland, but for best effect, a large patch of primroses along a watercourse is a delightful site in spring. Other primroses are grown as seasonal pot plants. The genus name is Latin for "first," referring to the early flowering of some primroses.

Propagation: Plants are usually multiplied by seed, but also can be divided in spring. Some types propagate from root cuttings. Most perennial cultivars are propagated by division. Acaulis, Polyanthus, and some Auricula types are propagated by seed, which needs cool germinating conditions and light and can benefit from chilling stratification.

Representative species and cultivars: There are more than 400 species in this large genus. Most are native to Asia, but they also occur in most other temperate regions of the world. Often, primroses are found in moist, alpine areas. Much hybridization has taken place in this genus, and many fine primulas of horticultural origin are available. Blue is not a dominant color in the genus, but is available, especially in the hybrid primulas.

Primula denticulata (drumstick primrose) produces rounded flower heads on plants usually less than 2 feet (60 cm) tall. It is native to the Himalayan mountains and usually produces yellow flowers; however, selections have been made for red, purple, white, and blue flowers.

Primula obconica is a tender perennial form China. Flower stems rise from a rosette of foliage to nearly cover the plant. Selections have been bred for early season pot plant sales from greenhouse-grown plants. Flower color can be white, pink, red, blue, or pastel shades. Series include Cantata, Juno, and Libre. Libre has become increasingly popular with a full range of colors and because it is primin-free. Primin is an allergin found in this species that can cause a skin irritation.

Primula ×*polyantha* is the Polyanthus type of primrose familiar to most gardeners. It includes complex hybrids from crosses with *P. elatior, P. vulgaris, P. veris,* and *P. juliae.* "Polyanthus" is a general term given to plants of horticultural origin that have multiple flowers on a flowering stem, a characteristic that separates them from the similar Acaulis hybrids. This flower cluster trait probably originated from natural hybrids in England from *P. vernis* and *P. vulgaris* in the mid-1600s. Modern Polyanthus hybrids owe their range of colors, large flower size, and short flowering stems to the Munstead strain originated by Gertrude Jekyll and the Spetchley strain by Mrs. Berkeley in the late 1800s. Breeders in the United States improved upon these earlier hybrids with increased flower colors in the Barhaven strain by Florence Bellis in Oregon, and particularly, the Pacific strain by Frank Reinelt in California in the 1930s and 40s. The Barhaven strain contributed improved blue color to the Polyanthus hybrids. These hybrids grow to about 1 foot (30 cm) tall and produce large flowers in almost every color and often with colorful central eyes. They are used in the shady perennial garden or even as bedding plants where the climate is suitable. *Primula ×polyantha* is also a popular pot plant for spring holidays. Some individuals have the added advantage of being scented. These are often grown from seed and listed as series of mixed or single colors. Popular series that include blue-colored flowers are Crescendo, Monarch, Pacific Giant, Rainbow, and Rumba.

Primula vulgaris (synonym *P. acaulis*) is a European native and one parent of the Polyanthus type primroses. Hybrids of *P. vulgaris* are similar to *P. ×polyantha,* but usually have only one flower per flower stem and are known horticulturally as Acaulis type primroses. They have come to dominate the seasonal pot plant market for greenhouse production of primroses. This dominance is partly due to breeding

Primula ×polyantha

efforts that provide early, mid-season, and late-flowering times for better greenhouse control of production for retail sales. Some of the current Acaulis strains that have blue flowers include Bellissima, Crayon, Danova, Gemini, Pageant, and Quantum.

Pulmonaria
Lungwort
BORAGINACEAE

Lungworts have become very popular herbaceous perennials for the shade garden, and the number of cultivars available to gardeners has increased substantially. These have been selected mostly for their varied leaf shape and green and silver patterning. Clusters of tubular flowers top each flowering spike and are produced as the foliage emerges in the spring. Flower color can be white, red, pink, or blue. Flowers often open pink and change to blue as they mature. Lungworts require a shaded location and a moist, organic soil. They are well-suited for planting with other shade-loving perennials like *Hosta*. Plants also work well as ground covers under spring-flowering shrubs. The genus name and the common name allude to the old association this plant had as a remedy for diseases of the lungs during the Middle Ages when medicinal properties were ascribed to plants based on the Doctrine of Signatures. This doctrine professed that the Creator put a "signature" on plants, suggesting their proper use. The spotted pattern on the leaves of lungwort provided its association with the lungs.

Propagation: Plants are multiplied by seed, but cultivars are more commonly propagated by division after the plants have flowered. Tissue culture is another method of propagation.

Representative species and cultivars: *Pulmonaria* is a genus of about 14 species native to Europe and Asia. Several species make excellent garden plants. Because these species hybridize freely in the garden, some selections may be of unknown hybrid origin, which has led to some confusion as to the way cultivars are listed in catalogs.

Pulmonaria angustifolia (blue lungwort) is a good flowering ground cover. Plants grow around 1.5 feet (45 cm) tall, and their leaves are not spotted. Flower color can be variable from seed, but good blue cultivars have been selected. These include 'Azurea', a bright blue selection sometimes listed as *Pulmonaria angustifolia* var. *azurea,* and 'Blaues Meer', a German selection with dark blue flowers fading to pink. Pink selections are also available.

Pulmonaria longifolia (long-leaved lungwort) is a native of Europe growing to about 1 foot (30 cm) tall. It is noted for its foliage that is longer and narrower than the foliage of other *Pulmonaria* species. Its flowers are a lavender-blue, and cultivars are selected more for unique foliage patterns. 'Bertram Anderson' has narrow leaves spotted with silver and cobalt blue flowers.

Pulmonaria officinalis (Jerusalem sage) is the European species of lungwort described by the Doctrine of Signatures. It produces a pink flower that matures blue. 'Cambrige Blue' is a selected blue-flowering cultivar. 'Sissinghurst White' has a clear white flower, and 'White Wings' is also white blooming with larger, longer lasting flowers that are less prone to mildew.

Pulmonaria longifolia 'Bertram Anderson' (long-leaved lungwort)

Pulmonaria saccharata (Bethlehem sage) has become a very popular lung-wort, because of the number of excellent foliage types. Native to southern Europe, it grows 1.5 feet (45 cm) tall and is clump forming. Cultivars with pink or blue flowers are available. Blue cultivars include 'Devrooman Pride', with an almost completely silver leaf; 'Highdown', with large, variegated leaves and bright blue flowers; 'Janet Fisk', with highly variegated foliage and pinkish blue flowers; 'Mrs. Moon', a popular selection with large silvery spots over green leaves; 'Roy Davidson', with longer, narrower leaves with silvery spots and good blue flowers; and 'Smokey Blue', with pale blue flowers and spotted leaves.

Cultivars of garden origin that have blue flowers: 'Apple Frost', silver variegation over lime-green foliage; 'Benediction', silver variegation and dark blue flowers that bloom over an extended period; 'Blue Mist', pale blue flowers and variegated leaves; 'Excaliber', metallic, silver leaves with only an outer edge of green; 'Glacier', rounded leaves with silvery spots and pale blue flowers; 'Leopard', early blue flowers on dark green leaves streaked with silver; 'Little Star', a small plant with good variegation and cobalt blue flowers; 'Mawson's Blue' (often listed with *P. angustifolia* because the leaves are solid green), excellent blue flowers on tall-flowering stems; 'Merlin', a long-blooming plant with blue and pink flowers and with variegated leaves; 'Milky Way', leaves spotted with silvery white, red buds opening to deep blue flowers; 'Regal Ruffles', flowers with ruffled edges to the petals and silver spotted foliage; and 'Spilled Milk', early blooming with leaves generously splashed with silvery white spots.

Puschkinia
Striped Squill
LILIACEAE

Puschkinia species are small bulbous plants similar to *Scilla* species. They are less familiar to many gardeners, but can be used in the same way as *Chionodoxa* and *Scilla*. The flowers are nodding and bell-shaped with several per spike. Flower color is pale blue or white with darker blue stripes along the tepals. These plants may not be as showy as other spring-flowering bulbs, but they have subtle charm. They should be planted in groups for best effect either used in rock gardens or massed in a naturalized setting. They prefer full sun or partial shade in a well-drained garden soil. Bulbs should be planted in the fall at a depth of 4 inches (10 cm). The genus name commemorates Apollos Puschkin, an eighteenth-century Russian botanist.

Puschkinia scilloides (striped squill)

Propagation: Plants are multiplied by seed or, more commonly, from bulb offsets. They increase naturally in the garden by both methods.

Representative species and cultivars: *Puschkinia* is a small genus containing only two species native to the Caucasus, Turkey, Iran, and Asia. *Puschkinia scilloides* (striped squill) is the only species available to gardeners. Plants grow about 6 inches (15 cm) when in bloom. Flowers are white stars with dark blue stripes. *Puschkinia scilloides* var. *libanotica* (Lebanon squill) is a botanical variety native to the Middle East. It usually has white flowers with longer tepals.

Ramonda
GESNERIACEAE

Ramonda is a winter-hardy genus of herbaceous perennials from a mainly tropical family. They are small plants less than 6 inches (15 cm) tall that grow from a rosette of dark green leaves. The flowers appear in spring and resemble African violets (*Saintpaulia* spp.). Each stem bears one to three flowers. Flower color is lavender-blue, purple, pink, or white. Ramondas are popular as rock garden plants or in containers for alpine collections. Plants can be difficult to grow without the proper environment. They prefer light shade in a well-drained, moist, organic soil and thrive only where the summers are cool. Water should not be allowed to collect in the rosette of leaves where it could cause crown rot. The genus name commemorates the nineteenth-century French botanist Louis F. E. von Ramond.

Propagation: Plants are multiplied by seed, division of the crown, or leaf cuttings.

Representative species and cultivars: The three species of *Ramonda* are native to Europe. Unlike other members of this popular family, they survive winter temperatures to −20°F (−29°C). They do not tolerate wet soils in winter.

Ramonda myconi (synonym *R. pyrenaica*) is the most commonly cultivated *Ramonda* species. Native to the Pyrenees, it grows about 6 inches (15 cm tall) tall with lavender-blue flowers. The yellow, pointed anthers contrast with the petal color. A white form is also available. The dark green, evergreen leaves have deep veins, giving them a crinkled appearance.

Ramonda nathealiae is similar to *R. myconi*, but with lavender-blue flowers that have an orange center. It is native from central Europe into Greece.

Ramonda serbica is the smallest plant in this genus, only reaching 4 inches (10 cm) tall with small leaves. It produces lilac blue flowers with a yellow center and is native to central Europe.

Ramonda myconi

Rosmarinus
Rosemary
LAMIACEAE

Rosemaries are tender, upright or prostrate woody shrubs. The flowers are pink, lavender, or blue and have the two-lipped shape typical of the mint family; they are produced in the leaf axils and appear in spring and summer. Rosemary can be an effective ornamental, but the plants are also grown for the pleasant, aromatic fragrance of the foliage. In mild climates, rosemary is an evergreen shrub to 5 feet (1.5 m) tall. Otherwise, it is grown as a container plant or a temporary garden plant that must be overwintered in a sheltered location. It has become fashionable to grow rosemary in topiary shapes. It is the common culinary

Rosmarinus officinalis 'Benenden Blue'
(rosemary)

herb, so it appears in herb gardens. Plants require full sun and must have a well-drained soil. The genus name means "rose of the sea," referring to the plants' native habitat. One story suggests that the Virgin Mary placed her blue cloak over a white-flowering plant to impart its blue color.

Propagation: Plants can be raised from seed, but stem cuttings are the most common form of propagation.

Representative species and cultivars: The two species of *Rosmarinus* are native to the Mediterranean region. Only one of them is commonly cultivated. *Rosmarinus officinalis* (rosemary) is an evergreen shrub that can grow to 5 feet (1.5 m) tall. Native to the Mediterranean region, it is not winter hardy in northern gardens. The trailing, prostrate form is *R. officinalis* 'Prostratus' (synonyms *R. eriocalyx*, *R. lavandulaceus*) and it only grows to about 6 inches (15 cm) tall. Several cultivars have been selected for a deeper blue flower color. These include 'Arp', selected for its lemon-scented foliage; 'Benenden Blue' (synonym 'Collingwood Ingram'), with dark green, fragrant foliage and bright blue flowers; 'Blue Boy', a prostrate type with tiny leaves, but heavy flowering, good in containers or baskets; 'Golden Rain', leaves streaked with golden yellow; 'Logee's Blue', with bright blue flowers; 'Madeline Hill', more winter hardy than other selections; 'Sissinghurst Blue', an upright grower with twisted stems, pine-scented foliage, and light blue flowers with speckles on the petals; and 'Tuscan Blue', an upright grower with dark blue flowers.

Saintpaulia

African Violet

GESNERIACEAE

Saintpaulia species are among the best-flowering houseplants. They are tender, herbaceous perennials that form as rosettes of leaves around a central crown. Flowers are held above the foliage on branched stems. Each flower is five-petaled with the upper two petals often slightly smaller. The stamens are yellow and contrast with the petal color. Many horticultural selections of African violets are available in many colors and color combinations including blue. African violets are common houseplants and are collected by many gardeners. They prefer bright but indirect light and a well-drained potting mix. Plants respond to supplemental light and fertilization to produce flowers all year long. An excessively moist potting medium should be avoided to prevent crown rot, and cold water can damage leaves. Many growers prefer to subirrigate African violets to avoid damaging the foliage. The genus name commemorates Baron Walter van Saint Paul-Illaire of Germany, who discovered the plants, and his father of the same name.

Propagation: Plants are multiplied by seed or leaf cuttings. Variegated foliage types need to be divided or have the crown stem rooted as a cutting to maintain the variegated leaf pattern.

Representative species and cultivars: Approximately 20 species of *Saintpaulia* are native to Africa around Tanzania. Today, the species are seldom grown, but the cultivars have become very popular plants because they flower indoors. Of the thousands of cultivars, most are derived from *S. ionantha*. They can be separated into five groups based on plant diameter. Miniatures have a diameter of around 3 inches (8 cm), while plants in the largest group are more than 16 inches (40 cm) in diameter. The first selections of African violet were all blue or purple. Then in 1940, the popular blue cultivar 'Blue Boy' showed a pink-flowering mutation, which was named 'Pink Beauty' and was patented by Holton and Hunkel nursery in Wisconsin. The first white was patented as 'White Lady' in 1942 by Peter Ruggeri from his hybridizing program in California. Today, all colors except yellow are represented. Some flower variants have double flowers or pinwheel coloration; others are iridescent or have frilled edges to the petals. Cultivars also have been selected for foliage shape or variegation. Blue-flowering cultivars can be purple-blue through light blue. A few of the many selected cultivars with blue flowers include 'Carmen', 'Concord', 'Crater Lake', 'Delft', 'Fox Trot', 'Idaho', 'Mickey Mouse', 'Rebecca', and 'Vienna'.

Salpiglossis
Painted Tongue
SOLANACEAE

Painted tongues are herbaceous annuals in the nightshade family. Loose, upright plants are topped with clusters of petunia-like flowers in a bright array of colors including blue, red, purple, orange, and yellow. Some cultivars have light streaks along the petals and a darker center. Painted tongues have been used traditionally as a summer bedding plant, but they also do well in containers as patio plants or for adding winter color to a greenhouse display. Because of their loose, upright habit, they mix well with lower-growing bedding plants, but can look lost if grown alone. Plants prefer full sun, but do not do well in extreme heat. In southern gardens, these plants do better in light shade. Otherwise, they are easy to grow, needing only a moderately fertile, well-drained soil. These colorful plants deserve wider acceptance by home gardeners. The genus name is Greek for "a tube and a tongue" and refers to the way the style and stigma protrude from the center of the flower.

Propagation: Plants are multiplied by seed or cuttings. The most common form of propagation is by seed sown in late winter for bedding out the following spring.

Representative species and cultivars: *Salpiglossis* consists of 2 or 18 species depending on the reference. All species are from the lower Andes mountains in Chile, Peru, and Argentina. Only *S. sinuata* (painted tongue) and its cultivars are extensively cultivated as ornamentals. This species has been extensively bred and selected to give mixed hybrids in a rainbow of colors including blue. The series include Bolero mix, from an older selection and in a range of colors; Casino mix, the current standard that includes a full range of colors, with plants more compact than older selections, only

Salpiglossis sinuata Casino mix
(painted tongue)

reaching 15 inches (38 cm) tall, and more weather tolerant; and Royale mix, with a full range of colors and better basal branching. 'Kew Blue' has purple-blue flowers with prominent streaking in the petals.

Salvia
Sage
LAMIACEAE

The interest in new species of *Salvia* for the garden has exploded in the last decades of the twentieth century. These herbaceous annuals and perennials as well as woody perennials produce whorls of flowers along the terminal flower spike. Individual flowers are tubular and inserted into prominent sepals (calyx) that can sometimes contrast with the petals and be ornamental. The upper lip of the flowers is straight or hooded, and the lower is sometimes spoon-shaped. Flower color is white, red, pink, purple, or blue. Several species bloom all summer. Plants are useful in mixed annual or perennial beds. Many tender perennials are grown as garden annuals and as container plants. *Salvia officinalis* is the culinary sage found in herb gardens. Some species make good fresh and dried cut flowers. One reason salvias have become so popular is they are easy-to-grow plants that prefer full sun and warm, summer weather. The soil should be well-drained, but with adequate moisture. The genus name is an old Latin word for "save" and refers to the supposed medicinal properties of some species. The common name is from the old-time belief that the use of this plant prolonged a person's life.

Propagation: As one might imagine in such a large genus, plants are propagated by seed, division, and stem cuttings depending on the species.

Representative species and cultivars: This very large genus has more than 700 species. Many of the finest garden types have blue flowers, but equally fine types have other colors. I find that red-flowered sages combine well with blue-flowered forms to make good garden displays.

Salvia azurea (blue sage; synonym *S. angustifolia*) grows to 3 feet (1 m) tall with blue flowers. It is native to Mexico, but if protected can overwinter as a perennial. *Salvia azurea* subsp. *pitcheri* has dark blue flowers on shorter plants with hairy stems; it is not as winter hardy as the species. 'Nekan' is a selection with azure blue flowers and white-tipped petals.

Salvia cacaliifolia produces deep blue, slightly fuzzy flowers on 3-foot (1-m) tall plants. This native of Mexico is treated as a tender perennial.

Salvia chamaedryoides (germander sage) is a prostrate 1-foot (30-cm) tall plant native to Texas and Mexico. This tender perennial has deep blue flowers that appear in midsummer.

Salvia farinacea (mealy-cup sage) is a tender perennial grown by most gardeners as an annual from seed. It is an upright plant to 2 feet (60 cm) tall with slender flower spikes. This native of Texas and Mexico is commonly grown for its fresh or dried cut flowers. 'Blue Bedder' is a tall selection with large flower spikes of dark blue flowers; it is an excellent choice for cutting. 'Rhea' has dark blue flowers on compact, uniform plants. 'Strata' is a former All America Selections and European Fleuroselect award winner with blue petals and white sepals. 'Victoria' is a former Fleuroselect winner with large spikes of violet-blue flowers.

Salvia forskaohlei is native to eastern Europe. It produces a 2-foot (60-cm) tall plant with violet-blue flowers that are streaked with white. Plants do well in full sun in any well-drained soil and are winter hardy.

Salvia guaranitica is a tender perennial developing from tuberous roots. Native to South America, it can grow 3 feet (1 m) or more in height with long flowering stems that appear in midsummer. Newer selections have made this plant very popular. 'Argentina Skies' has a lighter, sky blue flower and is shorter growing than the species. 'Black and Blue' has purple-blue petals and dark sepals. 'Omaha' has purple-blue flowers emerging from almost black sepals.

Salvia farinacea (mealy-cup sage)

Salvia hians is native to India and the Himalayan mountains. It is treated as a tender perennial. Plants grow to 2 feet (60 cm) tall with purple-blue flowers and a white spot on the lower petals.

Salvia jurisicii produces bright violet-blue flowers on 1.5-foot (45-cm) tall plants. Foliage is gray green and attractive, and flowers appear in late spring. The species is native to central Europe.

Salvia patens (gentian sage) is a tuberous-rooted tender perennial from Mexico that produces electric blue flowers. It grows to about 2 feet (60 cm) tall and blooms over a long period in the summer. 'Cambridge Blue' has a neat pale blue flower.

Salvia ×*superba* 'Blue Queen' (hardy sage)

Salvia pratensis (meadow sage; synonyms *S. pratensis* var. *haematodes, S. haematodes*) is a European species growing to 3 feet (1 m) tall. It produces lavender-blue flowers and is winter hardy. 'Indigo' has blue flowers in midsummer.

Salvia ×*superba* (hardy sage) is a hybrid resulting from several crosses between *S. nemorosa* and *S. pratensis*. Nomenclature here can be confused with some sources listing these plants as *S. nemorosa* or as *S.* ×*sylvestris*. Hardy sage grows to 3 feet (1 m) tall and is winter hardy, but can be short lived. Most cultivars like 'Blue Queen' and 'May Night' have violet-blue flowers. 'Blue Hill' is said to have petals that are a truer blue. 'Lubeca', a dwarf selection growing only half the size of other selections, has the same violet-blue flowers.

Salvia uliginosa (bog sage) is a gangly species to 6 feet (2.8 m) tall. This tender perennial from South America may overwinter in mild years. As its common name suggests, this plant likes a soil that is moister than the soil preferred by other sages, but it tolerates most garden sites. The flower color is a clear azure blue that cheers up a mixed perennial bed or even the shrub border. Plants bloom throughout the summer until frost.

Salvia viridis (synonym *S. horminum*) is the interesting annual clary sage. The bracts, which may be white, pink, purple, or shades of blue, expand and become the showy part of the plant rather than the flower. (Technically, then, this sage is not a blue-flowering species!) Originally native to the Mediterranean region, but now seen almost exclusively as one of its cultivars, this species grows to about 1 foot (30 cm) tall. 'Oxford Blue' has violet-blue bracts.

Salvia uliginosa (bog sage)

Scabiosa
Pincushion Flower
DIPSACACEAE

Scabiosa species are herbaceous annual and perennial plants that produce a composite flower head on a single flowering stem similar to members of the sunflower family. The outer florets are more petaloid and the inner ones are reduced, suggesting the "pincushion" analogy. Flower color can be white, yellow, pink, purple, or blue. Plants are used in annual or perennial beds and grown for their long-lasting cut flowers. Pincushion flowers should be sited in full sun and are easily grown in most well-drained garden soils, but prefer a slightly alkaline soil. Faded flowers should be removed to prolong flowering of the plant, and plants should be divided every three to four years. The genus name is Latin for "scabies" and suggests the plants' use in controlling itching.

Propagation: Plants are multiplied by seed or division. Seed requires light and is the common propagation method for the hybrids. Perennial cultivars are propagated by division of the dormant crown.

Representative species and cultivars: *Scabiosa* is a genus of about 100 species native to Asia, Africa, and Europe. Blue flowers are found in two commonly available, hardy, perennial species and in one annual species grown for dried cut flowers.

Scabiosa caucasica grows to about 1.5 feet (45 cm) tall and is very floriferous. It produces lavender-blue flowers in midsummer and is native from the Caucasus into Turkey and Iran. 'Compliment' (synonym 'Kompliment') is a compact selection to 2 feet (60 cm) tall with large lavender-blue flowers. 'Fama' has large dark lavender-blue flowers. 'Isaac House' (synonym 'House Hybrids') is less than 2 feet (60 cm) tall with lavender-blue or white flowers.

Scabiosa columbaria is similar to *S. caucasica* with slightly smaller flowers. Native to Europe and Asia, it grows to 3 feet (1 m) tall and produces lavender flowers in the summer. 'Butterfly Blue' and 'Nana' are bluer than the species, more compact, growing only 1.5 feet (45 cm) tall, and blooming over a long period beginning in summer until frost. 'Pink Mist' is also a popular pink-flowering selection.

Scabiosa stellata is an annual species native to Europe. It is grown for the interesting, papery seed heads that are prized by the cut flower industry. Plants grow about 1.5 feet (45 cm) tall and produce pale blue flowers that lead to rounded heads of papery seeds. 'Paper Moon' has seed heads with a hint of blue, while 'Ping Pong' is consistently white.

Scaevola
Fan Flower
GOODENIACEAE

Scaevola, a recent newcomer and an example of the renewed interest in Australian plants for U.S. and European gardens, is a group of tender, herbaceous and woody perennials. Only *S. aemula* is commonly available, but other members of this genus are also being developed for the ornamentals market. These trailing plants can be used as bedding plants, but are most often seen in hanging baskets. The flowers are distinctly fan-shaped and are produced in good number throughout the summer. Flower color is violet-blue. Plants do well in full sun or light shade in a well-drained but moist medium. The genus name is Latin for "left-handed" and may refer to the shape of the flower.

Propagation: Plants can be multiplied by seed or, more commonly, stem cuttings. Some species are propagated by tissue culture.

Representative species and cultivars: The more than 100 species of *Scaevola* are mostly from Australia and the Pacific Islands. Only one species is commonly available, but I expect other species to emerge as important ornamentals. *Scaevola aemula* (fairy fan flower) is a tender perennial treated like an annual in temperate gardens. Native to southern Australia, it can reach 2 feet (60 cm) tall in the garden. It produces lilac blue flowers and has a trailing habit. Plants are commonly grown in hanging baskets or containers. 'Blue Wonder' is grown more often than the species.

Scilla
Squill
LILIACEAE

Scilla species are bulbous plants that produce bell-shaped or spreading flowers. Some are winter hardy, while others must be considered tender perennials. Flower color can be white, pink, purple, or blue. Hardy forms are small bulbs suitable for use in the rock garden or for naturalizing. Tender forms are used as landscape plants where winters are mild. In colder climates, they are used as seasonal bulbs for spring color or as greenhouse specimens. They do well in full sun to light shade in a well-drained soil. Spring-blooming hardy forms are best planted in large numbers and allowed to multiply. The genus name is the old Greek name for this group of plants.

Propagation: Commercial growers propagate plants from bulb offsets, but plants self-sow in the garden.

Representative species and cultivars: Gardeners may be surprised that nearly 100 species belong to the genus *Scilla*. These are native to Asia, Africa, and Europe. Only a few species are cultivated.

Scilla bifolia (twin leaf squill) is a hardy form that is lesser known in the United States but commonly planted in Europe. It is similar to Siberian squill in size, but the flowers are a softer lavender-blue color. *Scilla bifolia* var. *taurica* has a deeper blue flower color. A white-flowering form exists. This species is excellent for naturalizing and deserves more consideration by North American gardeners. It is native from central Europe into Turkey.

Scilla peruviana (Cuban lily) is a half-hardy perennial that produces a large plant to 1 foot (30 cm) tall. The numerous (about 40) star-shaped flowers are borne in a flower head that is flatter than that of other cultivated squills. This species can be grown outdoors in the southern United States or makes an excellent container plant. 'Alba',

Scilla peruviana (Cuban lily)

a white-flowering form, is also popular. Interestingly, this species is not from South America, as the scientific name suggests; instead, it is native to southern Europe and northern Africa.

Scilla pratensis (meadow squill; synonym *S. litardieri*) is a late-flowering, hardy species that blooms in early June. It grows to 10 inches (25 cm) tall and has violet-blue star-shaped flowers that are held in upright spikes. Meadow squill is native to central Europe.

Scilla siberica (Siberian squill) is the most commonly cultivated squill. It is a small bulbous plant to about 6 inches (15 cm) tall and produces

Scilla pratensis (meadow squill)

Scilla siberica (Siberian squill)

deep blue, nodding, bell-shaped flowers. It is easy to establish and can spread to form large patches of flowering plants for early spring. As the species name implies, this squill is native from western Russia into northern Iran.

Scilla tubergeniana is an early blooming squill that produces white flowers with a blue stripe on the petals. It is native to Iran. 'Zwanenburg' has larger flowers.

Senecio
Cineraria, Ragwort, Dusty Miller
ASTERACEAE

Senecio is a varied group of herbaceous annual and perennials, but also includes woody plants. Some are grown for their colorful flowers and others for their foliage. Flower heads are the typical daisylike composites of the family. As a generalization, most *Senecio* flowers are yellow. For this discussion, *S.* ×*hybridus* is the only member with blue flowers. It is grown mostly as a pot plant for seasonal display, especially on Mother's Day. It does best in full sun or partial shade in a well-drained medium. The genus name is from Latin for "old man" and probably alludes to the grayish parts of the flowers in some species.

Propagation: Plants are multiplied by seed, division, and stem cuttings. *Senecio* ×*hybrida* is propagated from seed that needs light and a warm germination medium.

Representative species and cultivars: The arrangement of species in *Senecio* has been confusing over the years. Conservative botanists lump all possible species under an umbrella genus, which leaves *Senecio* with more than 2000 species! Other botanists tend to split large genera into smaller groups, which means that over the years florist's cineraria has been listed as *Senecio cruentus*, *S.* ×*hybrida*, *Cineraria cruentus*, and currently *Pericallis* ×*hybrida*. This plant can be a difficult plant to find in a catalog, where it is often listed under *Cineraria*. It was once more fashionable than it is today, but it is still a fairly common seasonal pot plant. Plants are usually listed as either grandiflora types with large flowers or multiflora types with smaller but more abundant flowers. Flower colors include white, red, pink, rose, and blue. Some selections have bicolored florets producing an attractive central eye. Several series have blue selections: Cindy mix, a medium-sized multiflora type for larger containers (including 'Cindy Blue Shades'); Cupid mix, a multiflora type with early blooming flowers on small plants; Festival mix, a grandiflora type with both solid and eyed blooms; 'Grandiflora Nana', a deservedly popular, dwarf grandiflora type for smaller 6-inch (15 cm) pots (includes blue with eye, cornflower blue, and marine blue); 'Jester Blue' from the Jester series, with blue flowers and a white center on compact plants; Sonnet mix, an early flowering grandiflora type; and 'Venus', a uniform, small multiflora type with bright flower colors (includes blue bicolor and blue shades).

Senecio ×hybrida (florist's cineraria)

Sisyrinchium
Blue-eyed Grass
IRIDACEAE

Sisyrinchium species are herbaceous perennials with grasslike foliage. They produce numerous star-shaped or bell-shaped flowers, singly or in groups, above the foliage in summer. Flower color can be white, yellow, red, purple, or blue. These plants are used in the rock garden or in the front of the border. They require full sun and do well in almost any moist, well-drained garden soil. The genus name is an old Greek name applied to some species related to iris.

Propagation: Plants are multiplied by seed or division.

Representative species and cultivars: *Sisyrinchium* has approximately 90 species native to North and South America. Although the common name for this genus is blue-eyed grass, one of the best garden plants in this genus is the yellow-flowered S. *striatum,* and many blue-flowering types have a yellow eye. This genus is an example of American natives returning home after selection in Europe.

Sisyrinchium angustifolium (synonyms S. *graminoides,* S. *bermudianum*) has violet-blue flowers with a yellow center on 6-inch to 1-foot (15- to 30-

Sisyrinchium angustifolium

cm) tall plants. This Californian native blooms in summer. It is a hardy, yet short-lived perennial that spreads by seeding itself in the garden. It has a white form.

Sisyrinchium bellum (California blue-eyed grass; synonym S. *idahoense*) is native along the West Coast of North America. It is similar in size and flower color to S. *angustifolium,* but not as winter hardy. In an appropriate environment, it can naturalize. A white form is also available.

Sisyrinchium littorale has a wider leaf than the

other blue-eyed grasses and produces a violet-blue flower with an
orange center. It may be the most winter-hardy species in the genus.

Sisyrinchium 'Quaint and Queer' is a hybrid of unknown garden origin
that has alternating blue and pink-mauve flowers.

Solanum
Potato Vine, Nightshade
SOLANACEAE

Solanum is a diverse group of herbaceous annual and perennial plants
as well as woody vines and shrubs. They are grown for their flowers or
fruits and include important vegetables like potato and eggplant. Flowers usually have fused petals shaped like saucers or bells. The anthers
are often bright yellow and form a pointed cone in the center of the
flower. Ornamental species are tender perennials grown as annuals in
the garden bed or more frequently as container plants for the patio or
greenhouse conservatory. In mild, frost-free climates, they can be
grown as landscape plants. Plants are fairly easy to grow. They require
full sun and adequate fertility for continued bloom. The soil or potting medium should be well drained. In greenhouse culture, some relief
from hot, summer sun is best. The genus name is from the Latin for
"sleep" and refers to the narcotic properties of some species.

Propagation: Plants are multiplied by seed and stem cuttings that can
be taken any time of year.

Representative species and cultivars: This large genus contains more
than 1500 species distributed throughout the world. Most of the ornamental species are from Central and South America. As is true for
blue flowers in other genera of the Solanaceae, most of the blue flowers
in *Solanum* have a purple or violet hue.

Solanum crispum (Chilean potato tree) is an evergreen shrub growing
to 15 feet (4.5 m) tall. Native to Chile and Peru, it bears purple-blue
flowers in clusters. 'Glasnevin' has larger flowers.

Solanum crispum (Chilean potato tree)

Solanum jasminoides (potato vine) is native to Brazil and is an attractive vine. Flowers form in clusters and are bluish white.

Solanum rantonnetii (blue potato bush) has become a common feature in most greenhouse conservatories at large botanic gardens. It is from Argentina and can grow to 6 feet (1.8 m) tall. Flowers occur in terminal clusters and are purple-blue. 'Royal Robe' is most commonly grown and has larger flowers than the species.

Solanum wendlandii, another vining type, is similar to *S. jasminoides* but larger. It is a native of Costa Rica and produces violet-blue flowers.

Solanum rantonnetii 'Royal Robe' (blue potato bush), Meersburg, Germany

Sophora

Texas Mountain Laurel, Pagoda Tree, Kowhai

FABACEAE

Sophora species are mostly woody trees and shrubs. As members of the pea family, they have the typical flowers of the family: the flowers are modified so that the upper petals form the banner, the lower petals form the keel, and the two middle petals form the wings. Flower color can be white, yellow, or blue. These species are used as landscape trees and shrubs that are adaptable to most well-drained soil. Only a few species are winter hardy. The genus name is a derivation of an Arab word for "trees with pealike flowers."

Propagation: Plants are multiplied by seed, grafting, or stem cuttings. Like the seed of other members of this family, *Sophora* seed requires scarification to allow water uptake.

Sophora secundiflora
(Texas mountain laurel)

Representative species and cultivars: *Sophora* is a genus of approximately 80 species, most native to temperate and tropical regions of the world. Several species form spectacular flowering trees and one (*S. tetraptera*) is the national flower of New Zealand. Two cultivated species have bluish flowers.

Sophora davidii (synonym *S. viciifolia*) is a deciduous shrub native to China. It can be marginally winter hardy in sheltered areas in northern gardens. Plants grow to about 10 feet (3 m) tall. The flowers are a pale, bluish white.

Sophora secundiflora (Texas mountain laurel) is more commonly available than *S. davidii*. It is an evergreen shrub hardy only in mild climates. The flowers are clustered within the foliage and are a purple-blue and white. They have the fragrance of grapes. The species is native from Texas into Mexico and can reach more than 20 feet (6 m) tall.

Stokesia
Stokes' Aster
ASTERACEAE

Stokesia is a herbaceous perennial that constitutes its own genus. It is suitable as a bedding plant and cut flower and produces large flower heads on individual flower stems. The flowers are composed of larger petaloid florets on the outside of the flower head and smaller internal florets. Flower color is lavender-blue or white. Stokes' aster is easy to grow, requiring full sun and a well-drained soil. The genus is named for Jonathan Stokes, a nineteenth-century English physician.

Propagation: Plants are multiplied by seed and division of the dormant crown. Seed needs chilling stratification for best germination.

Representative species and cultivars: *Stokesia* consists of one species native to the southeastern United States. *Stokesia laevis* grows about 1.5 feet (45 cm) tall and is clump forming. It is long blooming, from midsummer into fall. Flower color is white, pink, or lavender-blue, but several selections have been made for truer blue color. 'Blue Danube' produces large, mid-blue flowers. 'Blue Star' has flower heads with pale blue outer florets and almost white inner florets. 'Klaus Jellito' has very large, pale blue flower heads. 'Omega Skyrocket' has a flower color similar to that of the species, but a giant habit to almost twice the size of the species.

Streptocarpus
Cape Primrose
GESNERIACEAE

Streptocarpus species are tender, herbaceous perennials that produce tubular flowers on single or branched flower stems. The five-petaled flowers are two-lipped with the upper lip made from a pair of petals that are smaller than the petals in the lower lip. Flower color can be white, yellow, red, pink, violet, and blue. Cape primroses are mostly grown as greenhouse specimens or as houseplants. They also can be grown outdoors as a container or bedding annual. Hybrid forms are grown as a seasonal pot plant. Plants require filtered sun in the greenhouse or partial shade outdoors. The soil or potting medium should be well-drained and kept on the drier side to prevent crown rot. The genus name is Greek for "twisted fruit."

Propagation: Hybrids are multiplied by seed that benefits from light and a warm germination medium. Cultivars are propagated by stem cuttings or leaf cuttings.

Representative species and cultivars: The more than 100 species of *Streptocarpus* are native, for the most part, to tropical Africa. The most commonly cultivated plants are selections of S. ×*hybridus*. Several species with blue or violet-blue flowers are commonly grown by collectors of species in the Gesneriaceae; these include S. *candidus*, S. *cynandrus*, S. *primulifolius*, and S. *wendlandii*.

Streptocarpus holstii (synonym *Streptocarpella holstii*) is native to East Africa. It is an upright plant to 1.5 feet (45 cm) tall with glossy green foliage and small, 1-inch (2.5-cm) long blue flowers with a white throat.

Streptocarpus ×*hybridus* is the result of crosses and backcrosses of S. *dunnii*, S. *parviflorus*, S. *rexii*, and S. *wendlandii* at the Royal Botanic Gardens, Kew, in England. Flower color can be white, pink, and shades of blue. Blue cultivars include 'Concord Blue', with mid-blue flowers;

Streptocarpus ×hybridus

Streptocarpus wendlandii

'Constant Nymph', a very popular plant with several purple-blue, dark-veined flowers per flowering stem; 'Constant Nymph Cobalt', a selection of 'Constant Nymph' with lighter blue flowers; and 'Heidi', with flowers similar to those of 'Constant Nymph'.

Streptocarpus saxorum (synonym *Streptocarpella saxorum*) is a trailing species producing many small, terminal violet-blue flowers. Native to Africa, it makes a vigorous plant well-suited for a hanging basket. 'Blue Angel' has lavender-blue flowers. 'Good Hope' has light green leaves and sky blue flowers. 'Sparkle' has white flowers.

Streptocarpus wendlandii is quite impressive when seen for the first time. It has large, basal leaves that can be more than 2 feet (60 cm) long and 1 foot (30 cm) wide. It is one of four blue-flowered species grown by collectors.

Symphytum
Comfrey
BORAGINACEAE

Symphytum is an interesting group of hardy, herbaceous perennials that includes the herb comfrey (*S. officinalis*). Flowers are produced in terminal, nodding clusters in spring and are tubular. Flower color is white, yellow, red, purple, or blue. These species are appreciated for perennial gardens more in Europe than in the United States. They thrive in sun or partial shade in a moist, well-drained soil. They can colonize an area quickly and need attention to stay in bounds. The genus name is Greek for "to grow together" and refers to the way the leaf attaches to the stem. Comfrey was ascribed medicinal properties by the Doctrine of Signatures and was used as a cure for broken bones.

Propagation: Plants are multiplied by seed, division, or root cuttings. Cultivars are propagated by root cuttings taken from dormant plants.

Representative species and cultivars: *Symphytum* is a genus of approximately 25 species native to Europe and Asia. They can make excellent ground covers for a shady or woodland garden and are very aggressive, usually spreading rapidly. Plants can become a nuisance and very difficult to eradicate because they regenerate from any root pieces left in the garden.

Symphytum caucasicum is the most commonly grown ornamental comfrey with blue flowers. It reaches 2 feet (60 cm) tall on spreading stems with terminal clusters of flowers that are reddish in bud, opening to blue. As the species name suggests, plants are native to the Caucasus. 'Eminence' is a blue selection.

Symphytum ibericum (synonym *S. grandiflorum*) is normally a yellow-flowering comfrey growing to about 2 feet (60 cm) tall. It is native from the Republic of Georgia into Turkey. Catalogs sometimes list

Symphytum ×*uplandicum* (Russian comfrey)

the yellow-flowering cultivars as *S. grandiflorum* and the blue-flowering cultivars as *S. ibericum,* although these may be hybrids of garden origin. 'Hidcote Blue' has neat white and blue flowers. 'Goldsmith' (synonyms 'Variegatum', 'Jubilee') has a light blue flower with yellow and green variegated foliage. It has the advantage of not being as vigorous as the all-green-leaved species, but the reverted stems that will quickly take over must be removed.

Symphytum ×*uplandicum* (Russian comfrey; synonym *S. peregrinum*) is a cross between *S. asperum* and *S. officinalis.* It is an aggressive plant to 3 feet (1 m) tall. Flower color varies from purple to blue. Russian comfrey is grown either as an ornamental or in the herb garden.

Tecophilaea
Chilean Blue Crocus
LILIACEAE

Tecophilaea species are small, perennial plants produced from an underground corm. In the spring, the bright blue flowers appear between grasslike foliage. The flowers have six tepals that are deep blue with a white inner edge toward the center of the flower. Plants are well-suited for rock gardens but do not tolerate frost and are only hardy where winter temperatures do not fall below 0°F (−18°C). Chilean blue crocus is a bright addition to cool greenhouse displays or used in containers for the alpine house. Each corm produces only one to two flowers. The plants should be grown in full sun in a light, well-drained soil or potting medium. Watering should be reduced as the foliage dies back and is allowed to go dormant. The genus name commemorates Tecophila Billiotti, a flower painter and daughter of a nineteenth-century Italian botanist.

Propagation: Plants are multiplied by seed or division of the corm. They spread naturally by producing corm offsets (cormels). Seed, which should be sown as soon as the fruits are mature, may require chilling stratification.

Representative species and cultivars: *Tecophilaea* is a small genus of two species, only one of which is cultivated. *Tecophilaea cyanocrocus* was introduced into cultivation in 1872, but it is not common and its corms can be expensive to purchase. It is native to the mountains of Chile, where it is now rare. The flowers are fragrant and gentian blue. *Tecophilaea cyanocrocus* var. *leichtlinii* produces a lighter blue flower with a more pronounced white center. *Tecophilaea cyanocrocus* var. *elegans* has narrower leaves and tepals.

Teucrium
Germander
LAMIACEAE

Teucrium is a group of herbaceous and woody perennials grown mostly for their attractive, aromatic foliage, but they also can be effective in flower. Plant size in this genus varies from small 8-inch (20-cm) tall plants used in rock gardens to large 3-foot (1-m) tall shrubs that can be pruned into a hedge where the climate is mild. Some species can be pruned into topiary shapes, and germander has been a favorite plant for herb gardeners to clip into knot gardens. Plants prefer full sun in a well-drained soil. They tend to be very drought tolerant. The genus was named after Teucer, the first king of Troy who supposedly used this herb medicinally.

Propagation: Plants are multiplied by seed or, more commonly, stem cuttings taken in summer.

Representative species and cultivars: The more than 100 species of *Teucrium* are mostly native to the Mediterranean region. The best-known species is *T. chamaedrys,* used by herb growers for formal knot gardens. It is not blue flowering, however. *Teucrium fruticans* is the only species commonly grown for its showy blue flowers. This tender, small shrub grows to 3 feet (1 m) tall and can be sheared into a hedge or allowed to grow in the mixed shrub border. In northern gardens, it is treated as an annual. Plants produce pale blue flowers in abundance above silvery, aromatic foliage. 'Azurea' has flowers that are darker blue than those of the species.

Thunbergia
Trumpet Flower, Black-eyed Susan
ACANTHACEAE

Thunbergia is a tropical group of annual and perennial plants. Unfortunately, most gardeners only know this species from the common yellow-flowering black-eyed Susan vine (*T. alata*). The genus contains some of the most spectacular flowering vines with flowers that are white, yellow, orange, red, or blue and shaped like saucers or trumpets. These species are used to cover outdoor supports or as specimens for greenhouse conservatories. Perennial types respond to short days for flowering that cheers up the winter greenhouse. Plants do not tolerate frost, so those grown outdoors must be overwintered in a sheltered location. They do well in full sun or partial shade in a moist, well-drained medium. The genus name commemorates Carl Thunberg, an eighteenth-century Swedish botanist and plant collector in Africa and Japan.

Propagation: Plants are multiplied by seed or stem cuttings that root easily.

Thunbergia grandiflora
(blue trumpet vine)

Representative species and cultivars: The approximately 100 species of *Thunbergia* are native to tropical regions and are among the showiest of tropical vines. They are pluralistic in their choice of favorite colors. Several spectacular species have red, orange, yellow, and blue flowers. The long, hanging raceme of the yellow-flowered *T. mysorensis* is a show stopper in any spring greenhouse display.

Thunbergia battiscombei, a vigorous vine native to India, produces a more tubular flower than that of *T. grandiflora*. Flower color is blue-violet with a yellow throat.

Thunbergia grandiflora (blue trumpet vine) is the most common blue-flowering representative of this genus in cultivation. This vigorous woody vine is native to India and produces large pale blue flowers with a yellow throat. It brightens the winter scene in many large greenhouse conservatories. A white form is available.

Tillandsia
Air Plant
BROMELIACEAE

Tillandsia is the largest genus in the bromeliad family and occurs in warm temperate and tropical areas of North, Central, and South America. It represents the largest group of bromeliads in North America. Plants range in height from 1 inch to more than 14 feet (2.5 cm to 4.3 m) tall and consist of herbaceous perennials, most of which are epiphytic. Those species with showy flowers have a cylindrical or flat, compressed flower stalk consisting of alternating stiff bracts. The bracts are very showy and can be pigmented green, pink, or purple. Individual flowers begin to open at the bottom of the flower stalk and continue up to the tip. Only one or two of the twenty or more flowers are open at any time. Flowers have three petals and can be violet, blue, or yellow. Cultivated air plants are grown for their novel growth habit, interesting foliage, and colorful flowers. The common name, air plant, refers to the reduced or minimal root systems on these plants. In fact, the root system's main function is to hold the plant in place and is not critical for water absorption. Plants do not tolerate frost and are used in greenhouse displays, indoor dish gardens, and terrariums. Epiphytic types can be grown outdoors in the dappled shade of trees, but must not be exposed to frost. Terrestrial types are grown in containers with a well-drained medium similar to an orchid mix. They prefer light shade, high humidity, and minimal fertilization. Air plants make good companions to epiphytic orchids, *Aechmea* species, and other bromeliads. The Latin name commemorates Elias Tillands, a seventeenth-century physician and botanist.

Propagation: Plants are multiplied by seed or offshoots. The easiest method of propagation is to remove one of the offshoots. Seed can be sown on the surface of sphagnum moss as soon as the fruits are mature.

Representative species and cultivars: *Tillandsia* is a relatively large and diverse genus of approximately 400 species. All are of New World origin. Several epiphytic species are grown exclusively for their silver-green or brightly colored foliage. Like the flower clusters of other bromeliads, the flower clusters of *Tillandsia* have both showy bracts and in some cases showy flowers. Some of the more common species with blue flowers are listed here.

Tillandsia aeranthos, a native of Brazil, Paraguay, and Argentina, is an epiphytic species. It forms a dense cushion about 1 foot (30 cm) tall with scaly, silver-green leaves. The flowers are dark blue and emerge from rosy pink bracts.

Tillandsia cyanea is among the most commonly grown air plants. It is an epiphytic species native to Ecuador and can be grown attached to a wood or lava rock support. It also performs well when grown as a container plant in a light orchid mix. Plants reach about 1 foot (30 cm) tall and consist of a stemless rosette of narrow, pointed leaves. The flower spike is a flat, hand-shaped structure composed of attractive pink bracts from which the violet-blue flowers emerge.

Tillandsia lindenii (blue-flowered torch) is very similar in appearance and cultural requirements to *T. cyanea*. At one time both were considered a single species. Blue-flowered torch is native to Peru. The bract color is purple-pink and the flower color is bluer than that of *T. cyanea* with each petal having a white center.

Tillandsia multicaulis is an elegant bromeliad with rosettes of light green foliage. Plants reach 1.5 feet (40 cm) tall and produce numerous paddlelike flower stalks. The floral bracts are bright red, and the small tubular flowers are dark blackish blue.

Tillandsia usneoides (Spanish moss) is a familiar plant in southeastern U.S. gardens. It is a novel epiphyte that hangs from trees and does not produce roots. It also can be useful in greenhouse displays because of the gray green foliage. Individual plants are small but hang in clusters that can reach many feet long. Small 0.5-inch (1.3-cm) fragrant flowers are produced in either late spring or autumn and can be yellow or pale blue.

Torenia
Wishbone Flower
SCROPHULARIACEAE

Torenia species are herbaceous annual and perennial plants. The flowers are two-lipped, with the upper lip having two lobes and the lower lip having three lobes. Each lip can have a different color or the lower lip can be bicolored. Flower color is white, pink, purple, or blue. These species are used as annual bedding plants or grown in containers. They do well in partial shade in a moist, well-drained soil, and they respond to good fertilization. The genus name commemorates Olaf Toren, an eighteenth-century Swedish clergyman.

Propagation: Plants are multiplied most commonly from seed, but stem cuttings root easily. Seed needs a warm medium and light for best germination.

Representative species and cultivars: Of the approximately 50 species of *Torenia* native to Africa and Asia, only *T. fournieri* and *T. baillonii* are cultivated to any extent. *Torenia baillonii* (sometimes mislabeled as *T. flava*) is an interesting wishbone species, but has yellow flowers. *Torenia fournieri* is a useful bedding plant that can be relied upon to provide flowering in the shady part of the annual bed. It grows approximately 1 foot (30 cm) tall and produces lilac blue flowers. It is usually represented by 'Compacta', a selection that only grows to 8 inches (20 cm)

Torenia fournieri

tall. Breeding has resulted in compact, horticultural selections that have flowers in combinations of white, pink, violet, and blue. The Clown mix is a multicolored F_1 hybrid on compact well-branched plants that grow to 10 inches (25 cm) tall. Duchess series is available in light blue, blue and white, and deep blue colors. 'Panda Blue' is a selection from the Panda series with a light blue upper lip and dark purple-blue lower lips.

Trachelium
Throatwort
CAMPANULACEAE

Trachelium species are tender, herbaceous perennials often treated as annuals in gardens of the northern United States. Throatworts can be used in the rock garden, and the taller species are effective in the back of the border. They make long-lasting cut flowers. Plants should be grown in full sun in a well-drained, slightly alkaline soil. The genus name is Greek for "neck" and, like the common name, alludes to a former use of these plants in treating throat ailments.

Propagation: Multiplication is most common from seed, but plants can be rooted from stem cuttings.

Representative species and cultivars: *Trachelium* is a group of seven species native to the Mediterranean region. Flower color can be white, blue, or violet-blue. The only species commonly available is *T. caeruleum* (blue throatwort). It is a tall plant that can reach more than 3 feet (1 m) tall, but is usually represented by cultivars that grow between 2 and 2.5 feet (60 and 75 cm) tall. It can be grown as a pot plant, in the mixed border, or as a cut flower. Flower color in the species is violet-blue. Most plants seen in gardens are from the Umbrella series, which has white or purple flowers, or a mixture thereof.

Trachymene
Blue Lace Flower
APIACEAE

Trachymene species are herbaceous annual and perennial plants with flowers resembling Queen Anne's lace on wiry stems. Flower color in cultivated types is blue or lavender-blue. These plants can be grown in the annual bed, but are most often cultivated for the long-lasting cut flowers. Plants require full sun and a well-drained soil. The genus name is Greek for "rough membrane" and refers to the fruits.

Propagation: Plants are multiplied most commonly by seed, but they can be rooted from stem cuttings.

Representative species and cultivars: The approximately 10 species of *Trachymene* are native to Australia and the Pacific Islands. Only *T. coerulea* (synonym *Didiscus coeruleus*) is commonly available. Native to Australia, it grows about 2 feet (60 cm) tall. It blooms over a long period in the summer.

Tradescantia

Spiderwort, Wandering Jew

COMMELINACEAE

Tradescantia species are a group of hardy and tender, herbaceous perennials. They produce a characteristic three-petaled flower with conspicuous stamens in the center. Flower color can be white, pink, reddish purple, or blue. Plant habit can be upright or trailing. Spiderworts are used as long-flowering plants in the perennial bed. Tender types can be grown as annual ground covers or used as houseplants. Plants prefer light shade, but hybrids should be grown in full sun. The species can be native to moist areas, but hybrids do well in a well-drained soil. The common name, spiderwort, comes from the weblike threads that appear when the stem is broken and pulled apart gently. The genus name commemorates John Tradescant, gardener to the king of England in the seventeenth century.

Propagation: Plants are multiplied by seed, division, or stem cuttings. Most perennial cultivars are propagated by division of the dormant crown.

Representative species and cultivars: The approximately 60 species of *Tradescantia* are native to North and South America. *Tradescantia virginiana* and its hybrids can have blue flowers.

Tradescantia ×*andersoniana* is a group of hybrids derived from crosses between *T. virginiana* with *T. ohiensis* and *T. subaspera,* although some catalogs simply list them all as *T. virginiana.* Plants grow to 2 feet (60 cm) tall and can spread to form large patches. They bloom in late spring to midsummer. Flower color in the hybrids can be white, pink, purple, or blue. Blue selections include 'Barbel', an introduction from Germany with large blue flowers; 'Bluestone', with clear, lavender-blue flowers; 'Concord Grape', with purple-blue flowers over a long season; 'Isis', with dark blue flowers and extended blooming time; 'J. C. Weguelin', an excellent spiderwort with pale blue flowers; 'Osprey', a white-flowering selection with a center that appears blue because of the pigmentation of the anther filaments; 'Strausberg Blue', with deep blue flowers; and 'Zwanenburg Blue', with dark purple-blue flowers.

Tradescantia virginiana (common spiderwort) is native to moist wooded areas in North America. It produces a small blue or purple-blue flower. The species is useful for natural, woodland gardens, but its hybrids are superior hardy perennials.

Tradescantia ×*andersoniana*

Tricyrtis
Toad Lily
LILIACEAE

Tricyrtis species are fall-blooming herbaceous perennials that have become popular to gardeners in the twentieth century. The flowers are not showy from a distance, but are intriguing on close inspection. The six tepals are often heavily spotted. The three-branched styles are prominent in the center of the flower and compete for attention with the tepals. Flowers are produced in terminal clusters or all along the stem in the axils of the leaves. Flower color can be yellow, white, or lilac, and some flowers have spots of a separate color on the tepals. Plants are grown in the perennial bed to provide late fall interest. They prefer a shaded location with a moist, organic soil. Some species are so late blooming that they are best located in a sheltered site to avoid early fall frosts. The genus name is Greek for "three" and "convex" and refers to the nectar sacs on the tepals.

Propagation: Plants are multiplied by seed or division.

Representative species and cultivars: *Tricyrtis* is native from Asia (especially Japan) to the Himalayan mountains and has approximately 15

Tricyrtis formosana 'Amethystina'

species. Several species have found their way into cultivation. None of them produce a truly blue flower, but toad lilies are such wonderful garden plants that I was glad to find one with bluish flowers. *Tricyrtis formosana* (synonym *T. stolonifera*) is a wonderful creeping species from Japan. It grows to 2 feet (60 cm) tall and is topped with numerous late-blooming purple and white flowers. 'Amethystina' has star-shaped flowers that are light blue with dark reddish spots.

Triteleia
California Hyacinth
LILIACEAE

Triteleia (synonym *Brodiaea*) is a group of small flowering plants that develop from corms. These tender or marginally hardy perennials bloom in the spring above straplike leaves. The brightly colored flowers can make an interesting addition to the bulb or perennial bed. They are also grown as cut flowers and are small enough to complement rock garden plantings. In bloom, plants are between 1 and 2 feet (30 and 60 cm) tall. The tubular flowers are pink, purple, or blue in color. Plants grow well in full sun or partial shade. Corms need to be planted in the fall. The genus name is from the Greek words for "three" and "perfect" and refers to the number of floral parts.

Propagation: Plants are multiplied by seed, corm offsets (cormels), or tissue culture. Seed benefits from chilling stratification, but seed-grown plants require 3 or more years to reach flowering size. The most common form of propagation is to remove offsets from the corms.

Representative species and cultivars: Botanists have separated *Triteleia* from other similar species of the lily family to identify 15 distinct species native to coastal western North America. *Brodiaea* is the older and better-recognized name for this genus. One species is commonly cultivated for its bright blue flower color. *Triteleia laxa* (synonym *Brodiaea laxa*) is native to the Pacific coast of North America and grows to 18 inches (46 cm) tall in bloom. Upright, pale blue, tubular flowers appear in late spring in loose clusters. Plants are marginally hardy in northern gardens, surviving only to −10°F (−23°C) in winter. 'Königin Fabiola' (synonym 'Queen Fabiola') produces pale lavender-blue flowers.

Triteleia laxa

Verbena
Vervain
VERBENACEAE

Verbena is represented by herbaceous annuals and perennials, and some shrubs. Saucer-shaped flowers are produced in flat-topped clusters on thin upright spikes and are closely attached to the flower stalk. Flower color can be shades of white, pink, red, yellow, purple, and blue. Vervains are useful as bedding plants, for containers, or in hanging baskets. Hardy types can be used in the perennial bed. Some species freely self-sow in the garden and can become a nuisance. Plants need full sun and a moist, well-drained soil with moderate fertility. *Verbena* is the old Latin name for these plants. The common name, vervain, is a derivation of an old Celtic word for "to remove stones" and alludes to a former use of *Verbena* for treating bladder stones.

Verbena hastata (blue vervain)

Propagation: Plants are grown most often from seed, but stem cuttings can be rooted.

Representative species and cultivars: The approximately 250 species of *Verbena* are native to North and South America, with a few species found in Europe. They are most often represented by hybrids grown as annuals, but some perennial species can be found.

Verbena hastata (blue vervain) is a hardy perennial reaching to 5 feet (1.5 m) tall. It produces flowers in tight, upright spikes that can be shades of purple through violet-blue in midsummer. The species is native to eastern North America.

Verbena ×*hybrida* (synonym *V.* ×*hortensis*) is the common annual verbena grown as a bedding plant or found in hanging baskets. It is probably a cross between *V. peruviana* and *V. platensis.* These trailing plants grow less than 1.5 feet (45 cm) tall. Flower color can be white, pink, red, yellow, and shades of purple through blue. 'Amethyst' has blue flowers with a white eye and 'Blue Lagoon' has a light blue flower with a white eye. Available series containing blue selections include Novalis, with good tolerance to summer heat in compact plant, and Romance, a group of low-growing plants to only 6 inches (15 cm) in a full range of colors. 'Novalis Blue with Eye' in the Novalis series was a former All America Selections winner.

Verbena rigida (synonym *V. venosa*) is a tender perennial usually grown as an annual. Native to Brazil and Argentina, it reaches 2 feet (60 cm) tall and usually produces purple flower spikes. 'Polaris' is a compact plant with silvery blue flowers that are showy for most of the summer.

Verbena tenuisecta (moss vervain) is also a tender perennial from South

America grown in northern gardens as an annual. It is a mat-forming plant reaching about 1.5 feet (45 cm) tall. Flower color can be variable in either white or shades of blue. 'Imagination', an All America Selections and European Fleuroselect winner, produces heat-tolerant, violet-blue flowers and is a popular plant for a hanging basket. 'Sterling Star' is similar in plant stature, but produces a lighter lavender-blue flower.

Veronica
Speedwell
SCROPHULARIACEAE

The many fine blue-flowering species in *Veronica* are herbaceous annual and perennial plants, along with some deciduous shrubs. The evergreen shrubs previously listed in *Veronica* are now treated in *Hebe*. Flowers are typically produced in tight, upright spikes, but also may be produced in the leaf axils. Individual flowers are tubular with four or five spreading petals. Stamens are often longer than the petals. Flower color can be white, pink, purple, or blue. The flowers occur in spring and summer. Speedwells are commonly used as hardy perennials ranging in height from prostrate plants to large 4-foot (1.2-m) plants. Small plants are mainstays of rock gardens, while other *Veronica* species are used as ground covers for the front of borders or mixed with taller perennials. Compact selections also can be grown as container plants, and taller species are used as cut flowers. Plants prefer full sun and a well-drained soil. They may need division every 3 to 4 years, and taller species may need staking. The genus is named after St. Veronica, the woman who according to Roman Catholic tradition used her veil to wipe Christ's face as he walked to Calvary.

Propagation: Plants are multiplied by seed, division, and stem cuttings. Seed benefits from light for germination. Division of dormant crowns is a common method of propagating cultivars. Stem cuttings are taken before plants begin to flower.

Representative species and cultivars: If you are serious about blue flower color in your garden, *Veronica* is a good place to start. The more than 300 species are native to most temperate regions and include some excellent garden perennials in which blue is a dominant flower color. As might be expected with such a large genus, nomenclature can be confusing.

Veronica armena forms dense mats of foliage on creeping stems growing about 4 inches (10 cm) tall. Blue flowers are borne in short spikes in early summer. The species is native to dry sites in Asia Minor.

Veronica australis subsp. *teucrium* (Hungarian speedwell; synonyms *V. latifolia, V. teucrium*) has one of the deepest blue flowers in the genus. The plant is between 1 and 2 feet (30 and 60 cm) tall with spikes of dark blue open flowers. Exceptional cultivars include 'Crater Lake Blue', with gentian blue flowers on 1-foot (30-cm) tall plants; 'Kapi-

Veronica australis subsp. *teucrium* 'Kapitan' (Hungarian speedwell)

tan', with deep gentian blue flowers; 'Royal Blue', with dark blue flowers on 1.5-foot (45-cm) tall plants; and 'Shirley Blue', a compact form to only 8 inches (20 cm) tall with the same dark blue flowers as 'Royal Blue'.

Veronica beccabunga is an interesting speedwell growing in wet sites in central Europe and Asia. This creeping plant reaches 4 inches (10 cm) tall and has saucer-shaped flowers. 'Blue Spires' is a bluer selection.

Veronica chamaedrys (germander speedwell, baby blue eyes) is a low-growing plant to 6 inches (15 cm) tall with bright blue flowers. It is excellent for the rock garden. 'Miffy Brute' has the same blue flowers, but the leaf margin is white.

Veronica cinerea is a silver-leaved mat-forming plant that is ideal for rock gardens. Native to Turkey, it grows 6 inches (15 cm) tall. Flowers are deep blue on a short spike.

Veronica gentianoides is another low-growing speedwell that makes a spreading mat of 6-inch (15-cm) tall plants. Flowers are cup-shaped and pale blue. 'Variegata' has a white-edged leaf, and 'Alba' is a white-flowering form.

Veronica longiflora is a large speedwell that can become more than 3 feet (1 m) tall. It has large spikes of blue flowers and is native from northern Europe into Siberia. 'Foerster's Blue' (synonym 'Blauriesen') has dark blue flowers. *Veronica longiflora* var. *subsessilis* (synonym *V. subsessilis*) is a compact form with large blue flower spikes and leathery, glossy green leaves. Several selections of this variety are grown from seed for container or cut flower use: 'Blue Bouquet', with lavender-blue flowers; and 'Blue Pyramid', with bright blue flower spikes. 'Sunny Border Blue' is an exceptional speedwell for flower color, foliage characteristics, and length of bloom; it is often listed as a cultivar of *V. longiflora*, but is probably a hybrid of garden origin.

Veronica pectinata (comb speedwell) is a mat-forming plant suited for the rock garden. Native to the region surrounding Turkey, the species has dark blue flowers. The narrow foliage with a pointed tip leads to the common name.

Veronica peduncularis is another prostrate, mat-forming plant under 6 inches (15 cm) tall. It has saucer-shaped flowers and is native to the Caucasus and Turkey. 'Georgia Blue' is a newer, blue-flowering selection that currently represents this species in gardens.

Veronica prostrata (prostrate speedwell; synonym *V. rupestris*) is the most commonly available mat-forming speedwell. This European native forms 6-inch (15-cm) tall plants that creep slowly and make good rock garden specimens. Cultivars with blue flowers include 'Heavenly Blue' and 'Loddon Blue'. 'Trehane' has flowers similar to those of the species, but the foliage is yellow.

Veronica spicata (spiked speedwell) is an upright-growing plant similar to *V. longiflora* but reaching only to 1 or 2 feet (30 or 60 cm) tall. This variable species is native from central Europe into Asia with many cultivars that can display red, pink, white, or blue flowers. It is prob-

Veronica spicata subsp. *incana* (spiked speedwell)

ably best separated into the parent species (*V. spicata*) and two sub-species: *V. spicata* subsp. *nana* with smaller plants around 1 foot (30 cm) tall, and *V. spicata* subsp. *incana* with silver leaves, low-growing plants to 1 foot (30 cm) tall, and flowers in spikes. Garden catalogs and references may organize spiked speedwells this way. Blue selections of the species proper include 'Blue Charm', a large plant with lavender-blue flowers; and 'Blue Peter', a midsized plant with dark blue flowers. 'Goodness Grows', a very long blooming speedwell often listed under *V. spicata,* is probably a hybrid between *V. spicata* and *V. alpina.* Blue selections of *V. spicata* subsp. *nana* include 'Blau-teppich', with bright blue flowers, and a very small habit to only 6 inches (15 cm) tall; and 'Blue Fox', a compact plant to about 1 foot (30 cm) tall. *Veronica spicata* subsp. *incana* 'Saraband' and 'Silbersee' have bluer flowers.

Vinca
Periwinkle
APOCYNACEAE

Vinca species are herbaceous or woody perennials growing as trailing stems. The flowers are *Phlox*-like with five petals fused at the base. Flower color is white, purple, or blue. Flowers occur in abundance in the spring and then sporadically through the summer. These species are used as ground covers or in containers. They do well in full sun or partial shade in almost any well-drained garden soil. They can be very vigorous and spread quickly over a large area. The genus name is a form of the Latin word for "to wind around" and refers to a use of these plants at one time in making wreaths.

Propagation: Plants are multiplied by division or stem cuttings. Commercial growers use stem cuttings taken in early summer.

Representative species and cultivars: The seven species of *Vinca* are native to Africa, Asia, and Europe. Only the two vining species are usually grown in gardens.

Vinca major (large periwinkle) is an evergreen, trailing vine native to the Mediterranean region. It is not winter hardy in northern gardens. Where it is hardy, it is an aggressive ground cover. It is also used as a trailing element in mixed container plantings. Flower color is a violet-blue, and the flowers are larger than those of *V. minor*.

Vinca minor (common periwinkle, trailing myrtle) is also a trailing vine used as a ground cover. It has a smaller leaf than *V. major* and is winter hardy, being native to northern Europe and Russia. Its flower color is also a violet-blue, but cultivars have bluer flowers. 'Azurea Flore Pleno' (synonym 'Multiplex') is a blue double-flowering form. 'Bowles Variety' (synonym 'La Grave') is among the more popular forms and has a lavender-blue flower. 'Ralph Shugert' and 'Sterling Silver' have bright blue flowers and a variegated white margin on the leaf. 'Blue and Gold', 'Golden,' and 'Golden Heart' have green and yellow leaf variegation.

Vinca major (large periwinkle)

Viola

Violet, Heart's Ease
VIOLACEAE

Viola species are herbaceous annual, biennial, and perennial plants. They are garden favorites for their colorful flowers and the fragrance of some species. Interestingly, many species of *Viola* produce two types of flowers: a typical showy, violet flower with five petals of which the lower one is often larger and spurred, and a petal-less flower in summer. These flowers remain closed and are produced at or below the ground. They are self-fertile and produce an abundance of seeds. The technical term for this type of behavior is cleistogamous flowers. These species can become weedy, because of the volume of seeds. Violets are used in annual beds, as ground covers in naturalized areas, and in the front of perennial borders. Plants grow in full sun, but some prefer light shade. Many do well in typical garden soils, but some require a moister environment. Some types suffer in hot, summer heat. *Viola* is the old Latin name for "violet." The common name, heart's ease, comes from the use of violets in love potions. In fact, the name pansy is derived from the old French name for violet (*pensee*) which means "thought"; it refers to turning the thoughts of a perspective lover towards the bearer of the plant.

Propagation: Plants are multiplied by seed or division.

Representative species and cultivars: *Viola* is a large genus of possibly 500 species native throughout temperate regions worldwide. As might be expected with such a large genus and with species that so readily interbreed, nomenclature can be confusing. It is convenient to separate violets into two groups: the smaller-flowered perennials and the larger-flowered, short-lived, hybrid pansies.

Viola cornuta (horned violet, tufted violet) produces 1-inch (2.5-cm) flowers on "tufted" spreading plants that reach about 6 inches (15 cm) tall. The species is native to Spain. Flower color is violet, but some cultivars are blue, such as 'Azurella', 'Barford Blue', and 'Blue Perfection'. New hybrids are now being offered for fall and early spring flowering in a range of colors from white and yellow to purple and blue. Flowers usually have characteristic veins or streaks on the lower three petals. These hybrids are very floriferous, show uniform growth for bedding out, and are often more long-lived than standard pansies. The series with their representative blue selections include the Jewel series, with 'Jewel Blue'; the Penny series with 'Penny Azure Wing' and 'Penny Blue'; the Princess series with 'Blue Princess' and 'Lavender and Yellow Princess'; and the Sorbet series with 'Blueberry Cream'.

Viola cucullata (marsh blue violet; synonym *V. obliqua*) is native to North America and, as the common name suggests, prefers a moist, well-drained soil. This small violet is good for naturalizing. Two cultivars are often listed under this species. 'Freckles', more properly listed as *V. sororia,* has a white or light blue flower and dark spots on the petals. 'Royal Robe', more properly listed as *V. odorata,* has deep lavender-blue flowers on tightly bunched 6-inch (15-cm) tall plants.

Viola labradorica (Labrador violet) is a small plant suited for the rock garden. As the scientific and common names suggest, this violet is native to Canada. Plants spread quickly in a shaded, moist area. The flower color is violet-blue.

Viola sororia 'Freckles'

Viola odorata (sweet violet, English violet) produces fragrant, violet-blue or white flowers. It has been cultivated in Europe for centuries and was once part of a thriving perfume industry. Plants spread by rhizomes and bloom in late winter and early spring. 'Blue Remington' and 'Queen Charlotte' are fragrant, deep blue-flowering cultivars.

Viola pedata (bird's foot violet) is native to eastern North America. The common name does a good job of describing the shape of the leaves. The flowers appear in late spring and are lavender-blue. Plants are used in naturalized areas or in rock gardens.

Viola ×*wittrockiana* (pansy) has become one of the most popular seasonal flowering bedding plants. It is planted in the fall to provide color in fall, winter, and spring before being replaced by summer annuals. This complex hybrid between several *Viola* species including *V. cornuta, V. lutea,* and *V. tricolor* has large flowers and good garden performance. Colors range from solids and bicolors in white, yellow, red, purple, orange, and blue. Because so many pansy selections are available and these change quickly, it seems advisable simply to list the series (separate colors available) or mixes currently available from major seed producers. They are grouped here by flower size.

> **Large-flowering pansies** have flowers that are greater than 3 inches (7.5 cm) in diameter and can be solid colors or include a dark blotch on the "face" of the pansy. These include the following series: Atlas, Bingo, Colossal (synonym Super Majestic Giant) mix, Happy Face, Imperial strain, Swiss Giant strain, and Majestic Giant strain.
>
> **Medium-flowering pansies** have flowers that are between 2 and 3 inches (5 and 7.5 cm) in diameter. They show good landscape performance and can be plain-faced or blotched. These include the following series: Accord, Bingo, Crown, Crystal Bowl, Delta, Fama, Joker, Maxim, Melody, Rally, Regal, Rococo, Sky, Ultima, Universal, and Wink.
>
> **Small-flowering pansies** have flowers that are less than 2 inches (5 cm) in diameter. They include 'Baby Lucia' with blue flowers.

Vitex
Chaste Tree, Hemp Tree
VERBENACEAE

Vitex is a genus of woody trees and shrubs that are useful as landscape plants where they are winter hardy. Flowers are produced in terminal, branched flower spikes. Each individual flower is small, but the overall effect can be very showy in the late summer. Flower color can be white, yellow, purple, or blue. The leaves are five-lobed and can have a toothed edge, suggesting the common name hemp tree. These species are easy to grow in full sun in almost any well-drained garden soil. Since they bloom on new wood, they can be heavily pruned in the spring, if it is necessary to control growth or correct winter injury. *Vitex* is the old Latin name for "chaste tree."

Propagation: Plants are multiplied by stem cuttings taken in summer before flowers bloom.

Representative species and cultivars: *Vitex* is mostly a tropical genus of about 250 species. The hardy species are commonly cultivated as large landscape shrubs.

Vitex agnus-castus (chaste tree)

Vitex agnus-castus (chaste tree) is native to Europe and grows to 15 feet (4.5 m) tall. Flower color is a lilac blue, violet, pink, or white depending on the cultivar. 'Abbeville Blue' has a truer blue color than the species. 'Shoal Creek' shows some resistance to leaf spot diseases and is lilac blue in flower. *Vitex agnus-castus* var. *latifolia* has a broader leaf and is more winter hardy than the species.

Vitex negundo is an Asian species reaching 10 feet (3 m) tall. It also produces lilac blue flowers, but is more winter hardy and makes a better ornamental shrub than *V. agnus-castus*. 'Heterophylla' has a toothed leaf edge and is the form usually cultivated.

Vitex rotundifolia is not as commonly cultivated as the other *Vitex* species. Native to Asia, it is a smaller shrub than the other species, only reaching about 3 feet (1 m) tall. It produces round rather than five-lobed leaves that are typical for this genus. Flower color is blue or lilac blue.

Wahlenbergia
CAMPANULACEAE

Wahlenbergia species are annual and tender perennial plants that produce flowers shaped like funnels, stars, or saucers. Flower color is white or shades of blue, and the flowers appear in summer. These species are used as bedding plants, in containers, and in alpine or rock gardens. They prefer partial shade and an organic, well-drained soil. The genus name commemorates George Wahlenberg, a nineteenth-century Swedish botanist.

Propagation: Plants are multiplied by seed or division.

Representative species and cultivars: The approximately 150 species of *Wahlenbergia* are native to Europe, Asia, Africa, New Zealand, and Australia. Several diminutive plants from Australia and New Zealand are cultivated by collectors of alpine or rock garden plants, including *W. albomarginata*, *W. congesta*, *W. gloriosa*, and *W. saxicola*. These are similar, producing bell-shaped or star-shaped flowers on plants less than 8 inches (20 cm) tall. *Wahlenbergia melton* 'Blue Bird' is a relatively recent selection that can be grown as a summer-flowering bedding plant or as a container plant. It reaches about 1 foot (30 cm) tall and produces a sky blue flower on a *Campanula*-like plant.

Wisteria
FABACEAE

Wisteria is a genus of deciduous woody vines. These vigorous climbers produce long groups of pealike flowers in the spring. Flower color can be white, violet, or lilac blue. Wisterias are grown on supports, in trees, and along walls, or can be pruned into a small tree form or standard. They should have full sun and a well-drained soil. They need winter protection in northern gardens. The genus name commemorates Caspar Wistar, a professor at the University of Pennsylvania in the early nineteenth century.

Propagation: Plants are multiplied by seed or stem cuttings. Cultivars are propagated by stem cuttings taken in early summer.

Representative species and cultivars: The genus *Wisteria* constitutes 10 species. Most cultivated species are from Asia, but several are also native to the southeastern United States.

Wisteria floribunda (Japanese wisteria)

Wisteria floribunda (Japanese wisteria) is the most commonly grown wisteria because of its large groups of pendulous flowers in panicles. The size of the flower panicles and flower color can vary in seed-grown plants. Flower color can be lilac blue, pink, or white depending on the cultivar. 'Macrobotrys' produces lilac blue flower panicles that can be 4 feet (1.2 m) long! 'Violacea Plena' is a violet-blue, double-flowering form. 'Alba' and 'Snow Showers' have white flowers.

Wisteria ×*formosa*, a hybrid of *W. floribunda* and *W. sinensis,* is a vigorous vine with violet-blue flowers opening all at once in the flower cluster as they do in *W. sinensis*. Cultivars with mauve flower color include 'Burford', 'Caroline', and 'Lavender Lace'. 'Clara Mack' is a good white-flowering form.

Wisteria frutescens (American wisteria) is the representative of the genus from the United States that is occasionally cultivated. The species produces a violet-colored flower, but 'Amethyst Falls' has fragrant, lavender-blue flowers and 'Magnifica' has lilac blue flowers with yellow markings.

Wisteria macrostachys (Kentucky wisteria) is also native to the United States. It is more winter hardy and less aggressive than its more commonly planted Asian counterparts. The flower panicle is packed with many small flowers and can be up to 1 foot (30 cm) long. Flower color is lavender, but 'Abbeville Blue' and 'Pondside Blue' have bluer flowers.

Wisteria sinensis (Chinese wisteria) is native to China and usually has a shorter flowering panicle than *W. floribunda,* only reaching about 1 foot (30 cm) long. Flower color is usually lavender-blue, but cultivars can be white, purple, or pink. It is difficult to tell the Asian species apart, but in general *W. sinensis* has stems that twine counterclockwise and all the flowers in the panicle open at the same time. 'Prolific' was selected because it produces more flowers than the species. Selections with bluer flower color include 'Blue Moon' and 'Blue Sapphire'.

Worsleya
Blue Amaryllis
AMARYLLIDACEAE

Blue amaryllis is a herbaceous perennial grown from a bulb. It has straplike leaves similar to other members of the amaryllis family and grows to about 2 feet (60 cm) tall. Flowers are produced in a terminal cluster of 4 to 10 florets. Flower color is lilac blue and is unique for this family. Plants do not tolerate frost. They are suited for container production in the warm greenhouse or outdoors where the weather is warm. Blue amaryllis is not common in cultivation because it has a reputation for being difficult to flower. Plants also can be short lived and do not like to be transplanted. Bulbs are better left in the original container even though they appear crowded. Potting medium should be fairly organic and well drained. Plants prefer full sun and should be kept well watered and fertilized during the growing season, but water and fertilizer should be reduced in the winter. The genus name commemorates Arthington Worsley, an English botanist who died in 1943.

Propagation: Plants are multiplied by seed or offshoots. Seed can be sown as soon as the fruit is ripe.

Representative species and cultivars: *Worsleya rayneri* (synonym *Hippeastrum procerum*) is the only species in this genus. Native to the mountains of Brazil, it produces a large cluster of lilac blue flowers above straplike leaves during the winter. It is not a commonly cultivated plant, but worth the effort for those interested in this family because of the unique flower color and the challenge of getting plants to bloom each year.

Wulfenia
SCROPHULARIACEAE

Wulfenia is a genus of herbaceous perennials that produce small flowering stems of violet-blue flowers above a rosette of dark green leaves.

Plants bloom in early summer. They are not common perennials in the United States, but are interesting and easy to grow in full sun and a moist, well-drained soil. They make good plants in the rock garden or the front of the border. The genus name commemorates Franz von Wulfen, a sixteenth-century Austrian botanist.

Propagation: Plants are multiplied by seed or division.

The seven species of *Wulfenia* are native to alpine areas of central Europe and Asia. Only a few species are cultivated in gardens.

Wulfenia amherstiana produces an interesting flower stem with lilac blue flowers on one side of the stem. It is about 1 foot (30 cm) tall and native to the Himalayan mountains.

Wulfenia baldacii is similar to *W. carinthiaca,* but is an even smaller plant.

Wulfenia carinthiaca is the most commonly cultivated species. Native to the Alps, it grows less than 1 foot (30 cm) tall with a spike of purple-blue flowers. 'Alba' is a white form.

Wulfenia baldacii

Plants for Various Uses in the Landscape

Herbaceous Perennials for Sun or Part Shade

Early Spring Blooming
Ajuga
Anchusa
Aquilegia
Baptisia
Buglossoides
Camassia
Cynoglossum
Lindelofia
Symphytum
Vinca
Viola

Late Spring and Summer Blooming
Adenophora
Agastache

Allium
Amsonia
Campanula
Catananche
Centaurea
Clematis
Cynoglossum
Delphinium
Echinops
Eryngium
Gentiana
Geranium
Iris
Lavandula
Limonium
Linum
Lithodora
Lupinus
Nepeta
Perovskia
Phlox

Platycodon
Salvia
Scabiosa
Stokesia
Teucrium
Verbena
Veronica
Wulfenia

Late Summer and Fall Blooming
Aconitum
Aster
Caryopteris
Ceratostigma

Herbaceous Perennials for Shade

Brunnera
Collinsia

Herbaceous Perennials
for Shade, cont.

Hepatica
Hyacinthoides
Lobelia
Meehania
Mertensia
Myosotis
Pentaglottis
Phacelia
Polemonium
Primula
Pulmonaria
Tradescantia
Tricyrtis

Herbaceous Annuals Used as Bedding Plants

Achimenes
Aechmea
Ageratum
Anagallis
Borago
Brachycome
Browallia
Caryopteris
Centaurea
Clerodendrum
Coleus
Convolvulus
Cynara
Echium
Eustoma
Evolvulus
Exacum
Felicia
Heliophila
Lathyrus

Laurentia
Lobelia
Nemesis
Nemophila
Nierembergia
Nigella
Nolana
Otacanthus
Oxypetalum
Petunia
Phacelia
Plectranthus
Plumbago
Salpiglossis
Salvia
Scaevola
Senecio
Torenia
Verbena
Wahlenbergia

Bulbs, Corms, or Tubers for Mass Plantings or Specimens

Agapanthus
Allium
Babiana
Camassia
Chionodoxa
Commelina
Crocus
Gladiolus
Hyacinthoides
Hyacinthus
Ipheion
Iris
Muscari
Neomarica

Patersonia
Puschkinia
Tecophilaea
Triteleia
Worsleya

Rock Garden or Alpine Plants

Ajuga
Allium
Anchusa
Anemone
Aquilegia
Borago
Buglossoides
Campanula
Ceratostigma
Chionodoxa
Codonopsis
Corydalis
Crocus
Delphinium
Gentiana
Globularia
Hedyotis
Hepatica
Ipheion
Iris
Lindelofia
Linum
Lithodora
Meconopsis
Mertensia
Moltkia
Muscari
Myosotis
Nierembergia
Omphalodes
Phacelia

Phyteuma
Platycodon
Polygala
Primula
Puschkinia
Ramonda
Scilla
Sisyrinchium
Tecophilaea
Trachelium
Triteleia
Veronica
Wahlenbergia
Wulfenia

Plants That Make Good Cut Flowers

Ageratum
Anemone
Camassia
Centaurea
Echinops
Eryngium
Eustoma
Gladiolus
Hyacinthus
Hydrangea
Iris
Lathyrus
Lavandula
Limonium
Lupinus
Nepeta
Nigella
Otacanthus
Oxypetalum

Perovskia
Scabiosa
Stokesia
Trachelium
Trachymene
Viola

Climbing Vines for Trellises

Clematis
Clitoria
Ipomoea
Passiflora
Thunbergia
Wisteria

Plants for Hanging Baskets or Containers

Achimenes
Agapanthus
Brachycome
Browallia
Clerodendrum
Coleus
Convolvulus
Evolvulus
Exacum
Felicia
Laurentia
Lobelia
Petunia
Plectranthus
Plumbago
Primula

Saintpaulia
Scaevola
Senecio
Streptocarpus
Teucrium
Tillandsia
Verbena
Worsleya

Specimen Plants for Containers
(usually tender perennials)

Aechmea
Agapanthus
Brunfelsia
Clerodendrum
Dichorisandra
Duranta
Echium
Hibiscus
Hydrangea
Iochroma
Otacanthus
Petrea
Plumbago
Rosmarinus
Solanum
Vitex

Plants for In or Around a Pond

Iris
Nymphaea
Pontederia

Glossary

All America Selections. An organization that awards flower cultivars judged to be superior for garden performance.

Annual. A plant that (usually) completes its life cycle in one growing season.

Anther. The pollen-bearing part of the male reproductive structure in plants.

Biennial. A plant that completes its life cycle in two growing seasons. During the first year it grows vegetatively, and in the second it fruits and dies.

Bulb. An underground bud with a short stem.

Bulbous. Growing from a bulb.

Cleistogamous flowers. Closed flowers that self-pollinate.

Corm. A bulblike underground stem.

Cormel. An offset of a corm.

Cutting. A method of plant propagation by cutting a plant part that can develop into a new plant.

Day neutral. Applied to a plant that does not require a certain length of day for flowering to occur.

Disk floret. A small tubular flower surrounded by ray florets in a composite plant such as aster.

Division. A method of plant propagation by dividing parts that can produce roots and thus grow new plants.

Epiphyte, epiphytic. A plant that grows on another but obtains its nourishment from the air.

F_1 hybrid. A hybrid offspring of the first filial generation.

Fleuroselect. A promotional agency that evaluates flower cultivars in Europe and awards medals to plants that are superior to those currently available to consumers.

Hardy. Capable of withstanding cold temperatures.

Herbaceous. Having a soft, green stem with little or no woody tissue.

Nectary. A gland that produces a sweet liquid known as nectar.

Panicle. A branched spike.

Perennial. A plant that lives through three or more growing seasons.

Picotee. A flower with a ring in a contrasting color.

Pup. An offshoot.

Raceme. An unbranched flower stalk in which the flowers are borne on short stalks.

Ray floret. A small flower that, with other ray florets, forms a ring around the disk floret in a composite plant such as aster.

Rhizome. A horizontal underground stem that often stores food for the plant.

Scarify, scarification. To treat seed, often by scratching through the hard outer seed coat, to allow it to absorb water.

Seed propagation. A method of plant propagation by germinating seed.

Senescing. Becoming old; moving from maturity to death.

Stamen. The male part of a flower.

Stigma. The part of the female reproductive structure in plants that receives the pollen.

Stratify, stratification. To treat seed, often with cold or warm moisture, to overcome dormancy and improve rate of germination.

Stolon. A horizontal (usually) aboveground stem that produces new plants.

Strain. A group of plants with a common ancestry.

Style. The part of the female reproductive structure in plants that holds the stigma in position.

Tepal. The name given to a floral part in flowers with no distinct sepals or petals.

Terrestrial. A plant that grows in the soil.

Tetraploid. Having twice the normal chromosome number.

Tissue culture. A method of propagation in which small pieces of plant tissue are grown in an artificial medium under sterile conditions.

Tuber. An underground stem.

Umbel. A type of flower cluster in which the individual flowers arise from a common point on the stalk.

Vacuole, vacuolar. A compartment in a cell.

Bibliography

Armitage, A. M. 1997. *Herbaceous Perennial Plants: A Treatise on Their Identification, Culture and Garden Attributes.* Varsity Press, Athens, Georgia.

Austin, S. 1998. *Color in Garden Design.* Taunton Press, Newtown, Connecticut.

Bailey, L. H. 1939. *The Garden of Larkspurs; with Decorations.* Macmillan, New York.

Bailey, L. H. 1953. *The Garden of Bellflowers.* Macmillan, New York.

Bath, T., and J. Jones. 1994. *The Gardener's Guide to Growing Hardy Geraniums.* Timber Press, Portland, Oregon.

Brickell, C., and J. D. Zuk. 1996. *The American Horticultural Society A–Z Encyclopedia of Garden Plants.* DK Publishing, New York.

Bryan, J. (ed.). 1995. *Manual of Bulbs.* Timber Press, Portland, Oregon.

Chesshire, C. 1999. *Clematis.* DK Publishing, New York.

Clebsch, B. 1997. *A Book of Salvias: Sages for Every Garden.* Timber Press, Portland, Oregon.

Crook, H. C. 1951. *Campanulas: Their Cultivation and Classification.* Scribner, New York.

Davies, D. 1992. *Alliums: The Ornamental Onions.* Timber Press, Portland, Oregon.

Edwards, C. 1989. *Delphiniums: The Complete Guide.* Crowood Press, Marlborough, United Kingdom.

Evison, R. J. 1998. *The Gardener's Guide to Growing Clematis.* Timber Press, Portland, Oregon.

Fogg, H. G., and H. G. Witham. 1964. *Geraniums and Pelargoniums.* Garden Book Club, London.

Foster, H. L. 1968. *Rock Gardening: A Guide to Growing Alpines and Other Wildflowers in the American Garden.* Timber Press, Portland, Oregon.

Fretwell, B. 1989. *Clematis.* Capability's Books, Deer Park, Wisconsin.

Genders, R. 1963. *Delphiniums.* Garden Book Club, London.

Genders, R. 1973. *Bulbs: A Complete Handbook.* Robert Hale and Company. London.

Glasgow, K. 1996. *Irises: A Practical Gardening Guide.* Timber Press, Portland, Oregon.

Good, J. (ed.). 1993. *The Gardener's Color Guide: Designing the Flower Garden by Color and Season.* Camden House Publishers, Columbia, South Carolina.

Hay, R., and P. Synge. 1975. *The Color Dictionary of Flowers and Plants for Home and Garden.* Crown, New York.

Hecker, W. R. 1971. *Auriculas and Primroses.* Batsford, London.

Hobhouse, P. 1985. *Color in Your Garden.* Little Brown and Company, Boston.

Holttum, R. E., and I. Enoch. 1991. *Gardening in the Tropics.* Timber Press, Portland, Oregon.

Innes, C. 1995. *Alpines: The Illustrated Dictionary.* Timber Press, Portland, Oregon.

Jekyll, G. 1930. *Colour Schemes for the Flower Garden.* 7th ed. Scribner, New York.

Jekyll, G., and L. Weaver. 1924. *Gardens for Small Country Houses.* 5th ed. Country Life, London.

Jelitto, L., and W. Schacht. 1990. *Encyclopedia of the Hardy Herbaceous Perennials.* Timber Press, Portland, Oregon.

Köhlein, F. 1991. *Gentians.* Timber Press, Portland, Oregon.

Lawson, A. 1996. *The Gardener's Book of Color.* Reader's Digest Association, New York.

Lawson-Hall, T., and B. Rothera. 1995. *Hydrangeas: A Gardener's Guide.* Timber Press, Portland, Oregon.

Lewis, P., and M. Lynch. 1998. *Campanulas: A Gardener's Guide.* Timber Press, Portland, Oregon.

Lloyd, C., and T. Bennett. 1989. *Clematis.* Capability's Books, Deer Park, Wisconsin.

Mathew, B. 1990. *The Iris.* Timber Press, Portland, Oregon.

Mathew, B. 1997. *Growing Bulbs: The Complete Practical Guide.* Timber Press, Portland, Oregon.

Mineo, B. 1999. *Rock Garden Plants: A Color Encyclopedia.* Timber Press, Portland, Oregon.

Ortloff, H. S., and H. B. Raymore. 1951. *Color and Design for Every Garden.* Barrows, New York.

Oudolf, P. 1999. *Designing with Plants.* Timber Press, Portland, Oregon.

Padilla, V. 1966. *Bromeliads.* Crown, New York.

Phillips, G. A. 1933. *Delphiniums: Their History and Cultivation.* Butterworth, London.

Picton, P. 1999. *The Gardener's Guide to Growing Asters.* Timber Press, Portland, Oregon.

Pope, N., S. Pope, and P. Hobhouse. 1998. *Color by Design: Planting the Contemporary Garden.* Soma Books.

Saville, D. 1993. *Color (Letts Guides to Garden Design).* Abbeville Press, New York.

Slocum, P. D., and P. Robinson. 1996. *Water Gardening, Water Lilies and Lotuses.* Timber Press, Portland, Oregon.

Stebbings, G. 1997. *The Gardener's Guide to Growing Irises.* Timber Press, Portland, Oregon.

Still, S. 1987. *Manual of Herbaceous Ornamental Plants.* 3rd ed. Stipes, Champaign, Illinois.

Sutton, S. 1999. *The Gardener's Guide to Growing Salvias.* Timber Press, Portland, Oregon.

Symons-Jeune, B. H. B. 1953. *Phlox.* Collins Press, London.

Tinari, A. 1975. *Our African Violet Heritage.* Tinari Greenhouses, Pennsylvania.

Valder, P. 1995. *Wisterias.* Timber Press, Portland, Oregon.

Vanderplank, J. 1996. *Passion Flowers.* MIT Press, Cambridge, Massachusetts.

Wilkie, D. 1936. *Gentians.* Country Life, New York.

Wilson, H. V. P. 1970. *African-Violet Book.* Hawthorn Books, New York.

Yeo, P. 1985. *Hardy Geraniums.* Timber Press, Portland, Oregon.

Index

Boldfaced numbers indicate pages with color photos.